Visions of the Emerald City

Visions of the Emerald City

*Modernity, Tradition, and the
Formation of Porfirian Oaxaca, Mexico*

Mark Overmyer-Velázquez

Duke University Press
Durham and London 2006

© 2006 Duke University Press
All rights reserved
Printed in the United States of America on acid-free paper ∞
Typeset in Trinité by Tseng Information Systems, Inc.
Library of Congress Cataloging-in-Publication Data
appear on the last printed page of this book.

for Jordanna

Contents

Illustrations and Tables ix
Preface xi

Introduction
Writing the Emerald City 1

1. *La Vallistocracia:*
The Formation of Oaxaca's Ruling Class 17

2. The Legible City:
Constructed, Symbolic, and Disciplined Spaces 40

3. "A New Political Religious Order":
Church, State, and Workers 70

4. "A Necessary Evil":
Regulating Public Space and Public Women 98

5. Portraits of a Lady:
Visions of Modernity 122

Conclusions
The Consequences of Modernity 153

Appendix
Articles Cited from the 1857 Constitution 161

Notes 163
Bibliography 203
Index 221

Illustrations and Tables

MAPS

Map 1. Mexico and Oaxaca State   3
Map 2. State of Oaxaca: District Capitals and Oaxaca City   4
Map 3. Oaxaca City   5
Map 4. "Red Zone" of Prostitution   117

FIGURES

Figure 1. "The Races in the State of Oaxaca"   58
Figure 2. Petrona O., 1896   123
Figure 3. Page from *Registro de mujeres públicas*   125
Figure 4. Amado J., 1905   138
Figure 5. Victoriano R., 1903   138
Figure 6. Anastacio B., 1891   138
Figure 7. Alberto H., 1901   139
Figure 8. Cirilio L., 1903   139
Figure 9. Orfino D., 1907   139
Figure 10. Matilde C.   140
Figure 11. Isabel R.   140
Figure 12. Gregoria M.   140
Figure 13. Angela H.   140
Figure 14. Mercedes P., 1895 (Sevilla, Spain)   142
Figure 15. Francisca G., 1901 (Mexico City)   142
Figure 16. Rosa B., 1905 (Barcelona, Spain)   142
Figure 17. Rosaura S., 1895 (Austria)   142
Figure 18. Fashion Page from *El centenario: Revista mensual ilustrada*, 1910   144
Figure 19. Fashion Page from *El centenario: Revista mensual ilustrada*, 1910   144
Figure 20. Josefina R., AHMO, Registry of Prostitution, 1895   144
Figure 21. Herlinda M., AHMO, Registry of Prostitution, 1901   144
Figure 22. Rafaela O., 1896 (Oaxaca City)   145
Figure 23. Luisa M., 1901 (Oaxaca City)   145

Figure 24. Rosa N., 1905 (Oaxaca City) 145
Figure 25. Violeta G., 1895 (Havana, Cuba) 147
Figure 26. Juana A., 1892 (Ixtlán, Oaxaca) 147
Figure 27. Guadalupe F., 1892 (Oaxaca City) 147
Figure 28. Rosario M., 1902 (Mexico City) 147

TABLES

Table 1. Number of Properties Owned
by Prominent Families in Oaxaca City 29
Table 2. Number of Registered Sex Workers 111
Table 3. Origin of Registered Sex Workers 143

Preface

For most tourists, Oaxaca City is a place that time forgot, a magical fusion of pre-Columbian and colonial eras. Of course, these anachronistic yearnings say more about the traveler than about the city and its people. Oaxaca City, now consigned to the margins of both national politics and historical scholarship, played a central role in Mexico's history until the beginning of the twentieth century. I conceived of my project at the tail end of that same century in Mexico, while it was yet again seeking to assert itself as a modern nation. As the country's exiled president, Carlos Salinas de Gortari, submitted to public scrutiny his fourteen-hundred-page memoir, *Mexico: A Difficult Step toward Modernity*, Mexico reeled from the effects of a devalued peso, an economic crisis, and the North American Free Trade Agreement (NAFTA). Meanwhile, a relatively small group of indigenous campesinos rallied under the banner of Emiliano Zapata, Mexico's historical and mythologized agrarian revolutionary, to put the government's latest version of modernity on trial. It is within that context that, thanks to some sound advice, I turned to Oaxaca City and its rich and fascinating history to ask questions about the nature of modernity and how it was imagined and constructed by elites and commoners alike.

I could begin to answer those questions and complete this study only because I was fortunate enough to have the generous help and support of many people and institutions. It is a pleasure to thank all of those friends and colleagues.

This project would have remained a starry-eyed PhD prospectus had it not been for the financial assistance of several agencies, programs, and institutions. A Yale University Fellowship, the Program in Agrarian Studies at Yale University, an Albert J. Beveridge Grant from the American Historical Association, a Mexican Secretaría de Relaciones Exteriores (Ministry of Foreign Relations) Fellowship, a Henry Hart Rice Research Fellowship at the Yale Center for International and Area Studies, a Toni Roothbert Doctoral Fellowship, and a Social Sciences and Humanities Research Council of Canada Doctoral Fellowship all funded various stages of my research. A Giles Whiting Fellowship in the Humanities and a National Research Council–Ford Foundation Fellowship for Minorities granted funds for the writing of the dissertation. A César E. Chávez Fellowship at Dartmouth College provided me with the wherewithal to finish the dissertation and gave me a chance to share some of my work with new colleagues. Here I am especially grateful to Christina Gómez, Mary Kelley, Silvia Spitta, Sheila Laplante, Gary Hutchins, Alex Hernandez-Siegel, and the students in the Latin American, Latino, and Caribbean Studies Program for easing me through the transition from graduate student to faculty member. Thanks also to the Program in Native American Studies for finding me an office.

The process of transforming the dissertation into this book accumulated some additional debts. An Andrew W. Mellon Postdoctoral Fellowship at Wesleyan University's Center for the Humanities afforded me the time and space to make revisions, and my colleagues at the Center and its interim director, Jill Morawski, helped me think about and express my work across disciplinary divides. A Faculty Small Research Grant from the University of Connecticut allowed me to gather up the remaining archival material I needed. New colleagues at the University of Connecticut in the History Department, the Center for Latin American and Caribbean Studies, and the Institute of Puerto Rican and Latino Studies have provided a very welcoming and intellectually vibrant academic home for me and my work. I have especially appreciated the support and encouragement from Melina Pappademos, Blanca Silvestrini, Karen Spalding, and Altina Waller.

My personal and intellectual debts extend back many years to locations throughout Mexico, Canada, and the United States. While I was an undergraduate at the University of British Columbia, William French challenged and inspired me to search for truth in historical inquiry. His scholarship, carnivalesque lectures, insightful and exhaustive editorial advice, continued commitment to my work, and friendship all have been invaluable in the writing of this book.

This study is based on eighteen months of research in various archives and libraries in Mexico and the United States. Archivists and historians in these two countries helped me immeasurably in my search for documents and Oaxacan cognoscenti. Javier Garcíadiego at the Colegio de México supplied me with much-needed institutional support while I was in Mexico. Tere Matabuena at the Universidad Iberoamericana's Porfirio Díaz archive kindly put up with my many questions about the location of don Porfirio's uncataloged letters. Archivists at the Archivo General de la Nación, the Biblioteca Miguel Lerdo de Tejada, the Centro de Estudios de la Historia de México, and the Hemeroteca General de la Nación also helped me find material. In Oaxaca City, where I spent most of my time, Rosalba Montiel at the Notary Archive and Tere Bustamante at the Fundación Bustamante allowed me to arrive early and stay late in exchange for some cataloging of their collections. The Archivo Histórico Municipal "Manuel R. Palacios" de Oaxaca became my second home for the better part of a year and its archivists have become my close friends and urban guides. The then-director, Carlos

Sánchez Silva, generously offered me hours upon hours of scholarly wisdom and entertained me with his wonderful stories and excellent taste in jazz. I had the unique opportunity to be the first researcher to use the archive's Porfirian collection in a comprehensive way. The archivists, Aarón Martínez García, Jesús ("Chucho") Mendoza Ferrer, Gloria Irma Méndez, Edith Rojo Guerrero, and Manuel Guadalupe Villafáes, and I simultaneously discovered the wealth of the collection. My relationships with all of them extended well beyond the archive to the streets of the capital city and its homes, markets, taquerías, and soccer fields. Throughout my study in Oaxaca City, Francisco José ("Paco Pepe") Ruiz Cervantes doled out ample good advice and not a few bibliographic suggestions. I also appreciate the assistance of the staff and archivists at the Archivo General del Poder Ejecutivo del Estado de Oaxaca, the Archivo Poder Judicial, the Archivo de la Arquidiócesis, and the Hemeroteca de la Ciudad de Oaxaca de Juárez, all in Oaxaca City. While in Oaxaca City, my friend and colleague Yanna Yannakakis shared in the mysteries and wonders of archival research in southern Mexico. Back in the United States, César Rodríguez, the tireless and cheerful director of Yale's Latin American collection, found the time and money to bring material to New Haven for my perusal.

Along the way I have had the good fortune to receive comments on and critiques of my written work and papers presented at academic conferences. Emilia Viotti da Costa, Deborah Poole, John Mraz, John Womack, Friedrich Katz, Miguel Tinker Salas, Jeffrey Rubin, John Lear, Stephen O'Brien, Dain Borges, Daniela Traffano, Ronald Spores, Patrick McNamara, Katherine Bliss, Martin Nesvig, Eddie Wright-Rios, Jordanna Hertz, Manuel Esparza, Gloria Medina Gómez, and Anselmo Arellanes have all contributed to the better parts of this work. The members of my dissertation writing group — Jay Garcia, Michael Cohen, Amy Chazkel, Fiona Vernal, and Victoria Langland — took time away from their own work to read chapter drafts patiently and offer rich suggestions, as well as invaluable companionship and cariño, during our monthly rendezvous. Amy and Tori deserve special praise for their last-minute edits and stress-reducing advice. Raymond Craib and Rick López have directed me through the nuances of academia. More important than their judicious scholarly guidance, they reminded me how to be a good neighbor and combine work with the joys of fatherhood. Two anonymous readers for Duke University Press wrote extensive, astute, and invaluable comments on an early draft of this work. Valerie Millholland has been a wonderful guide and cheerleader throughout the publication process.

At the same time that they kept me focused on the task at hand, the members of my dissertation committee guided me past innumerable intellectual obstacles and conceptual pitfalls. I was always able to turn to Stuart Schwartz for generous doses of common sense and good leads. As is obvious by the numerous citations of James Scott in the study that follows, his influence on my work is pervasive. He not only supported my training as a young graduate student but also shared his office with me. That space provided me with a refuge to write a critical mass of chapters and to find a balance between work and home. A phone call to Francie Chassen-López more years ago than I care to recall inspired me to work on Oaxaca City in the first place. Since then Francie has introduced me to her coterie of Oaxacan colleagues, shared her work with me, and, through her corrections and suggestions, greatly improved my own. It is well known among historians of Latin America that Gil Joseph is a superlative mentor and scholar. I still cannot understand how Gil does all the excellent and important work that he does and still finds the time to be such an incredible mentor, mensch, and friend. I imagine that the best way to thank him is to promise to try and be as devoted and inspiring a teacher to my own students in the years to come as he has been to me.

Although my dissertation tends to portray administrators in an unfavorable light, the truth is that many of the hard-working administrators in my life have been invaluable guides through the seemingly impenetrable thickets of institutional bureaucracy. Kay Mansfield at the Program in Agrarian Studies, Beatriz Riefkohl at the Council on Latin American and Iberian Studies, and Florence Thomas in the history department, all at Yale, Brenda Keating and Susan Ferris at Wesleyan University's Center for the Humanities, and Rosi Quiroz at the Colegio de México have each been my *santa patrona* at one time or another.

Throughout this long process, my extended family has surrounded me with love and support and provided my immediate family and me with a home away from home whenever it was needed. In addition to some careful editing, my dear friend and *compadre* Grant Sheppard cheered me on and offered solace in times of doubt and frustration. My *suegros*, Claire and Martin Hertz, have been truly magnanimous souls. I could never measure (nor would I want to) the abundance of care, affection, and good food with which they have filled me over the years. Sharing an apartment in Mexico City with my sister, Rebecca Overmyer-Velázquez, made a daily three-hour commute seem worthwhile. Despite our residence on opposite coasts of the United States, it has been a blessing to know that I could always call her to help me decipher the latest peculiarities of the academic experience. My parents, Estella and Daniel Overmyer, have done more to bring me to this point in my life than all of the others combined, and then some. I have been deeply influenced by my mother's enthusiasm for Mexico and my father's commitment to a passion for learning. At different stages of writing this book, *mis hijitos*, Sarai Dov and Maceo Ilan, joined us. I thank them both *con un abrazo cariñoso* for teaching me about the preciousness of life and the value of experiencing the world in awe.

Although this seemingly interminable list of acknowledgments clearly bears out the fact that my project has been an exercise of collaboration and discussion with many people, there is but one person who shared it all. She came with me to Mexico, endured with great patience and support the insecurities of a young academic, showered me with love and affection, paid the bills, and shared in the alternately exasperating and exhilarating experiences of parenthood: Jordanna, this is for you.

I wrote the bulk of this study in the shadow of the horrific events of September 11, 2001. At a time when government officials, pundits, and the media continue to re-inforce rigid dichotomies of us and them, civilized and tribal, modern and tradi-tional, I have found it all the more crucial to look to history for the contexts and contingencies that have shaped the present world.[1] In an age when hundreds of Oaxacans continue to leave their capital city and state each year for the uncertain hopes of el Norte—despite the promises of NAFTA and the threats of increasing "security" along the Mexican-U.S. border—I can only speculate uneasily what the consequences of this latest encounter with modernity might be for the women and men making that arduous journey. While it is a commonplace that we now live in a "modern" time, it is vital to consider how we arrived here in the first place. Perhaps taking into account the histories of locations like Oaxaca City will help us to reconsider marginalized peoples and places at the center of our visions and practices of modernity.

Writing the Emerald City

The anxiety of modernity creates the desire for new myths and traditions — beliefs that will bring under control the changes that have undermined all seemingly fixed and stable cultural, political, and economic relations.
— Gregory Grandin, *The Blood of Guatemala*, 2000

The beautiful city of Oaxaca is being adorned with new and beautiful avenues like Porfirio Díaz Avenue, with new buildings like the school of the same name; and the improvements are occurring without interruption not only in the capital, but also in the towns of the districts. Public morality is becoming established, vices are being persecuted . . . [and] new schools are being erected . . . in order not to detain the course of civilization for the masses, who are struggling incessantly with difficulties and innumerable hardships.
— Francisco Belmar, *Breve reseña histórica y geográfica del Estado de Oaxaca*, 1901

In its early-twenty-first-century incarnation, Oaxaca City appears to the uninitiated (at least to those who restrict their touristic movements to the *centro histórico*) to be a relic of Mexico's colonial past. Yet beneath the palimpsest of the present city lies a neglected history. Much of what the contemporary visitor sees of this Mexican provincial city was constructed or reconstructed during the late nineteenth century and early twentieth, under the reign of President Porfirio Díaz.[1] When Francisco Belmar, a philologist and Mexican Supreme Court judge, wrote the above passage in the introduction to his *Breve reseña* (*Brief Historical and Geographical Outline of Oaxaca State*), he, like other elites of his era, envisioned the state capital as part of Mexico's transformation into a new and modern era. Paying homage to the state's theatrically elected (read, presidentially selected) governor, General Martín González, Belmar extolled the government's efforts to rebuild, expand, and regulate the city after its bellicose days in the nineteenth century.

The particular form that this southern provincial city took, however, depended on more than the lofty visions of the ruling elite.

In this study I explore a critical feature of nineteenth- and twentieth-century Mexican history: how Mexicans constructed and experienced the processes of modernity. I examine the city of Oaxaca de Juárez, an important site in Mexico's encounter with modernity at the turn of the century. Elites and commoners alike constructed modernity physically in the streets, plazas, neighborhoods, and buildings of the Emerald City (structures whose *cantera* stone – volcanic tuff mined from local quarries – made the city famously green), and discursively through notions of class, race, gender, sexuality, and religion as displayed in things like civic regulations, newspapers, and public rituals.[2] Different urban groups – including governmental elites, church leaders, and popular groups, each characterized by specific and contested understandings of class, race, and gender – simultaneously constituted modernity. These groups mobilized ideas and practices of modernity in their struggles over social, cultural, and political power in Oaxaca City.

The construction of modernity depended in large part on its representation or "staging" of reality.[3] For elites, notions of legibility and visual order were central. Elite visions and representations of modernity in the Emerald City attempted to simplify and, hence, make legible the complexities of the capital's Porfirian-era historical transformation. The practices of envisioning and ordering the state capital and its population took shape in areas such as urban planning and architecture, social engineering, the organization and mapping of public and private spaces, and most prominently in the photographic registries of the city's workers. Although these practices drew on and transformed colonial and early-nineteenth-century traditions, the Porfirian era uniquely intensified Mexico's encounter with modernity as it deepened the nation's engagement with international capitalism, increased the proliferation of mass media and industrialization, and, through the dictates of an authoritarian regime, extended the technological reach of the state to reshape urban areas.[4]

As did elites, commoners possessed their own visions of the Emerald City. They also used the technological and juridical innovations of the Porfirian era to transform the ways in which they experienced life in the capital. In one example, sex workers appropriated aspects of the expanding municipal regulatory apparatus and rhetoric from Mexico's liberal constitution to lay claim to respectability and certain elements of a "modern" lifestyle considered by many in the elite to pertain only to themselves. What emerged from these multiple and competing currents in Porfirian Oaxaca City was not an abrupt end to "traditional" society and

Map 1. Mexico and Oaxaca State

the beginning of a "modern" one but the simultaneous and mutual construction of both.

Oaxaca de Juárez is located 350 miles southeast of Mexico City (see maps 1, 2, and 3). During the Porfiriato, that period between 1877 and 1911 during which Porfirio Díaz served as president, the country, for the first time since it won independence in 1821, maintained a large measure of political stability and industrialization. Díaz and the political elite carefully orchestrated this period of relative peace through a combination of juridical manipulation, patronage politics, and violent coercion.

The anxiety of modernity experienced by Oaxaca City's inhabitants resulted from a related and rapidly occurring series of developments in the state capital. During the Porfiriato, economic expansion based on a boom in the state's mining industry, the concomitant arrival of the national railroad and thousands of new residents, newly defined and shaped urban spaces, and increasingly muscular and intrusive government and ecclesiastic bureaucracies fundamentally altered the relationship of the city's inhabitants with one another. Specifically, these new developments unsettled the seemingly fixed and stable relations within and among the elite, the church hierarchy, and the urban popular classes.

Similar to the ways observed by Gregory Grandin in the case of Guatemala, Oaxaca City's residents, both elite and commoners, generated new myths and

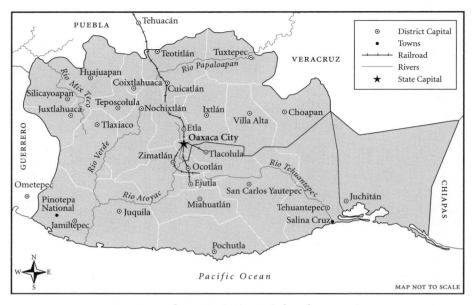

Map 2. State of Oaxaca: District Capitals and Oaxaca City

traditions to give meaning and lend stability to the radical changes occurring around them. Key among these techniques was the myth of modernity, one that simultaneously lauded the creation of a "modern," white, masculine city and seemingly rejected its "traditional," indigenous, female, rural correlate. Imagining the city in this way allowed inhabitants to situate the state capital within a national narrative of "Order and Progress" while suspending the obvious: that these two sides of the same city depended on each other for their discursive and physical construction.

As a provincial city and a commercial hub of southern Mexico, Oaxaca City not only acted as the locus of modernity for a population much greater than that housed within its limits but also typified, in many ways, the construction and experience of modernity in a much vaster area, making conclusions drawn here more broadly applicable. Although Oaxaca City experienced only moderate demographic growth during the period (its population increased from 25,948 in 1876 to 38,011 in 1910),[5] it served as the state's economic, political, and cultural center. During the Porfiriato, Mexico's population increased by 61 percent. By comparison, the population of the country's provincial cities rose by 88 percent. In 1900, no urban area in Latin America had a million inhabitants; in the entire region, only fourteen had a population of over one hundred thousand. Like Oaxaca City, most cities were much smaller, and their rates of demographic increase, largely

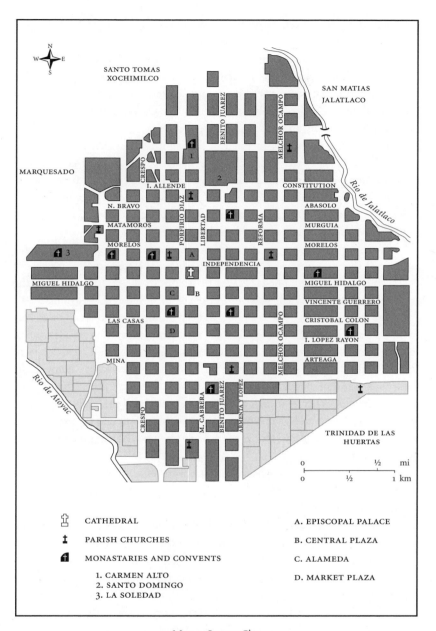

SANTO TOMAS
XOCHIMILCO

SAN MATIAS
JALATLACO

MARQUESADO

Rio de Jalatlaco

BENITO JUAREZ

MELCHOR OCAMPO

CRESPO

I. ALLENDE

CONSTITUTION

N. BRAVO

ABASOLO

PORFIRIO DIAZ

LIBERTAD

REFORMA

MATAMOROS

MURGUIA

MORELOS

MORELOS

MIGUEL HIDALGO

INDEPENDENCIA

MIGUEL HIDALGO

VINCENTE GUERRERO

LAS CASAS

CRISTOBAL COLON

MELCHOR OCAMPO

I. LOPEZ RAYON

MINA

ARTEAGA

Rio de Atoyac

CRESPO

M. CABRERA

BENITO JUAREZ

ARMENTA Y LOPEZ

TRINIDAD DE LAS
HUERTAS

| 0 | | ½ | mi |
| 0 | ½ | 1 | km |

🏛 CATHEDRAL

✝ PARISH CHURCHES

⛪ MONASTARIES AND CONVENTS

   1. CARMEN ALTO
   2. SANTO DOMINGO
   3. LA SOLEDAD

A. EPISCOPAL PALACE

B. CENTRAL PLAZA

C. ALAMEDA

D. MARKET PLAZA

Map 3. Oaxaca City

due to natural growth, rose slowly. In that same year, 4.4 percent of Mexico's total population (13,607,000) lived in its four major urban centers, whereas 8.3 percent of the country's population lived in one of fifty-four provincial cities like Oaxaca de Juárez.[6] Despite its lack of industrialization, Oaxaca's capital played an important role in mediating the experience of modernity in Mexico's South. Connecting the "periphery" to the "center," provincial capitals like Oaxaca City were showcases for Díaz's modernizing and state-building projects.[7]

Oaxaca, in the narrative generated in Mexico City, has been constructed as the "traditional" backwater that enables the "center" to define itself as "modern." Until the mid-1980s, historical studies of Oaxaca depicted the southern state as Mexico's backward frontier. Because of its primarily indigenous population and geographic isolation—Oaxaca is separated from Mexico City by the vast ridge of the Sierra Madre—scholars assumed that the forces of modernity passed by the state and its capital. Writing in the mid-seventies and early eighties, some scholars argued that the state was "immunized against the epidemic of progress."[8] Furthermore, they maintained, because of its ties to the Porfirian regime, the state's population remained "passive" in the face of revolutionary currents.[9]

Before those scholars, local cronistas had been telling the historical tale of Porfirian Oaxaca City for decades. While their treatments provide a useful sketch of the city's political figures and material changes, they tend to elide local details in favor of a more heroic version of their home city from the vantage point of the governor's mansion. In his work Apuntes históricos de Oaxaca, for example, Angel Taracena concludes his treatment of Porfirian Oaxaca with the simple statement that the state's governors were almost all "honorable people and sincere lovers of their homeland who did all that they could to finance peace and materially improve the state."[10]

Visions of the Emerald City builds on the work of a small, dedicated cadre of scholars who are currently revising the modern historiography of the oft-neglected and misunderstood state. The group has expanded and enriched the research on Mexico's regions, continuing to prove that "fuera de México, [no] todo es Cuauhtitlán," or, in other words, that to understand Mexico's complex history we need to look beyond the nation's capital.[11] In their different historical approaches to the state, these oaxacólogos argue that, the conventional wisdom notwithstanding, Oaxaca was not an ideological, economic, and political backwater of the late nineteenth century. Francie Chassen-López, the doyenne of this group, has convincingly argued that Mexico City-centered stereotypes of Mexican history must be challenged and our historical view redirected to places like Oaxaca, Guerrero, Chiapas, and Yucatán. Chassen-López challenges representations of Mexico's South that consider the region as an impediment to progress because of its predominantly indigenous population.[12] Studies by other scholars also have helped open up the examination of the politics, society, and culture of Oaxaca's past. Monographs and articles on precursors to the Mexican Revolution, on education, religion, gender, race, labor, and liberalism have firmly inserted Oaxaca into Mexico's modern historical narrative.[13] Access to previously closed or restricted private and public archives has fueled the research and publication of several new studies on Oaxaca and its capital city.[14]

Don Porfirio and his predecessor, Benito Juárez, had more than sixty years of family ties to Oaxaca City, underscoring the importance of this state in Mexico's history. Before his presidential rule became "permanent," Díaz interrupted his tenure for a four-year period (1880–84), during which he governed Oaxaca.[15] It is largely because of Oaxaca's intimate connection to Díaz that the state and especially Oaxaca City were so involved in the modernizing activities of the era. Although often oppositely characterized, the inhabitants of Oaxaca state and its capital directly experienced the economic and social transformations occurring throughout Mexico and Latin America in the late nineteenth and early twentieth century.

Constructing Modernity

At the heart of this study is the elusive concept of modernity. For well over a century now, scholars and others have imagined and defined the world around them as in a state of "progress" toward a "modern" end.[16] As Latin American countries emerged from the founding violence of their independence struggles and as the unequal division of land ownership and labor continued along new socioeconomic lines, proponents of modernity celebrated the processes of industrial capitalism and nation building as the natural developments of an increasingly secular and industrialized world.

Early critics of modernity, including Marx and Weber, saw the darker side of this equation. In their view, along with the increasing rationalization and specialization of knowledge and skills came a world increasingly diminished in meaning, a place where "all that is solid melts into air" and human lives are transformed into commodified, powerless objects.[17] Both apologists and critics of the notion of modernity agree that a society becomes quintessentially "modern" when it becomes consumed by a notion of interminable development and the "restless forward movement of time and history."[18]

Yet, all of these approaches to understanding the phenomenon of modernity take for granted its genesis as a universal force of the "West."[19] This all too common formulation has been central to the theories of development articulated by scholars framing the relationships between developed and less-developed countries. In turn, these theories, premised on Western-centered assumptions of modernity, have helped shape the views of Latin America held by both scholars and policy makers. Beginning in the 1960s, critical theoreticians such as André Gunder Frank, Fernando Henrique Cardoso, and Enzo Falleto posited a radical revision of the diffusionist model of development in Latin America.[20] The diffusionist model maintained that the introduction of capital, technology, and trade would necessarily beget political and economic development in the region. The "dependency" or "world systems" models essentially established the inverse of diffusionism. While the newer theories acknowledged the agency of local actors and their history, they continued to do so within the same master narrative of dependency. Dependentistas retained the presupposition that the North/South, bipolar relationship elided regional, class, racial/ethnic, gender, and generational differences in favor of an overarching superstructure that controlled social and economic development. Based on metropolitan notions of modernity, both diffusionist and dependency theory discourses have situated the United States and other "central" countries at the helm of a "neocolonial" system.[21]

Moreover, including "peripheral" sites such as Oaxaca City as an area of capitalist development undoes Eurocentric notions that relate modernity to the metropolis alone. It illustrates that, whereas metropolitan modernity may be dominant, it should not serve as the self-proclaimed universal standard of modernity.[22] Theorists of development have viewed national capitals in Latin America as critical "insertion points" for the dissemination of modern economic and cultural capital. Consequently, academics have focused their research on large metropolitan areas. In Mexico, Mexico City has been viewed as the primary location of the country's encounter with modernity.[23] This profusion of Mexico City–centered literature has neglected provincial cities like Oaxaca de Juárez. The preferential treatment of national capitals over their provincial complements essentially recasts on an internal level the center/periphery and civilization/barbarism dichotomies asserted in theories of development.

In addition to undermining the notion of a universal standard, viewing modernity from the perspective of Oaxaca City also challenges the rigid polarity usually drawn between sites of "modernity" and sites of "tradition." The work of François-Xavier Guerra exemplifies this binary model. Guerra's powerful analysis of the political structures and transformations occurring during the Porfiriato posits individuals and institutions seeking a compromise between a Mexico that is, on the one hand, modern, individualist, and masculine and, on the other, collective, traditional, and feminine. The failure of these "two heterogeneous worlds" to reconcile ultimately led, in Guerra's formulation, to revolution.[24]

It is these rigid bipolarities of "modernity" and "tradition" that this study seeks to undo. Viewing modernity through a Oaxaca City–centered lens challenges and recasts the state capital's definition as a homogeneous, monolithic, and reified system. Inhabitants of the Emerald City simultaneously and mutually constructed modernity historically *with* tradition. Oaxacans, both elites and commoners, crafted and manipulated practices and notions of tradition and modernity in relation to one another to define themselves and their city as integral parts of a modern Mexico.

Modernity's central paradox lies in the fact that its proponents proclaim modernity as a universal and singular certainty while they elide its fundamental ties to tradition. This paradox also fuels modernity's enormous historical power to reproduce and expand itself. Cast as the only universal history, Western notions of modernity have successfully colonized the world insofar as every society must contend with the West's framing of civilization and progress.[25] Yet in an ironic inversion, modernity depends on the denigration of phenomena heterogeneous to itself, what Timothy Mitchell has called the "constitutive outside": the non-Western, the local, the other.[26] In other words, modernity is not somehow ontologically prior to tradition, but both are made in reference to each other.[27] Notions of the civilized and modern have been constructed in dialectic with images of the uncivilized and barbaric. More to the point, the disruption and dislocation of cultural and social practices caused by the processes of capitalist development generate the desire to construct new frameworks of modernity and tradition that will create meaning for those disruptions and dislocations.[28] It follows, then, that in order to understand the historically and geographically specific iterations of modernity we must examine the multiple ways modernity is negotiated at the local level and among so-called peripheral places and peoples. The "periphery" is an increasingly unsuitable term as it is incorporated into the fundamental definition of the "center." It is thus critical to integrate the universal metanarrative of modernity and its myriad constituent parts.[29]

The term *modernity* serves as an incomplete yet unavoidable all-inclusive shorthand for this complex historical process. Far from monolithic, Oaxaca's Porfirian modernity was fragmented along multiple lines characterized by contested understandings of class, gender, and race. The capital's inhabitants attempted to rebuild these fragments into a coherent structure and narrative that would signal and lead them into a more prosperous future. Yet, it was its fragmented nature in Oaxaca that disrupted modernity's claim to universality.[30] Modernity's dependence on local forms of difference undermined its unity, revealing the inherent weakness of dominant discourses and practices.[31]

Individuals and groups in Oaxaca City employed the practical and discursive elements of modernity to gain power in Porfirian society. While a dominant (but

not universal) modernity from Mexico City persisted during the Porfiriato, the
notion took on particular characteristics and outcomes when mediated by the inhabitants of Oaxaca City.[32] Throughout the era, city residents utilized the term
modern and its cognates, *civilization* and *progress*, when representing themselves in
the capital's transforming historical landscape. For the city's ruling elite, modernity was an essential part of Mexico's state formation, which involved including
the city in national projects of economic development.

In addition to describing the rational and ordered qualities of what they believed modernity was, elites also directly and indirectly worked to remove what
they believed modernity was not. In order to reinforce and maintain their hegemony in the state capital, Oaxaca City's ruling elites sought to construct a class-,
gender-, sexuality-, and race-specific modernity. Secular elites attempted to place
the city's workers, the lower-middle classes, women, and Indians at the margins
of their visions of the Emerald City.[33] They strove to control the city's popular
classes and the spaces in which they moved and lived.

The clearest expression of the elite attempt to relocate inhabitants within an
imagined space that was specifically Mexican and modern came in the characterization of, on the one hand, the city and its mestizo/white inhabitants as central
to the achievement of progress and, on the other, rural areas and their indigenous
populations as their supposedly traditional (and, by definition, "unmodern") opposite. With few exceptions, Mexico's elites – animated by Darwinian notions of
racial evolution – cast the country's contemporary rural and indigenous elements
as impediments to progress.[34] At the same time, Porfirian elites portrayed "traditional," pre-Columbian indigenous society as the unique, "authentic," and unchanged historical foundation of Mexico.[35] Although Guillermo Bonfil Batalla argues that the elites of "imaginary" Mexico could be found only in certain corners
of the larger cities, the same ambivalent "civilizing" rhetoric and practice he describes was prevalent in provincial Oaxaca City.[36]

Elites in Oaxaca City, influenced by foreign models and ideas but eager to assert their own visions of modernity, sought ways to attract capitalist investment.
They believed that in order to showcase their city and state to foreign governments in venues like the Crystal Palace at the 1908 World's Fair in London, they
needed to extirpate obstacles like vice, vagrancy, and sloth (supposed characteristics of the state capital's indigenous population and lower classes) and promote
"traditional" domestic values and a heroic interpretation of the nation's past.[37]
With this in mind, municipal politicians enacted reforms that sought, on the one
hand, to inculcate a work ethic among the city's laborers, and, on the other, to
stimulate consumer values broadly to drive the growing economy.[38]

If *modernity* was an ideological or cultural framework for Porfirian Mexicans, then the term *modernization* meant its implementation in the country's streets and institutions. To become "modern" the Porfirian government attempted to radically restructure ("modernize") all aspects of Mexican society. The Díaz government promoted advances in technology (transportation, communication, mechanization), economic liberalization, and the reform of the military and education. In constant negotiation with all sectors of the population, it rebuilt urban spaces and attempted to redefine their use (new public rituals and holidays) and restructure social and political relations in the hope of aligning citizens (white and male) to the emerging nation-state. Yet underlying all of this "Order and Progress" was a contradictory dependence on old social and political arrangements. This contradiction ultimately served to delegitimize Díaz's regime and fuel opposition groups, leading to the outbreak of the Mexican Revolution in 1910.[39] The uneven pace of economic development and the concentration of political power in the capital city prompted a disaffected, inchoate lower-middle class to demand more equal rights. That group's actions and the military opposition by peasant rebels from the neighboring Sierra Madre challenged the dominance of ruling elites.

The Eve of the Porfiriato

In the decade before Díaz became president of Mexico, Oaxaca City continued to suffer the effects of continuing skirmishes and battles initiated in the Reform era of the mid-nineteenth century.[40] During this period, L. L. Lawrence, the U.S. commercial agent in Oaxaca, wrote frequent dispatches to the Department of State in Washington describing the capital's precarious nature and warning U.S. citizens to stay clear of the ongoing imbroglio.[41]

Although Oaxaca's Porfirian-era historian Father José Antonio Gay wrote that the physical appearance of Oaxaca City had not changed significantly since the colonial period, its relative economic condition had.[42] Over half a century of bloodshed and political and economic instability had left the state capital in disrepair. In 1876, when Díaz triumphantly passed through Oaxaca City on his way to claim the presidency in Mexico City, his general, Fidencio Hernández, reported that a meager thirteen pesos and eighty centavos remained in the city coffers.[43] In the years prior, the central district's *jefe político* (political boss), Joaquín Mauleón, lamented the dismal condition of the state capital.[44] On the eve of the Porfiriato, Mauleón's annual report noted the lack of formal education of the city's poor, the rudimentary skills of workers, the absence of transportation routes and systems, and the general economic insecurity of all inhabitants. Furthermore, due to increased secularization and inadequate education, the citizens were demoralized, which, Mauleón claimed, often led to drunkenness and crime.[45]

During the Porfiriato the people of Oaxaca de Juárez experienced the transformation of their city. After years of renewed political stability and moderate financial recovery, the arrival of the Mexican Southern Railway supported a mining boom in the region and a period of economic and demographic growth. Amid much hoopla and fanfare, the first train pulled into the Oaxaca City station from Mexico City via Puebla on November 12, 1892. Local, national, and international politicians and dignitaries presided over three days of inaugural speeches and celebrations in the capital.[46] Governor Gregorio Chávez praised the new railroad and its potential to connect Oaxaca to world markets. "From today forward," Chávez wrote, "Oaxaca will no longer live in isolation from the world, forgotten by commerce, science, and the arts. The event [of the arrival of the Mexican Southern Railway], celebrated by all of Oaxaca, will be extraordinary in the state's history!"[47] Francisco Belmar's subsequent assessment of the moment went a step further. Belmar equated the arrival of the railroad with the advent of civilization itself: "After the last internal revolutions laid the foundation of peace in all the states of the Republic, the people, guided by the powerful and intelligent hand of General Porfirio Díaz, initiated an era of progress in all the branches of industry and human knowledge. The railroads broadened their dominions, and the locomotive's whistle was heard throughout the beautiful Valley of Antequera [Oaxaca], proclaiming the arrival of civilization in our land."[48]

The Mexican Southern Railway exemplified the integration of Mexico into the world capitalist marketplace.[49] Díaz and other Oaxacan natives invested heavily in the British-owned railroad. In addition to the mainline, several spurs reached out from Oaxaca City to connect with mining operations in the Central Valley. By 1910 and the end of the Porfiriato, the state counted 1,829 kilometers of new track.[50]

Yet it was not the train itself but what it carried that brought economic resurgence to the region. Oaxaca's mining industry had waxed and waned since the colonial era. During the Porfiriato, however, Díaz's government opened the country's mineral deposits to the world, igniting a boom in mining and bringing new economic prosperity to Mexico. Also in 1892, the federal government reformed the country's mining code to permit foreign ownership of the subsoil. This new clause reversed centuries of protectionism and sparked a flood in foreign investment.

The industry's owners depended for the most part on local indigenous labor to extract the gold, silver, and iron for export.[51] J. R. Southworth's touting of Oaxaca's "cheap" and "effective" Indian labor ignored the mine workers' miserable working conditions. At the same time, the mine owners and prospectors who made their home in Oaxaca City benefited from the large pool of indigenous laborers and artisans living in the capital, many forced there after the state subdivided and commodified a large portion of their communal lands during the Reform era of the mid-nineteenth century.

In Oaxaca, as elsewhere in the republic, entrepreneurs from the United States, France, and Britain dominated the mining industry. Although the size of Oaxaca's mines paled in comparison with their northern Mexican counterparts, mining greatly impacted the state capital by linking it more closely to international markets and the influence of foreign capital.[52] More than a hundred businesses had their mining offices in Oaxaca City.[53] Connecting the state to national and international markets, the mining industry radically shaped the capital's Porfirian history.

Method and Structure

In the chapters that follow, I analyze a series of interrelated and contingent themes within the Porfirian history of the city. I have tried to relate this history from multiple points of view without relinquishing the responsibilities and prerogatives of a narrator.[54] Although, for the purpose of analysis, I have separated into one chapter, for example, an examination of the formation of the capital's ruling elite and, into another, a discussion of the role of the Catholic Church and the city's workers, it is essential to keep in mind that each of these aspects of life in the city influenced the others and that all played out simultaneously.[55]

As the commercial and political hub for the region, the city was the site of much social and economic interchange. As municipal administrators expanded the capital into the surrounding areas, they hoped to tame the "uncivilized" character of the countryside. Although I focus on Oaxaca City as the site where the majority of the region's population interacted with the forces of modernity, I am not implying that the countryside was therefore its barbaric opposite.[56] Far from passive historical actors, citizens of indigenous towns and villages in the state's Central Valley mediated the forces of modernity in their own unique ways.[57]

I distinguish the eras before and after the arrival of the Mexican Southern Railway in 1892 as well as the years of Emilio Pimentel's governorship (1902–11). Each of these three periods witnessed an increasing interaction with the government's efforts to modernize the state capital.

The chapters that follow integrate multiple approaches to studying and "writing" the city. Chapter 1 examines how administrators on the city council interacted with state government officials and foreign and Mexican capitalists to forge an elite vision of modernity and a sustained hegemony. In addition to intermarriage and territorial and industrial ascendancy, ruling urban elites utilized tourism, print culture, and recreational activities to bolster their social status.

Chapter 2 turns to how elites conceptualized and implemented a class- and race-exclusive form of modernity in the streets and neighborhoods of the city. Officials utilized regulations and surveillance to confine the popular classes to increasingly peripheral areas. City administrators introduced new legislation, policing, mapping, and urban expansion to establish a visual order and rationalize the city in the positivist and nationalist spirit of the times, thereby rendering it more "legible."

Chapter 3 analyzes the little studied, renewed presence of the Catholic Church after years of anticlerical repression in the mid-nineteenth century and examines the critical role that the church played in shaping the modernity of the city, especially among the capital's workers. During the Porfiriato, scores of city dwellers renewed their faith in, and returned once-disentailed urban properties to, the Catholic Church. Drawing on a wide selection of documents, including church bulletins, newspapers, and the personal writings of Archbishop Eulogio Gillow, the chapter explores the critical relationship church leaders maintained with government officials and members of the Catholic Workers Circle in their attempts to resuscitate the church by integrating it into elite Mexican designs of modernity.

The next two chapters explore how new economic and political developments in the city upset the seemingly fixed and stable notions of gender, race, and sexuality. The chapters study in detail the development of the commercial sex trade and its integral role in the construction of the mutually defining discourses and practices of tradition and modernity. Chapter 4 examines the city government's attempts to define and regulate the trade. The industry's regulation reveals the attempt of Porfirian administrators to construct new myths along lines of race, gender, and sexuality. After discussing the era's reigning medical-legal notions of crime and deviance, the chapter explores how religious and political elites rendered the image of the "proper" woman and man. City officials debated ways to control the rapid influx of "dangerous sexualities" and to preserve the "decency" of the precarious institution of the family. Chapter 5 shifts the analytical focus to the different ways city officials and female sex workers utilized photographs in registries of prostitution and other elements of the capital's regulatory apparatus to harness dominant notions of modernity for their own separate ends. The chapter also disaggregates the different roles prostitutes and madams played in the sex trade; in so doing it provides an alternative to homogeneous descriptions of subaltern groups.

The year 1911 marked the beginning of the Mexican Revolution in Oaxaca City and the end of the Porfirian drive to modernize the state capital. The concluding chapter discusses the rapid decline of the city's industrial base and the growing divisions among local political groups leading to the Revolution. It also reflects on the historically determined use of public space in contemporary Oaxaca de Juárez. At a time when its elites and popular classes are struggling to construct meaning and order out of the seemingly incongruous phenomena of international tourism and movements for indigenous rights (both central forces in the daily life of the capital city), issues of legibility and visual order continue to be critical to the construction of modernity in the twenty-first-century Emerald City.

CHAPTER ONE

La Vallistocracia
The Formation of Oaxaca's Ruling Class

Let it be known to our people that in September the Caudillo of our Freedoms will
be among us.

— *Periódico oficial de Oaxaca*, 1892

In order to demonstrate how this class is a *ruling* class, it is necessary to specify
the modes in which its economic hegemony is translated into political domination: which means examining, among other things, processes of recruitment to
elite positions in the major institutional spheres, the relations between economic,
political and other elites, and the use of effective power to further define class
interests.

— Anthony Giddens, *Elites and Power in British Society*, 1974

The Emerald City's *Vallistocracia*, members of the state capital's upper and upper-
middle classes, put their visions of modernity into practice by mobilizing old and
developing new social and cultural forms to strengthen and perpetuate their rule.
By coordinating long-standing practices such as transnational business relationships and elite family intermarriage with modern cultural and media events as
diverse as playing baseball, engaging in tourism, and reading the newspaper, the
city's ruling elites moved beyond coercive methods to secure their positions of
privilege in the Porfirian city. The elite vision of modernity in Oaxaca City also
involved a simultaneous erasure of the capital's contemporary "traditional" (i.e.,
indigenous) elements and a celebration of the region's autochthonous past. City
elites incorporated long-standing and modern political practices with newly constructed cultural forms and discourses to become *ruling* elites.

This chapter is the first of two that explore the social, political, economic, and
ideological aspects of the elite class in the state capital. During the Porfiriato,
Oaxaca City elites translated economic and social privilege into dominant politi-

cal power to become ruling elites. The capital's ruling class, those in command of the local bureaucracy and tied into Díaz's federal political structure, consisted of members of both the upper and upper-middle class.[1] Anthony Giddens's study of elites in Britain and Romana Falcón's work on Mexican *jefaturas políticas* provide powerful conceptual frameworks for understanding the process of recruitment and the structure of the city's elite class through long-standing patron-client ties. Their work is also relevant here for its examination of how elites distributed power via "modern" cultural projects and affiliations.[2] Central to the formation of the capital's ruling class was the "governmentality" of Oaxacan elites, that is, as Colin Gordon glosses Foucault's term, the "way or system of thinking about the nature of the practice of government (who can govern; what governing is; what or who is governed), capable of making some form of that activity thinkable and practicable both to its practitioners and to those upon whom it was practised."[3] In other words, not only was the administrative structure of political power in the state capital critical to the formation of ruling elites, but so was its nature, how it was maintained through sociopolitical ties and cultural practices.

In chapter 2 we will see how elites reshaped the city according to their specific race-, class-, and gender-biased visions and practices of modernity to fortify their dominant status. Like the city's popular groups, elites neither comprised a unified block of individuals nor articulated a coherent vision of modernity. These two chapters also provide an on-the-ground, local case study of state formation and government power in modern Mexico. As showcases of Díaz's modernizing regime, state capitals like Oaxaca de Juárez were also regional power centers for the Porfirian government. For over thirty years Díaz built and maintained his regime from Mexico City through an interconnected hierarchy of political appointments from the presidency down to city administrators. Emphasizing economic prosperity and modernization, Díaz eagerly supported national and foreign business people in their efforts to bring world capitalism to Mexico.

Porfirian Politics in Díaz's Backyard

In 1866, the year following the bloody battle and fall of Antequera (Oaxaca City) to the troops of French imperial commander Marshal Bazaine, General Porfirio Díaz returned to reclaim the city of his birth. After securing a victory there he continued north to lead the final defeat of the occupation armies in the state of Puebla. Díaz was on his way to becoming Oaxaca's most celebrated son. A decade later in 1876, after his country had survived more than a decade of civil war, foreign interventions, lost elections, and the death of President Benito Juárez, Díaz seized the reigns of liberalism and rode triumphantly into Mexico City to begin his thirty-four-year rule over the republic.[4] Díaz's military and political credentials would make a lasting impression on the inhabitants of Oaxaca's state capital.

This chapter's first epigraph, celebrating the presence of President Díaz at the inauguration of the Mexican Southern Railway in September 1892, captures the dominant Porfirian attitude of the Emerald City's ruling elites toward Díaz. Recipients of Oaxaca's Juarista and Porfirian "dual legacy," elites in the capital city championed programs of economic modernization fostered by Díaz and his predecessor, Benito Juárez. Oaxaca's government leaders manufactured this unifying liberal myth to legitimize the rule of Porfirio Díaz as perpetuator of the Juárez legacy despite the historical antagonism between these two Oaxaqueños.[5] Díaz sustained his multidecade dictatorship largely by circumventing official electoral procedures and appointing loyal friends and colleagues to positions of political authority in federal and state governments. As the Porfiriato progressed, elites in Oaxaca City both benefited and suffered from their links to Díaz's federal government in Mexico City. Although following "official" state elections Díaz handpicked all of Oaxaca's governors, it was the election of Emilio Pimentel in 1902 that fused the most successful and debilitating aspects of the Díaz presidency. Pimentel was part of the new *científico* elite—a coterie of technocratic lawyers and officials that held prominent and influential positions (including four governorships)[6]—closely connected to Díaz and well supported by the state capital's foreign community.[7] During his tenure as governor (1902–11), Pimentel worked to recast the state and its capital into a showcase of modernity for the Porfirian regime. Owing to his modernizing plans, he and the state's oligarchy alienated and embittered the city's growing professional and commercial sectors, which would eventually rally against the excesses of the regime.

Although President Díaz claimed that he led a modern and democratic government, for most of its reign the Porfirian regime effectively closed the political system to opposition and, in positions like the *jefatura política* (office of district political boss), condensed and integrated functions usually differentiated in a modern state.[8] While espousing liberal values of autonomy and self-representation, it simultaneously supported long-standing structures of corporatism and patronage that had existed since the colonial era. In favor of economic development, Díaz and his government neglected the country's political democratization. The integration of paternalistic political structures and democratic political rhetoric characterized the history of Porfirian politics in Oaxaca City and helped to sustain Díaz's regime in the state capital and throughout Mexico for over three decades.

Like Mérida and other state capitals in Mexico, Oaxaca City played a critical role in the political architecture of the nation. State capitals were both the insertion points for federal policies and the centers of the states' political and economic cultures.[9] Because Oaxaca City was also the hometown of Díaz and Benito Juárez, its connection to Mexico City's political center was particularly strong. As president of Mexico in 1877, Díaz adeptly integrated members of the local and national Juarista opposition and groups of supporters into his new government. Díaz's ability to incorporate diverse liberal factions into one, pro-Díaz coalition grew in sophistication as he secured his political tenure for more than three decades. By 1902 Díaz had placed several of his Oaxacan *compadres* (to be sure, they were all men) in federal and state posts of authority throughout the republic.[10] Indeed, one pro-Díaz historian wrote that Oaxacans were for Díaz "what the Jesuits have been for the Pope, charged with sustaining the faith in the hero of peace, the doctrine of grace by reelection. . . . The Oaxacan privilege has lasted from 1858 to 1911, fifty-three years dominating Mexico!"[11]

In Oaxaca the president established a local version of his national oligarchy. Díaz structured his system of political power so that it emanated from his centralized position in Mexico City. The federal capital dominated the country's economic and political landscape. During the Porfiriato the federal government reclaimed Mexico City's economic primacy, which had been compromised during the nineteenth century's wars and struggles with the church, by locating all of the national banks and the Monetary Commission in the capital. Taxation of the states allowed this financial dominance. Mexico City attained its financial supremacy at the expense of the remainder of the country.[12]

As in other Mexican states, Oaxaca's elaborate government hierarchy facilitated Díaz's rule on the local level. Adopted from Oaxaca's state constitution, the *Manual de gobernadores y de jefes políticos* (Manual for Governors and Political Bosses) clearly outlined the different positions and responsibilities in the state's government. Mexico's states were (and continue to be) geopolitically divided into districts and municipalities. City councilmen (*regidores*) and trustees (*síndicos*) responded to a municipal president who, in turn, answered to a district's political boss (*jefe político*).[13] Appointed by President Díaz, the jefe político and state governor worked in conjunction to carry out the mandates of the federal government. Between 1876 and 1902 Díaz named loyal generals to the governorship of his home state.[14] Except for a four-month leave in 1882, Díaz himself governed the state from December 1881 to October 1883. During his tenure as governor, Díaz never broke stride as the de facto ruler of the country. Among the thousands of letters in the Porfirio Díaz Collection in Mexico City are dozens addressed to Díaz in Oaxaca City from 1881 to 1883. Top-level federal officials like Matías Romero and Manuel Romero Rubio continued to consult the governor on matters of national importance. For example, Matías Romero sought Díaz's help in obtaining initial financing for the Mexican Southern Railway from U.S. President Ulysses S. Grant, and

Romero Rubio queried the governor about the recent election of Mexican President Manuel González (1880–84).[15]

As president again after 1884, Díaz's influence over local Oaxacan affairs continued to increase. In January 1889, Díaz and Governor Albino Zertuche corresponded about material improvements in Oaxaca City. The letters provide an excellent example of the extent of Díaz's control over developments in the state capital. Speaking for the municipal councilman Francisco Colmenares, Zertuche requested assistance in improving the city's lighting system and slaughterhouse. Díaz's response was definitive: contact the American Gas and Water Company to carry out its recent contract with the government to better municipal public works and instruct Oaxaca City's council to construct their own slaughterhouse.[16] Many letters like these demonstrate President Díaz's role as arbitrator in local affairs. Ordinary citizens petitioned Díaz as both governor and president. In scores of notes, city residents requested financial assistance and employment for themselves and their relatives.[17] With the power to connect residents and city officials with the state government and international businesses, Díaz cemented his political dominance.

As residents of the state capital, Porfirian-era governors personally oversaw the expansion and reconstruction of the city. Annual reports by the governors attest to their intimate involvement in city affairs. More than just a recounting of the previous year's successes and failures, these reports prescribed actions for the coming year. In his administrative report of 1904, Governor Emilio Pimentel, emphasizing sanitation, discussed ways to improve public hygiene and outlined the contractual agreement with the Mexico City engineer Robert Gayol to conduct a preliminary study of the city's drainage system.[18]

Further complementing Díaz's personal extension of power in Oaxaca, the system of jefaturas políticas acted in conjunction with the governor to monitor and maintain control over local politics.[19] Díaz revamped the colonial-era jefaturas políticas system during his reign, using it to bolster his centralized, personalist rule in the state's districts and municipalities. As a former jefe político himself, Díaz realized how the position could bridge the local to the national, aiding the integration of states into the developing Mexican nation.[20] Although formally legalized in the Constitution of 1857, jefes políticos utilized patronage ties and informal methods of coercion to gain consent and power in state politics.[21] In Oaxaca's Central District, the location of Oaxaca City, President Díaz directly appointed the jefe político. Often military men or government administrators closely allied with Don Porfirio, jefes políticos of Oaxaca's Central District like Mariano Bonavides (1879–94), Colonel Priciliano M. Benítez (1898–1902), and Tirso Iñurreta (1902–8) influenced almost every aspect of life in the state capital. They directly controlled education, taxation, and public works, as well as oversaw the police force, prison system, and census reports.[22]

Jefes políticos also intervened directly in the lives of ordinary people. As mediators between municipalities and the federal government, jefes políticos played crucial roles in Mexico's inchoate process of state formation. In one case exemplifying their frequent involvement on the popular level, Tirso Iñurreta, the principal jefe político during Pimentel's term as governor, insisted on behalf of the residents of the sixth block of Armenta y López that the municipal government install a drainage pipe along the street. The urban railroad had been causing mud to build up in front of their homes. After a typical flurry of administrative wrangling, city officials agreed to have the railroad company construct the much needed drainage pipe.[23]

The Central District's jefes políticos played commanding roles vis-à-vis Oaxaca City's government. Before Tirso Iñurreta left the state for Mexico City on business in June 1907, he appointed the municipal president, Gildardo Gómez, to act as interim jefe político. In turn, Gómez temporarily assigned a city síndico to replace himself.[24] A decade earlier Priciliano Benítez had attempted to appoint the municipal president, Francisco Vasconcelos, to his position as jefe político. Benítez had hoped that Vasconcelos could take over the jefatura while simultaneously maintaining his original post as the head of the city's government. Although state authorities, including the governor, uncharacteristically rejected Benítez's administrative move, the effort was indicative of the tight political connections at the state and municipal levels. This fluid exchange of political positions enhanced the control by the jefes políticos and, hence, Díaz of the municipal government.

Intimately linked to Díaz's dictatorship, the municipal presidents of Oaxaca City not only closely followed the dictates of their jefes políticos but also participated in a corrupt municipal electoral system. Although in theory elected by a democratic majority (of men), municipal presidents were in fact installed by a small group of ruling elites. Municipal electoral records reveal that election counts considered only a minority of male voters in the capital's affluent center. In the 1905 municipal elections only 552 of 9,660 eligible voters cast their vote in 18 of the city's 66 electoral wards. Absent from the election rolls were votes from the city's lower-class neighborhoods. Tereso Villasante took the election over Gildardo Gómez with 534 votes to 18.[25] The mandates of the Federal Electoral Law concerning municipal elections further linked the fate of local political positions to national demands and aided in the manipulation of election results. According to Articles 13 and 14 of the 1901 Federal Electoral Law, the municipal president himself was the first to receive the uncounted ballots during an election. After the city secretaries counted the votes, the municipal president would review the count and announce the victor. Thus, these procedures provided the municipal president clear access to uncounted votes and a strong hand in determining the results.[26]

President Díaz's presence both directly and indirectly dominated local Oaxacan politics. His long reach was further strengthened by the loyalty of the city's politicians and elite industrialists, often one in the same.

La Vallistocracia and the Foreign Elite

At the beginning of the Porfiriato, a small but influential mixture of individuals from the upper and upper-middle class sectors formed the capital city's ruling class. This group, instrumental in shaping the city's encounter with modernity, included merchants (with ties dating back to the colonial era), liberal politicians, and two waves of European and North American immigrants.[27] This group occupied key positions in the city government. Oaxacan historians have dubbed this tight-knit group "la Vallistocracia" because of its location in the state's Central Valley and its extended position of political power in the capital city, throughout the state, and in the federal government.[28]

Drawn by the lucrative cochineal dye and textiles trade, foreign and Mexican merchants came to Oaxaca City in the colonial period and during the nineteenth century. Victorious military and political figures, emerging from the era of liberal reforms and government secularization promoted by Díaz, further populated the Emerald City's new Porfirian bureaucracy. Finally, foreigners, arriving in a first wave during the 1830s and a second in the 1890s, filled the ranks of the city's ruling class. Although predominantly from Spain, immigrants also arrived from Germany, Britain, France, Italy, Canada, and the United States.[29]

Throughout Porfirian Mexico, foreigners joined the ranks of local industrialists in large numbers.[30] In Oaxaca as elsewhere, the mining industry brought the vast majority of foreign nationals to the capital. Eager to acquire their own *pertenencias* (mineral rights equaling one hectare), foreigners arrived in droves at the beginning of the mining boom in 1892.[31] Before leaving the governorship of his home state, Díaz made sure to open the city and state to foreign investors. Díaz believed that the success of capitalist development depended on the "civilizing" touch of foreign industrialists and financiers. In his 1882 gubernatorial speech to the state executive he noted:

> The people of Oaxaca, like those of the entire Republic, have great competence in the arts and sciences. We should hope that the day is not far off when an extensive immigration of the sons of commerce from more civi-

lized countries arrives in our state. There will be a vast study of the many industries important to us. Those citizens [conducting the study] will provide us with the first step in the life of true progress, acquiring the good work habits and tastes that characterize the people of Europe.[32]

While foreign industrialists had long been welcome in the state, it was not until 1901 that interim governor Miguel Bolaños Cacho promulgated a new law granting financial concessions to individuals and companies that sought to expand industry in Oaxaca.[33] Succeeding Bolaños Cacho, Governor Emilio Pimentel accelerated the creation of new companies, principally mining enterprises, well into the final decade of the Porfiriato. The Vallistocracia eagerly welcomed foreign entrepreneurs they believed would bring vital technology and capital to the region. Indeed, like their counterparts in the state of Chihuahua, Oaxaca City elites served not only as intermediaries with foreign investors but also as independent entrepreneurs and active partners.[34] An article in the city newspaper La unión extolled the arrival of foreigners, their languages, and the "civilization" they symbolized:

> In the past, no other language was known in Oaxaca . . . today people can be heard speaking more than four languages, [a fact that] is ending the vulgar habit of our grandparents. In the past, signs for rooms for rent would read, "se alquila [for rent]." Nowadays [one reads]: "Chambres à louer," "Rooms to Rent," "Zimmer zu vermiten [sic]," all in the style of Europe's capital cities. Not everyone understands the terse phrases, but that is not the point. It is more important to hear that the words are harmonious, rich, and elegant, that they vibrate with cadences of civilization. . . . In effect, "Zimmer zu vermiten" is the sound of progress, advancement, and glory.[35]

The article ignores the diverse indigenous languages spoken throughout Oaxaca. Consistent with elite efforts to erase the capital's contemporary "traditional" elements (constructed as belonging to Oaxaca's past), the inclusion of only European languages implies that the state's indigenous languages could not be included in its measure of progress.[36] Furthermore, the emphasis on Europe's languages and capitals underscores the importance of national identity and Mexico's place in the world of nations.

Sons of the first wave of foreigners began to populate the ranks of industrialists in the city. Members of the Zorrilla, Trápaga, Allende, Grandison, and Baigts families, as well as new arrivals from the United States and Europe, contributed to the city's economic development. Foreigners occupied key posts in the capital. The U.S. consular agent, Charles Arthur, owned railroad lines in the Central District; British entrepreneur Constantino Rickards headed the buyers of La Natividad, the state's largest mine; and a German, Heinrich Heinrichs, worked as a merchant and as the German vice consul in Oaxaca. Several prominent French industrialists remained in the Central Valley following the Franco-Mexican War of the 1860s.[37]

Foreign Elites: The Case of the Zorrilla Family

The example of José Zorrilla Trápaga's family allows us to inspect closely the rise and diffusion of foreigners and their Oaxacan-born families into the capital's elite business and political life. As we have seen, Porfirio Díaz skillfully developed and took advantage of an extensive network of patron-client relationships. This system of *personalismo* enabled Díaz to maintain centralized control by having a hand in the local governments of Mexico's many regions. Local elites, negotiating this personalist system, strengthened Díaz's provincial ties and their own political power and thus fostered the political stability critical for Porfirian economic development.[38] The Zorrilla family was one of many such local power brokers.[39]

Unaware that he would start a family in Oaxaca City and spend the rest of his life there, José Zorrilla arrived in 1846 from Santander, Spain, and, as an experienced textile worker, joined his uncle, Juan Sáenz Trápaga, in the cochineal dye business.[40] Zorrilla managed to raise enough funds during the waning years of the cochineal industry to purchase the San Nicolas hacienda in the district of Zimatlán and later, with Trápaga, the textile factory San José in San Agustín Etla, seventeen kilometers from the state capital.[41] Zorrilla also partnered with the British entrepreneur Thomas Grandison and opened the San Agustín factory, La Soledad de Vista Hermosa, in 1884. On May 11, 1885, Zorrilla made his first delivery of blankets to Governor Luis Mier y Terán to distribute to the city hospital and orphanage.[42] Zorrilla's factory paid over six thousand pesos in taxes to the state government that year.[43] Located in the beautiful, lush hills of San Agustín Etla, the factory contributed to the development of the immediate area, which served (and continues to serve) as a favorite holiday spot for the city's affluent classes.[44]

Central to the consolidation of his family's economic and political power, Zorrilla widely diversified his business activities and socially integrated into other elite Oaxacan families. After marrying Josefa Tejada, inheritor of a sizeable family fortune, and parenting seven children (all Oaxacan born), Zorrilla started a second business, José Zorrilla and Company. Zorrilla's marriage into another wealthy family underscores the importance of gender in the formation of the capital's elite social networks. Although the city's business and political elites were predominantly male, many of them married prosperous women to expand their social and political power. Furthermore, these women, often active in the city's well-heeled social circles, devoted much of their time and energy to mothering the sons that would inherit their father's posts. Thanks to the adoption of new legal codes in the late nineteenth century, some women owned land and businesses in the city (see below). Although usually limited by their husbands' power, wives, widows, and single women participated in Oaxaca's growing economic climate.

Following the deaths of Zorrilla and Company's original cofounders, Juan Trápaga and Thomas Grandison, Zorrilla partnered with two of his sons, José Jr. and Federico. Backed by the Banco Nacional de México, José Zorrilla and Company helped to finance projects such as the Mexican Southern Railway and the Banco de Oaxaca and served as an import/export business in the city for products like coffee and tobacco.[45] The two brothers also married into wealthy and powerful Oaxacan families. When Zorrilla senior died in 1897, his sons took over and expanded the family business.[46] In 1903 Federico Zorrilla joined with Juan Baigts, a prosperous hacendado and miner from France,[47] to form yet another company. The two men signed a contract with the city to install a system of electric generators and lights in the capital.[48] That same year Federico Zorrilla, taking advantage of Governor Bolaños Cacho's taxation exemption law, also contributed to the construction of the Luis Mier y Terán Theater and Casino. The theater would become the capital's flagship of modernity, showcasing highbrow events and an in-vogue (i.e., French) architectural design.[49]

It was during these years of prosperity and relentless entrepreneurial activity that the Zorrilla family merged its business interests with prominent positions in city politics. After acting as *regidores* (councilmen) and state deputies, Federico and brother José later served as municipal presidents (Federico, 1900 and 1901; José, 1904) while simultaneously negotiating their family businesses. José Zorrilla Jr. also served as a federal deputy, became president of the Central Reelection Club of Oaxaca in 1910, an organization that defended the governorship of Emilio Pimentel, and served a term as state treasurer in 1915, when Oaxaca fought again to claim sovereignty from the republic.[50] The integration of politics and business was de rigueur in Oaxaca City politics. A list of commissioners for city projects like the Luis Mier y Terán Theater and Casino reads like a who's who of ruling elites. In addition to the Zorrilla family, the theater's board members included Emilio Pimentel, the Trápaga and Grandison sons, Miguel Bolaños Cacho, Juan Baigts, Guillermo Trinker, Constantino Rickards, and Jesús Acevedo.[51]

The story of the Zorrilla family demonstrates how foreign and Oaxacan elites combined politics and economics to become ruling elites in the state capital.[52] Intimately connected to the state and its leaders, elites like José Zorrilla and his relatives actively promoted the modern development of the city through projects such as electric municipal lighting and the elegant Mier y Terán Theater and Casino.

The Middle Sectors

Beneficiaries of elite patronage, a small and homogeneous group of professionals from the upper-middle class filled in the remaining ranks of the Vallistocracia. This group drew its members primarily from the medical and legal professions, a section of the population that expanded with Mexico's rapid economic growth during the Porfiriato. Most members of the city's upper-middle class were graduates of the prestigious Instituto de Ciencias y Artes del Estado de Oaxaca (Institute of Science and Art of the State of Oaxaca, or ICA); like their upper-class patrons, they were predominantly male. Founded in 1827, the ICA replaced the Catholic Seminario Conciliar as a key postsecondary institution in southern Mexico. As governor, Díaz increased funding to the school, as did Governor Pimentel, who also allocated two hundred thousand pesos for renovations. Prominent graduates of the Instituto included Benito Juárez, Porfirio Díaz, and Emilio Pimentel. Part of an expanding, more powerful Mexican middle class, ICA alumni served in key government and judicial positions in Oaxaca City and throughout the state. In the years before the Mexican Revolution (1910–20), Porfirian elites, ever restricting their ranks, began to exclude some of the up-and-coming graduates. Dissatisfied with their limited political mobility, many of these individuals helped to form the opposition to Díaz.[53]

Once hopeful to obtain access to political and social power, the city's lower-middle-class sectors, like their upper-middle-class counterparts, became disaffected with the Porfirian regime. Largely small-scale merchants and teachers, many of whom were immigrants, members of this heterogeneous sector possessed the educational and financial profile that allowed them to experience directly the exclusionary characteristics of Porfirian plans to modernize Mexico. It was during the years of Emilio Pimentel's governorship that the Vallistocracia both strengthened its political power and saw this challenged largely by the discontented lower-middle class, many of whose members joined the Mexican Liberal Party and Oaxaca's Juárez Association. This discontent would eventually lead to the undoing of the capital's ruling class on the eve of the Revolution.[54]

Recruiting Members, Reinforcing Rule

The ruling elite reinforced its political and economic dominance by developing and participating in a number of social and cultural aspects of life in the state capital. Principal residents of homes in the city's secular and sacred center and owners of the majority of the capital's property, elites recruited and retained their places in these exclusive ranks through social networks enabled by marriage as well as by athletic, artistic, and touristic events. Announcements and editorials in the Porfirian city's flourishing periodical literature further supported this cohesion by linking elites to one another and to larger currents of nationalism and capitalism.

Owning City Space

A list of key city government employees (deputies, councilmen, and legislators) in 1894 revealed that most lived within a one-block radius of the city square, or *zócalo*.[55] Moreover, an analysis of Andrés Portillo's masterwork *Oaxaca en el centenario de la independencia nacional* (1910) clearly demonstrates that a small number of ruling elites, many from the same families, dominated the ownership of land and properties throughout the state capital. In his block-by-block study of Oaxaca City, Portillo enumerates the properties in the capital, indicating their usage, ownership, and value. The work also compares statistics on property ownership from their study to a city census conducted in 1848. *Oaxaca en el centenario* reveals that 219 people owned 704 houses, or 35 percent of the city's 1,942 homes. In fact, a mere 25 families owned nearly 300 of those 704 houses (see table 1).

Although men certainly dominated the administration of the city's government, they by no means had exclusive control of economic life in the capital. A second look at Portillo's statistics shows that women accounted for almost 20 percent of the 219 prominent municipal property owners. Postindependence Mexico inherited a Spanish legal system that permitted women to sell property and enter into business partnerships. Emancipated single women and widows such as Guadalupe Fernández de Vasconcelos, Juana García Velasco, and the anonymously named "widow of Unda" all bought and sold property in the Porfirian capital.[56] Married women and daughters, however, remained legally beholden to their husbands and fathers. In 1870 and 1884 new legal codes recognized widows as legal heads of household and gave them guardianship (*patria potestad*) over children or wards.[57]

Findings in *Oaxaca en el centenario* underscore the dominant Porfirian trend in the city: thanks to a sustained period of economic growth, elites modernized the image of the capital by constructing new buildings and reordering spaces.[58] Both male and female members of the ruling class secured their exclusive status in the Porfiriato through ownership of most of the land and buildings in the city. A select group of families and individuals thus controlled the capital's property in addition to its political, economic, social, and cultural life.

Table 1. Number of Properties Owned by Prominent Families in Oaxaca City

Family	Number of Properties	Family	Number of Properties
Alvarez	9	Fenochio	16
Berges	11	Figueroa	6
Bonavides	26	Franco	7
Bustamante	9	Gil	16
Cajiga	8	Gris	4
Candiani	7	Heredia	16
Canesco	16	Hernández	11
Castro	9	Larrañaga	6
Cruz	15	Martínez	10
Cuevas	9	Meixueiro	9
Chapital	5	Mimiaga	10
Chávez	6	Zorrilla	3[a]
Esperón	37	Total	281

Sources: Portillo, Oaxaca en el centenario; Lira, "La ciudad de Oaxaca," appendix 9.
[a] The Zorrilla family also owned homes and factories elsewhere in the state.

Cultural and Social Networks

Oaxaca City's ruling elites employed a wide range of social and cultural networks to recruit and retain their members. As we saw with the Zorrilla family, marriage ties among elites and between foreign males and Oaxacan women reinforced their exclusive positions in the capital's society. Local newspapers celebrated the nuptials in lengthy articles describing the backgrounds and pedigrees of the married couples. The predominantly male foreign population in the capital strengthened its social ties by marrying local women and occasionally the daughters of other prominent foreigners. On July 26, 1908, the North American manager of the Detroit-Taviche Mining Company, Frederic Wallace Woolrich, married Annie Heinrichs, the daughter of the German consul, at the city's Episcopal Church. Many members of the German and U.S. colonies as well as local Oaxacan officials attended the wedding.[59]

Tourism

During the Porfiriato city elites also considered what incentives, in addition to economic ones, they could offer to lure foreigners to the provincial city. Touristic visions of the Emerald City depended on mutually constructed notions of tradition and modernity, discourses that came into existence at the same time and against each other. By simultaneously promoting and juxtaposing the state's "traditional" indigenous cultures and "modern" economic and infrastructural developments, the government turned the capital itself into a touristic commodity that attracted foreign visitors and highlighted the modern cast of the state capital.[60] The tourist industry in Oaxaca City began to develop after the arrival of the Mexican Southern Railway in 1892. An article in the newspaper El Estado de Oaxaca celebrated the arrival of twenty-five American tourists to the capital and provided details of their itinerary.[61] Hoping to lure travelers to the southern city, the Mexican Southern Railway Company as well as local business and hotel owners printed advertisements in Mexico City newspapers celebrating the vestiges of the region's indigenous temples and population centers. One advertisement appeared daily in the Mexican Herald, Mexico's most prominent English-language newspaper. It read:

> Mexican Southern Railway. Daily Service to Tehuacán, Oax. and Southern Mexico. Only route to the famous ruins of Mitla. The Mexican Southern traverses beautiful scenery and Oaxaca City is situated in a perfect climate 5000 feet above sea level; is never subject to extremes of temperature, and coast fevers are unknown. It is within easy reach of the Big Tree of Tule, the Ruins of Mitla and Monte Albán, and the many prosperous mining camps of the state. Cheap round trip tickets, good for fifteen days, entitle holder to stay off in Tehuacán, which is becoming better known daily on account of its mineral waters and bathing establishments.[62]

The advertisement seamlessly imbeds a promotion for the state's mining industry with images of natural (climatic) beauty and the indigenous past. This effective intersection of natural tropes — a pristine nature ripe for exploitation — is a clear example of the elite discourse of modernity that creates or imagines zones of "tradition" that can then be appropriated, consumed, and exploited.

In his El Estado de Oaxaca (1901), J. R. Southworth reported that, thanks to the railroad, thousands of visitors came annually to the capital, many of whom stayed and became investors in the mining industry.[63] Of course, the impact of tourism extended beyond the city's moneyed classes. As we will see, like tourism promoters, elites attempted to remove traces of the popular classes from the city's center. Yet, the arrival of wealthy tourists ironically attracted "vagrants." Alongside touristic announcements in local newspapers, articles ran describing the public "nuisance" of vagrants approaching tourists for money. The Oaxaca Herald reprinted one article from the San Antonio Express that referred to

> a peon lad with a mangy pup under his arm [who had] stopped this friend (who believes he is fully familiar with all of the customs of this land) on the

street recently, and offered the whining canine for the absurd price of five dollars. My friend looked like a "tourista" and any peon boy or girl over six years of age knows the significance of the title, as well as Americans' liberality, and will resort to genuine grifting principles to extract a few reales from the stranger.[64]

Although Oaxaca City had been a favorite stop for European and North American travelers since the colonial era,[65] it was during the Porfiriato that elites first developed tourism to attract foreigners and their money. Throughout Mexico, tourism was encouraged as a means not only to bring foreign dollars to the republic but also to increase the "civilizing" foreign presence.[66] Decades before the archaeologist Alfonso Caso "discovered" Monte Albán and the riches of Tomb Seven, the region's most notable precolonial sites, Oaxacan elites had begun to typecast the capital and its surroundings as a timeless locale of precolonial delights, hypocritically celebrating the state's "traditional" indigenous "past" while erasing its present existence. The *Oaxaca Herald* described excursions to see "the wonderful monuments of a forgotten race so wonderfully preserved on Monte Albán."[67] These stereotypes persist to this day, reinforced by the annual Guelaguetza extravaganza and fueling what is now the state's most lucrative industry.[68]

Sports and Leisure Activities

Nineteenth-century Latin American policymakers recognized the importance of entertainments and public diversions to the creation of cultural modernisms in their new nations. Like the colonial "social engineers" of the Bourbon period, the new Latin American elites sought to inculcate values they considered more compatible with the ideology of the time, namely, positivism and a fascination with European culture. The new pastimes, generally promoted in the capital cities and often linked to issues of hygiene and public safety, were devised to control the passions of the lower orders and encourage rational and ostensibly modern behavior.

—Fanni Muñoz Cabrejo, "The New Order: Diversions and Modernization in Turn-of-the-Century Lima," 2000

Participation in leisure and athletic activities helped foreign and domestic Porfirian elites to cultivate their exclusive social status in the city. Common pursuits among the ruling classes throughout Mexico, European and North American pastimes increasingly filled the recreational schedules of Oaxaca City's ruling class.[69] These events simultaneously helped to unite the capital's elites into a cohesive social group and provided the means with which to display ostentatiously their notions of a modern society while simultaneously positioning themselves apart from activities they deemed as "uncivilized."

Unlike its counterpart in Mérida, the capital of the state of Yucatán, where, by the end of the Porfiriato, baseball had become a regional pastime for elite and popular classes alike, baseball and most other organized sports in the Emerald City remained events for the *gente decente*.[70] In his study on sport in Latin America, Joseph Arbena contends that athletic events provide us with a lens through which to view the development of capitalism in the region.[71] In Oaxaca, elites utilized sports to showcase their developing relationship with capitalism and modernity, juxtaposing certain "modern" events against other "uncivilized" ones. While the city's affluent class trumpeted baseball and *automovilismo* (automobile touring) as the epitome of civilized and civilizing activities, they contrasted them with other "barbaric" sports such as soccer, which they disparaged as "violent and occasionally brutal." According to an article titled "Sport and Its Utility" in *Oaxaca progresista*, a conservative magazine published during the Pimentel era, baseball was "the most complete and pure of sports," and automovilismo reigned as the "aristocratic sport par excellence." Furthermore, automovilismo connected the wealthy with technological modernization. It "introduced rich people to the physics of mechanics, brought them in contact with the factory, and encouraged them to appreciate and protect engineering." The same article espoused the civilizing and revitalizing properties of sport: "Rooted in every social class, today sports form a part of our education. Men and even women have begun to practice them, adding to their grace and refinement. Thanks to tourism and automobile touring, the roads have been open to the pueblos allowing us to get to know the countryside, saturating us with air, sun, and freedom. Sports have brought with them exercise. All sports strengthen the muscles and calm and stretch the nerves."[72] Tourism and the automobile thus provided elites the means with which to "know" the city's surroundings, to interact temporarily with the indigenous villages on the outskirts before returning to the civilization of the Emerald City. As such, these "leisure activities" had an important side or "instrument-effect," as they also served to extend the geographic reach of the Vallistocracia.[73]

After the beginning of the twentieth century, elites began to celebrate baseball, which had been brought to Oaxaca in the late nineteenth century by North American investors, as the capital's most popular sporting event. Baseball teams formed in the city and around the Central Valleys with names like Sur, Ocotlán, Filadelfia, and Los Gillow (named for the city's archbishop). On January 13, 1907, the first game between an entirely Mexican squad and a North American team took place in the capital. In an unusual reversal of fortune, the Mexicans handily defeated their foreign rivals. Matches regularly drew large crowds of "distinguished ladies and gentlemen" from Oaxaca's high society.[74] Elites sponsored other athletic activities including tennis and bowling. Sporting events became so popular in the city that, in February 1907, Marcelino Muciño, a baseball enthusiast and journalist from the state of Puebla, published the magazine, El score, which he claimed was the first sporting paper in Mexico not entirely dedicated to bullfighting.[75] In 1909 North American and British residents formed the Oaxaca Tennis Club to promote this game in the capital.[76]

By the end of the Porfiriato yet another elite pastime had hit the streets of the Emerald City: bicycling. Advertisements for the latest imported models began to appear in city newspapers. Although shipped from Europe and the United States via Mexico City, enough bicycles made it to Oaxaca to allow affluent residents to start the Oaxacan Cycling Club for "committed young folk and casual riders."[77] Bicycles must have appeared ostentatious and even strange to the majority of citizens in provincial Oaxaca. In Porfirian Mexico City, the bicycle came to represent modernity and with it notions of technology and progress. Cycling clubs in Mexico City promoted the bicycle's speed and the competitive and rational aspects of racing and record keeping.[78] The bicycle eventually became "a metaphor for the dictator's policy of modernism [and] remained a safe target for criticism." In his mordant political cartoons in Mexico City newspapers like El hijo de Ahuizote, José Guadalupe Posada employed images of the bicycle to ridicule the decadent habits of the ruling class.[79]

During the Porfiriato, Oaxaca City elites reinforced their dominant status in the state capital by developing social ties and through activities with other members of the ruling class. Foreign and domestic elites cultivated leisure activities such as sports and social events in places like the new Mier y Terán Theater in order to display and inculcate values of "civilization" and "progress."[80] As Muñoz Cabrejo argues, "The enthusiasm for sports . . . came to signify not only modernizing elites' emulation of European society, but also their program for using modern sports to form the ideal bourgeois man: autonomous, virile, healthy, slender, and clean (because sports became linked to personal hygiene)."[81] There was, of course, a pronounced gender dimension to the development of modern sporting activities in the city. For elites, sports like automovilismo and bicycling provided an "institutional setting" in which to display a more refined sense of masculinity in contrast with "uncivilized" sports like soccer.[82] If the middle and upper classes wished to keep abreast of all the sport, tourist, and leisure activities that the city had to offer, they could turn to the state capital's increasingly numerous periodicals.

Periodicals

No one, wise Kuublai, knows better than you that the city must never be confused with the words that describe it. And yet between the one and the other there is a connection.

— Italo Calvino, *Invisible Cities*, 1972

This is the age of the newspaper in Mexico. Ten times as many printed sheets are sold here as was the case 20 years ago. The coachman on his box reads his paper, often the same journal as that which meets the eye of the banker or the merchant. [As] the rural parish priest takes his morning chocolate he turns over the pages of his favorite clerical journal, which consults his prejudices, attacks the foes of his faith, and combats modern tendencies.

— *Oaxaca Herald*, July 1, 1909

The above quotation from the *Oaxaca Herald*, although perhaps overzealous in its attempt to claim a wide readership, speaks to the eruption of print media in Mexico during the Porfiriato.[83] During the Díaz era, at least 171 separate periodicals, a fivefold increase over the previous half-century, were published in the state of Oaxaca, the majority in the capital.[84] The proliferation of print media in the provincial city of Oaxaca de Juárez not only allowed elites to "read" the city and to imagine themselves as part of a coherent entity and as part of the broader Mexican nation and world; it also provided a venue for elites to invent and assert themselves as modern citizens. Furthermore, periodicals, by introducing readers to a culture of consumption, connected them to the expansion of capitalism. As the epigraph by Italo Calvino suggests, there is an intimate link between a city and its texts. As we will see in the cases of the photograph and the camera, periodicals emerged in full force in Oaxaca during the Porfiriato. The newspaper and its glossy cousin, the magazine, at once represented elite designs to modernize the capital and were an integral part of them. As Benedict Anderson has argued, mass media provided literate citizens with a vehicle through which to imagine and participate in a shared community.[85] Aside from a relatively minor politically liberal voice, the particular community in question was one articulated by and for the ruling class. Mobilizing the Emerald City's media along the lines of modernity, politics, and religion, government and church leaders utilized periodicals to promote and sustain their positions of power. Indeed, the sheer quantity of print material littering the streets and newsstands of the capital must have been a compelling visual reminder of the elites' privileged place in society.

After Mexico City and Puebla, Oaxaca de Juárez was the third municipality in

New Spain to begin printing its own publications. As early as 1720, Doña Francisca Flores, under the auspices of the Dominican order, established a printing press in the city's San Pablo convent to produce ecclesiastical literature.[86] In 1823 Lorenzo Aldeco set up the first government press in the capital. Aldeco used the press to print a series of decrees and orders by the state government. Although other small presses existed during the nineteenth century, it was not until the early 1870s that men like Lorenzo San Germán and Ignacio Candiani started the wave of modern printing. By 1890 there were more than a dozen printers in the city publishing a wide range of periodical materials.[87]

Newspapers and magazines were not the only forms of printed material that abounded during the Porfiriato. Broadsheets, posters, photographs, and, eventually, illustrated periodicals also found their place in the surge of new urban texts in the state capital. These texts helped to make the city more legible for their readers by orienting them in relationship to one another and to the city spaces in which they lived and worked. As David Henkin has pointed out, it is not simply academic fetishism for the written text that makes the periodical so attractive. The sheer number of periodicals published during the Porfiriato makes them invaluable primary sources for the urban historian. For historians (like the Porfirian Oaxacans themselves) periodicals serve as "indispensable guides and apt symbols for a new kind of public life."[88]

There is a central paradox to the dramatic increase in periodical publications in Oaxaca. Unlike places such as New York City, which during the antebellum era claimed close to 96 percent literacy,[89] during the Porfiriato the state of Oaxaca was one of the most illiterate in the country. In 1910, not only did the state register a 91 percent illiteracy rate, it also had the highest percentage of monolingual speakers of indigenous languages in Mexico.[90] Yet conditions were different in the state capital. According to city census records, even in the poor, peripheral sections of the city, approximately one-quarter of the population was at least semiliterate (i.e., it could read but not write). In central areas around the zócalo the only illiterate people were the servants in elite households.[91] The 1895 federal census recorded that of the city's 27,730 inhabitants over the age of six, 14,782 could read.[92] Therefore, in Oaxaca City there existed sufficient literate and semiliterate individuals to sustain an expansion of the publication industry. The largest papers of the era claimed a circulation of two thousand to three thousand readers.

Taken as a whole, publications in Porfirian Oaxaca City can be organized around three central themes: modernity, politics, and religion. Publications such as the state's and city's official government papers and *Oaxaca moderno*, *Oaxaca progresista*, and the *Oaxaca Herald* were written by and for the ruling class. Although these types of papers existed throughout the Porfiriato, their heyday was during Pimentel's governorship in the first decade of the twentieth century. The periodicals focused on the description, celebration, and development of the city's "modern" quality. Stories and editorials on the "new and improved" Oaxaca abounded alongside pages of advertisements for the latest consumer product and highbrow affair. One commentator from La unión captured the moment dramatically: "Oh civilization! In our impure times, loaded with rancid concerns and disturbing atavisms, we work just to watch it all go by. However, it is a question of waiting patiently for what heralds our future. Newspapers and more newspapers; advertisements and more advertisements; mines, banks, machines; all of these lead us undoubtedly toward our future well-being."[93]

Weekly papers and magazines provided ruling-class Oaxacans with a medium to imagine their city in the abstract. The continual literary reconstruction of the city provided an "imagined community" in which the elite saw themselves.

The city's only English-language paper, the Oaxaca Herald, epitomizes the papers that highlighted modernity and progress. Started by representatives from its Mexico City counterpart, the Mexican Herald, the Oaxaca Herald claimed to be "published further South than any other publication in [English] and . . . the only publication in English between Mexico City and Buenos Aires."[94] As with other newspapers of its kind, the Oaxaca Herald centered its reporting and editorials on the mining industry. The paper's editors, Paul Wooton and A. J. Morcom, credited the state's mining boom with increasing the number of subscribers and the amount of purchased advertisement space. In addition to information on the business of mining, the Oaxaca Herald ran editorials on upcoming sporting events and leisure activities, gave advice on the "proper" behavior of women, celebrated the social and political lives of the capital's ruling elite, and promoted the latest consumer goods.[95]

Porfirian-era periodicals played a key role in propagating a new consumer culture among the middle and upper classes. Newspapers encouraged consumers to purchase the "correct" goods, those that would promote their "modern" image. In turn, manufacturers tied products to notions of nationalism and progress. This deliberate construction of a consumer paradise became another aspect of modernity, one accessible only to the moneyed classes.[96] While most Oaxacan papers were riddled with advertisements for clothes, furniture, machinery, services, and the newest luxury items from the United States and Europe, one paper, El eco mercantil: Semanario de comercio, noticias, variedades y avisos (The Commercial News: Weekly of Commerce, News, Variety, and Ads), paid specific homage to the growing consumer society. Its editors dedicated over half of each edition to advertisements and national and international stock market reports.

Newspapers were in many respects the quintessential modern urban form. Designed for mass consumption, they contained the unique marketing value of a single-day shelf life. Furthermore, newspapers embodied the simultaneous display of "traditional" and "modern" forms of communication. The daily replaced once-intimate exchanges of gossip with provocative columns and editorials.[97] Indeed, Oaxaca's papers were rife with tabloid-style sections on the day's social transgressions, criminal activities, and lists of attendees at the most recent gala. All of these qualities, reflected in the majority of Oaxaca's periodicals, simultaneously constructed and then juxtaposed notions of tradition and modernity in order to support the ruling class's self-presentation as the champion of progress. Rare was the publication of an article challenging, let alone criticizing, the city, state, or federal government. These papers served as strategic apologists for the Porfirian regime.

Although some short-run government opposition papers such as El amigo del pueblo (1879) and El cometa (1878) were published in Oaxaca during the Porfiriato, most opposition was ephemeral. Victims of the Porfirian municipal government, opposition periodicals had a short life. When Víctor Vargas published El huarache (1881), a paper at odds with Governor Martín González's administration, the government closed the press, threw him in jail, and forced him to serve as a soldier in a battalion of the state's army.[98] Worker's papers also were short-lived in the capital city. Oaxaca labor organizations lacked what María Elena Díaz calls Porfirian Mexico City's "vigorous sense of working-class consciousness." Dominated by the Catholic Church and government elites, workers in the state capital remained relatively powerless in city politics and thus unprepared to produce any publications.[99]

It was not until the advent of newspapers like El bien público (1905) and La voz de la justicia (1907) that opposition weeklies managed to gain a tentative foothold in the city's print culture.[100] Responding to the graft and corruption in Pimentel's positivist government, these papers sought to give voice to growing and increasingly disgruntled middle-class groups. They struggled to stay in print as they came under constant attack from the city administration. The editors of La voz de la justicia admitted that editions would "come out when possible since being a liberal paper we come up against many difficulties."[101] Originally the official organ for the liberal, upper-middle-class Juárez Association, the paper eventually radicalized against the Pimentel regime. Articles from El bien público appeared in Filomeno Mata's well-known Mexico City paper, El diario del hogar, as well as other national oppositionist periodicals. Ismael Puga y Colmenares and Heliodoro Díaz Quintas, members of its editorial board, rose to become key figures in the

Oaxacan revolutionary movement. The government eventually fired them from their posts in the Instituto de Ciencias y Artes because of their writings and anti-Pimentelista leanings.[102]

Explicitly progovernment papers were, of course, abundant. Supporters in re-election clubs published several papers during Pimentel's governorship. Periodicals like La unión and La democracia extolled the governor's policies and celebrated him as a modern man of letters. Unsurprisingly, it was José Zorrilla along with Fausto Moguel who started the pro-Pimentelista paper El voto público: Organo del Club central reeleccionista de la ciudad de Oaxaca (The Public Vote: Organ of the Central Reelection Club of the City of Oaxaca). The paper also supported the 1910 re-election of Porfirio Díaz and Ramón Corral for president and vice president.[103]

Religious newspapers produced by both the Catholic and Protestant communities of Oaxaca de Juárez comprise the third thematic group of periodicals published during the Porfiriato. In his description of the arrival of the national paper El país to the town of San José de Gracia in the state of Michoacán in 1900, Luis González echoes the tensions that existed between religious and secular publications in Oaxaca City. He writes:

> Padre Castillo tried to hold back the avalanche of news and inventions. He absolutely forbade women to read the newspaper. For those who enjoyed such things he provided religious texts. But both men and women who could read continued, with no diminution of piety, to pursue El país and astound themselves with the gramophone, the sewing machine, the "views" of the stereoscope, and the camera. It was probably the newspaper that brought the new styles in dress and ornament to San José. It was undoubtedly because of El país that political arguments sprang up among the villagers.[104]

Religious papers like the Protestant La bandera del evangelio and the Catholic La voz de la verdad engaged in caustic diatribes against each other's faith and rhetoric. Periodicals from both religions fought what they perceived as a dangerous attack on the time-tested traditions that held Oaxacan society together. For them modernity meant foreign imposition (European and North American) and the erosion of fundamental morals and values. The most popular paper of this category, La voz de la verdad, served as the official voice of the influential Archbishop Eulogio Gillow and the city's largest worker association, El Círculo de Obreros Católicos (the Catholic Workers Circle).

Conclusions

Despite repeated claims of recreating Oaxaca City in the modernist vision of the times, the capital's ruling class perpetuated and reinforced long-standing socio-political structures passed down from the colonial and independence eras. This approach to politics ultimately helped seal the ruling class's fate as disaffected middle sectors began to feel that their short-lived power and status in society had been eroded by the Porfirian and Pimentelista regimes. Workers had even less access to power within this exclusivist regime.

The elites of Oaxaca City used not just coercion but also an alliance of social relations and cultural practices to fashion their governmentality. The city's ruling class did much more than simply appear on the scene; throughout the Porfiriato it took part in its own formation, simultaneously constructing and mobilizing discourses and practices of tradition and modernity to secure its privileged place in society. Through an intricate combination of foreign and local business partnerships and family alliances, the elite controlled city politics and the flourishing mining industry. The elites' use of tourism, sports, leisure activities, and a burgeoning print media reinforced their dominant presence in the state capital. As ruling elites these individuals also imbued the city's spaces with the characteristics of Díaz's modernizing regime.

CHAPTER TWO

The Legible City

Constructed, Symbolic, and Disciplined Spaces

Walking through Oaxaca City's streets at the beginning of the twentieth century, a veteran of the devastating 1870 earthquake would have been amazed at the ongoing changes.[1] Government and private investors had constructed new buildings, roads, parks, and sewer systems. Lighting and telegraph poles dotted parts of the city while tramlines crisscrossed neighborhoods on their way from the Mexican Southern Railway station to newly developed suburbs. Increasingly throughout the Porfiriato, government officials, through new regulations and public works, sought to transform the urban spaces of the state's capital. In so doing, they attempted, in the words of James Scott, to make the city "legible," to simplify it into an "administratively more convenient form."[2] Furthermore, increasingly rationalizing the city's spatial arrangements meant countering the perceived problematic illegibility, the politically autonomous, decentered, and ungovernable quality of unregulated spaces.[3] Elites hoped to ease their anxieties generated by Porfirian modernization. They envisioned that the advent of new neighborhoods, buildings, maps, regulations, police forces, and the like would tame the disorder inherent along the city's path to "progress."

Elites sought, in a sense, to rewrite the city as a readable text infused with the nationhood and modernity they so desired for their country. Therefore, officials did not merely extend streets into new *colonias* (municipal districts) past the city's frontier; they renamed, adorned, and celebrated them with symbols of a heroic past and a prosperous future. In other words, in order to lend meaning to Oaxaca City's modernity, they simultaneously invented historical traditions that linked them to their precolonial ancestors and untied them from the religious symbols of the preindependence period. Elites, attempting to reinforce their positions of power, conceived of and organized city spaces to reflect their dominant, class- and race-exclusive form of modernity. For them, spaces in the capital (constructed and cleaned with the labor of the popular class!) were to be hygienic, orderly, secularized, didactic, and, above all, rational. City police forces were formed and expanded to surveil sections of the city while urban planners mapped and re-mapped the urban landscape, each time reinventing it as more modern than the time before. As city coffers grew, officials enlarged their bureaucracy and endeavored to increase their control over the inhabitants of the Emerald City with scores of new regulations. Elites reshaped and increasingly regulated the city as part of a vision of modernity that confined nonwhite workers to the city's margins. Although government officials carried out these modernization projects throughout the Díaz era, the projects became increasingly important following the arrival of the Mexican Southern Railway and the boom in the mining industry in 1892. It was, however, during the governorship of Emilio Pimentel (1902–11) that the schemes to modernize the city took hold. In order to highlight the government's attempts to implement these projects, this chapter focuses on central themes in urbanization while moving across this time period. By the end of the Porfiriato these exclusionary projects served to alienate further the disaffected middle-class groups and to galvanize their opposition to the aging Porfirian regime.

For Porfirian elites (like their independence- and colonial-era predecessors), cities were the apotheosis of their modernizing ideals.[4] While urban planners in the United States adhered to Jeffersonian notions of American pastoralism, a predominantly agrarian bias that sought to balance the benefits of rural living in an urban context, Mexican elites viewed the city as the sole site of civilization.[5] In his path-breaking study of Mexico City, Mauricio Tenorio-Trillo points out that "the ideal view of modernity [was] understood as harmonious and peaceful economic development, progress and science. The best embodiment of this ideal was the modern city—which contained the proofs of the nation's pedigree: economic progress and cultural greatness, but which was also sanitary, comfortable and beautiful."[6] While the state of Oaxaca's new factories, haciendas, and plantations like the Vista Hermosa factory in San Agustín Etla existed as smaller, discrete sites of economic development, for provincial elites, Oaxaca City was the prime example of the modern urban center for the region.

Elites in Oaxaca City altered and adorned the city's spaces and imbued those spaces with symbols of progress, nationhood, and modernity in relationship to the capital's human geography. The ideological hallmarks of Porfirian state formation reached well beyond the nation's metropolis to small state capitals like Oaxaca City, relatively contained spaces in which state government officials could promote their ideals of modernity and progress. After expanding, sanitizing, and adorning spaces in the capital, city officials treated the city symbolically by organizing secular celebrations, by mapping, by erecting street signs, and by disciplining urban spaces through police surveillance and administrative regulations.

Time and Space in the Emerald City

Space does not merely display itself to the world, as if it were somehow ontologically prior to the cultural and semiotic codes through which its existence is expressed. Such myths of mimesis turn the historical into the natural, concealing its
social, cultural and political underpinnings.
                    —Raymond Craib, *Cartographic Mexico*, 2004

Space, too often considered as always already there, is in fact a socially constructed
phenomenon, garnering meaning through a multiplicity of human practices.[7]
David Harvey argues that "space . . . gets treated as a fact of nature, 'naturalized'
through the assignment of common-sense everyday meanings. In some ways
more complex than time—it has direction, area, shape, pattern and volume as key
attributes, as well as distance—we typically treat it as an objective attribute of
things which can be measured and thus pinned down."[8] Space is far from an in-
consequential aspect of society's historical development. The historical construction of space critically determines relations of power and discipline and helps to
infuse daily life with political and ideological meaning.[9] As we will see in chapters 4 and 5, space was also organized along gendered lines, where the personal
became political in the contested site of the prostitute's body.

More so than with time, the alteration of urban spatial arrangements was essential to the experience of modernity in the Porfirian state capital. While systems
and rhythms of time began to change with the advent of train schedules, secular
civic festivals, electric lighting, and the like, Oaxaca City largely retained its pre-
Porfirian sense of diurnal and nocturnal meter. Since the city's workforce was still
largely preindustrial, the deliberately regimented fragments of time that characterize industrial societies barely existed. This is made all the more apparent by the
dearth of documents in the municipal archive concerning the regulation of work
according to time schedules.[10] E. P. Thompson notes that "attention to time in
labour depends in large degree upon the need for the synchronization of labour.
But insofar as manufacturing industry remained conducted upon a domestic or
small workshop scale, without intricate subdivision of processes, the degree of
synchronization demanded was slight, and task-orientation was still prevalent."[11]
Cycles of the ecclesiastical calendar continued to dictate the daily ebb and flow of
time in the city. The regular sounding of church bells and the perpetual agenda
of Catholic festivals persisted throughout the Porfirian era. In May 1890, the city
government posted a placard displaying a regulation on bell ringing. The ordi-
nance indicated that church bells "can ring the hour of day (6:00 a.m., 8:00 a.m.,
12:00 p.m., 2:00 p.m., 3:00 p.m.), as well as in case of fire, calls to Mass, and for

national festivals. Any other ringing cannot last more than five minutes."[12] This
moderate temporal pace in the capital city remained largely unchanged from the
mid-nineteenth century until the Porfiriato.[13]

By contrast, the organization of space by elites and city planners in Oaxaca City
was a deliberate political act designed to reinforce their dominance in society. In
their daily lives, depending on their position in the urban landscape, residents
of the city experienced spatial arrangements in different ways. By the eve of the
Revolution, alterations to municipal roads, building facades, private houses, and
public parks had transformed the capital city's appearance radically from the early
days of the Porfiriato.

Constructing Space

When government officials envisioned the city's first urban expansion area or
suburb (ensanche) in 1898, they did not argue over its social impact on the capital's
population but over how to establish the most "rational" system of land division
and evaluation (the adjective appears repeatedly in the documents). Throughout
Mexico's provincial cities and state capitals, Porfirian urbanistas sought to reproduce the "chilango blueprints" of the country's capital. Following patterns similar to those of their counterparts in provincial cities of the states of Michoacán
and Yucatán, city officials in Oaxaca City looked to Mexico City when design-
ing the new fraccionamientos (urban developments) and avenues of their provincial urban center.[14] Indeed, in June 1907, Oaxaca City's municipal president, Gildardo Gómez, returned from a tour of Mexico City and five state capitals having
"noted all the important public and municipal buildings of each place." The
newspaper La unión reported hopefully that he would in turn "introduce [to the
city of Oaxaca] much of the good he had learned during his fruitful voyage."[15]
For elites in Oaxaca City, "mejoramiento urbano" (improvement of urban spaces)
meant not only constructing new buildings and beautifying and sanitizing city
streets, but also removing what they considered to be urban blight – such as cantinas, vagrants, and prostitutes – to the capital's margins.

Elite Spaces: The Colonia Díaz-Ordaz

In 1898, unable to build in any other direction because of natural obstacles (two
rivers and a mountain range), city officials decided to expand the city beyond its
northern border. The development of the Colonia Díaz-Ordaz clearly spelled out
what Tenorio-Trillo has described as the urban Porfirian colonization of the "uncivilized 'emptiness' of the countryside."[16] Documents concerning the Colonia

Díaz-Ordaz entirely neglect the rural area being developed and instead focus on ways to subdivide the land into coherent parcels. The development of the city's northern frontier was also part of a larger Porfirian project to "survey and fix" previously unregulated (nonrationalized) spaces. An example of this type of aggressive spatial intervention occurred with Don Porfirio's decision to use the surveying and mapping prowess of the Comisión Geográfico-Exploradora (Geographic Exploration Commission) to forcibly settle and divide the land in order to pacify rebellious Yaqui Indians in the northern state of Sonora in 1887.[17]

Named for the famous liberal general José María Díaz Ordaz,[18] the Colonia Díaz-Ordaz consisted of eleven divisions with sixty-six carefully demarcated lots each precisely enumerated, situated, and valued. City planners, following the "well-ordered" positivist logic of Porfirian governance, had crafted an exclusive and rational extension of the city. These geometrical and uniform lots also facilitated their purchase and sale. Disassociated from their ecological surroundings, the lots transformed space into an ideal commodity, the value of which could be exploited equally by city planners and salespeople.[19]

In addition to establishing a rational subdivision on the city's northern outskirts, officials developed an exclusive living space for upper-class residents, thereby reinforcing notions of modernity and elite privilege. The city government auctioned off the lots according to first-, second-, third-, and fourth-class categories. Although at first glance the government seemed to be generously creating financially accessible land divisions, the high price of even the fourth-class lots prevented workers from becoming part of the neighborhood. Furthermore, of the sixty-six lots, developers set aside only three as fourth-class units.[20] Following the expansion, the department of the municipal secretary was flooded with bids from the city's ruling elite on lots in the new colonia. Politicians and business leaders such as Albino Zertuche, Heliodoro Díaz Quintas, Cassiano Conzatti, Francisco Salazar, and the Zorrilla brothers quickly purchased lots throughout the subdivision. The future municipal president Gildardo Gómez also had his home there, as did members of the city's foreign community.[21] Although the city government turned down developer Manuel Arenas's request to build a velodrome in the colonia's division of fourth-class lots, Max Lange, a member of the British colony, enjoyed success with his proposal of a lawn tennis club. The city administration, excited at the prospect of having a "modern" recreational facility (for elites), agreed to charge Lange only nominal rent for the land. Playing to the modern aspirations of city elites, Lange wrote: "It is well proven that this game is one of the most cultured [culto] and hygienic and is enjoyed only by people in high society; for this reason I do not doubt that my request will be seriously considered, knowing well the lively interest you have in the progress of this cultured city."[22]

The City from Without

On May 1, 1909, when the city of Oaxaca annexed the neighboring village of Santa María del Marquesado (named for the valley's original marquis and Mexico's primary Spanish conquistador, Hernando Cortés), it was not to provide another exclusive space for the capital's ruling class. Instead, city officials expanded Oaxaca City's urban boundaries in order to bring an "unruly" worker district under centralized control. City officials vilified the village's inhabitants as rebellious enemies of progress and argued that the annexation would bring them into line while simultaneously offering them increased prosperity. This was not the experience of citizens of El Marquesado (as it was known commonly): they bitterly complained that the annexation of their village brought only an increased tax burden and an oppressive police presence.

Throughout the Porfiriato, the local press portrayed El Marquesado and its inhabitants as degenerate and troublesome pariahs bordering on the state capital. The establishment paper, El *correo del sur*, compared El Marquesado to "la Colonia de la Bolsa de la Metrópoli," referring to a suburb in Mexico City notorious for its thieves and beggars.[23] City lawmakers complained earlier that a clandestine *pulquería* in El Marquesado had been sending its agents into the city to sell illegally its "El Mexicano" pulque.[24] City officials protested that the unregistered vendors avoided taxes and contributed to generalized degeneracy.[25] By 1907 the concern over the "disturbance" caused by the sale of alcohol in El Marquesado prompted La *unión* to advocate for the jurisdictional expansion of the city's police force: "We wish that the respective authorities would be allowed to conduct the necessary surveillance [of El Marquesado] in order to avoid the disorder that always starts among the clientele that frequents these immoral establishments."[26] No doubt the city's promulgation of a regulation for prostitution in 1907 was another response to the village's "delinquency."

Situated along the northwestern border of the city and up against the Cerro Fortín, El Marquesado, despite being the location of three small gold mines, provided little financial revenue to its larger neighbor.[27] Before its annexation the state capital was already spending funds on the administration of El Marquesado's transportation and water services. In 1904 the Compañía de Ferrocarriles Urbanos y Agricolas de Oaxaca, S.A. (Urban and Agricultural Railway Company of Oaxaca, Ltd.), constructed a 745-meter tramline along Avenida Hidalgo connecting El Marquesado to the city.[28] In 1906 the Oaxaca Smelting and Refining Company linked the station of the Mexican Southern Railway in El Marquesado to the mining areas in San Juan Chapultepec and San Martín Mexicapam.[29] Water mains also passed through the village on their way from San Felipe del Agua to the capital. In 1876 Oaxaca City residents complained that villagers from El Marquesado were pilfering water from the public fountain at the Plaza de la Soledad.[30] Although the city was in charge of El Marquesado's water supply, it waited until 1889 to grant a request for an additional public fountain in the village.[31]

A series of electoral registries and census records provide detailed information about the inhabitants of El Marquesado.[32] Throughout the Porfiriato the village experienced very little change in its population.[33] The social and economic statistics of El Marquesado, like that of many of the surrounding towns and villages, are remarkably homogeneous.[34] The average inhabitant was born and never moved from the village, worked as a baker, laborer, or tortilla maker, practiced Catholicism, identified as mestizo,[35] and spoke Spanish. If a man, the inhabitant typically could read and perhaps write; a woman could perhaps read. The village had fifteen small bakeries and one sugar mill (trapiche).[36]

In May 1909, El Marquesado became part of the city of Oaxaca as its ninth quarter. The capital's government assumed control of El Marquesado's public lands and took over all its fiscal responsibilities.[37] Yet the transition was far from tranquil. A fortnight after the annexation took effect, El correo del sur's headline read, "The Rebellious of El Marquesado on the Threshold of an Uprising." Throughout May increasing numbers of disgruntled inhabitants of the newly annexed village complained to Joaquín Sandoval, the interim governor of the state, that their new status brought only higher taxes.[38] The city's English language newspaper, the Oaxaca Herald, wrote that "fifty residents of the Marquesado, the newly annexed suburb of Oaxaca, were given an audience with the governor yesterday. Their plea was that the decree annexing Marquesado be revoked. The governor advised them that it was not in his power to set aside the action of the state legislature and that the plea would have to be taken up with it. The reason advanced for nonannexation was additional taxes."[39] The city, in an attempt to extend its control over the newly acquired territory, installed a new police headquarters in the former village. According to an interviewee in El correo del sur, many villagers, accustomed to only neighborhood watchmen, were uncomfortable with the increase in police surveillance.[40]

Elites and the local press dismissed the allegedly rebellious members of El Marquesado as "disturbing . . . enemies of all ideas of progress" and "social vermin." Finding little audience in Oaxaca, a group of fifty discontented inhabitants left for Mexico City to petition Díaz himself.[41] Unsuccessful, the group returned to Oaxaca, where news of any further protest is absent from the historical record. Labeling protestors as throwbacks to an uncivilized era, city elites had managed to expand the capital's borders and assert their notion of progress beyond previous frontiers.

The story of El Marquesado's annexation is not only the first example of the colonizing actions of the Oaxaca city government (the city continued to expand its borders in the 1930s and until the present day); it also provides us with a glimpse of how people from surrounding villages perceived the modernizing strategies of the state capital from "without." Cities are never self-contained or fixed in space. They must be viewed from a multitude of perspectives both within and outside their boundaries.[42]

While the city expanded into new colonias and neighboring villages, officials allocated substantial funds and exerted considerable effort to alter the physical presence of the state capital. It is to the development of this Porfirian visual order and aesthetic of modernity that we now turn.

The Shape of Modernity: Streets, Gardens, and Secular Architecture

By 1905 the budget for adornment and gardens (*ornato y jardines*) in the state capital reached a staggering 10 percent (10,021 pesos) of the city's annual budget. The adornment and gardens category first appeared in the city's budget of 1891. Around that same year, expenses for sanitation, lighting, and public works began to rise rapidly as urban planners attempted to modernize the city. In order to re-construct the city in the positivist vision of the times epitomized by planners in Mexico City, Porfirian Oaxaca City planners rebuilt and constructed dozens of new parks, buildings, streets, tramways, and lamp and telegraph posts. Elites gave a strategic shape to their vision of modernity. New city spaces underscored existing class and race divisions, forming increasingly separate areas for rich and poor, white and nonwhite.

Streets

In his 1890 annual report, municipal president Ramón Castillo announced that the city's streets and public spaces were in need of immediate repair. For Castillo, the city's form would ultimately follow its function as an important site of civilization: "The cleanliness of the city streets is not only an indication of the capital's level of civilization, but also a necessity and convenience for public health. Good and sufficient lighting, in addition to being indispensable to the security and comfort of the residents, contributes to the city's beautification."[43] These aesthetic and hygienic changes would, however, benefit only a select group of urban residents. A 1907 effort to pave the streets around the central plaza (*zócalo*) symbolized the elite and Mexico City–inspired designs for the city's spaces. Roberto Gayol, the engineer who earlier had developed Mexico City's sewage system, planned the street-paving project for Oaxaca's capital. Old stones from the city's central avenues were to be removed and used to patch up streets in peripheral areas while the areas in and around the zócalo would be newly paved.[44] The condition of the municipality's avenues would reflect prescribed class divisions in the capital. Yet according to a letter that the American consular agent in Oaxaca City, Ezra M. Lawton, wrote to the Reo Motor Car Company in Lansing, Michigan, the following year, the paving project never got off the ground:

> I have your letter of the 31st and in reply would say that there are no dealers in motor cars here, and I am a little doubtful as to whether you would be able to work up a trade here. The country around here is extremely mountainous. The streets of this city have not been paved more than the rough stone pavements, which with the open sewers make it very bad for use of motor cars. In order to be useful too, the cars would have to be rather heavy power, as there are some pretty stiff grades around the city. There are very few vehicles in use even, most all travel being done with horse back riding.[45]

Despite other successes in segregating the city's space, officials would wait until after the Revolution to pave streets in the affluent neighborhoods of the capital. The initial failure of the paving project demonstrates how plans to develop and expand the city were contingent on the administration's financial resources and priorities. Furthermore, the delayed implementation of the project shows that elites lacked a unified and coherent vision of modernity. Ruling elites disagreed over how best to alter the city's spaces.

Gardens

While efforts to gentrify the city streets floundered, city officials made sure that the capital's gardens became the cornerstone of their Porfirian spatial designs. Although gardens had existed in the capital since colonial times, it was during the Porfiriato that officials transformed the public city plazas into relatively private manicured garden spaces.[46] Originally, city plazas had a wide-ranging, popular use. They were the location of public water sources (fountains); market stalls for meat, poultry, tortillas, and coal; and job fairs for tradesmen. Zapoteca women frequently would come down from the neighboring town of San Felipe del Agua to sell blanditas, giant seasoned tortillas. Most of all, the plazas were places for popular social interaction.[47]

During the Porfiriato, city administrators completely altered the use, image, and meaning of the plazas. City officials forced water carriers, milkmen, and a host of other vendors to abandon these central areas, leaving them no choice but to work as street peddlers (*vendedores ambulantes*) in officially designated market spaces. In 1897 officials developed regulations that effectively displaced these laborers and transformed the use of these lands. Manuel Martínez Gracida, a prominent Oaxacan bureaucrat and intellectual, summarized the transition of the capital's green spaces:

> It is undeniable that Oaxaca continues toward its betterment. It has been a while since the material improvements have made the city beautiful and located it in a place of honor among the cities of the Mexican Confederation.
>
> Soon the conclusion of the central garden will be celebrated in the annals of history. Even now in the nights of the full moon before the Zócalo has been finished, the best families that society has to offer come to visit. The young women are enchanted by its spells, the children revel in its freshness, and the men and everyone, in a word, breathes the spirit of peace and progress.[48]

The workaday and social plazas became exclusive gardens, florid and fragrant areas through which the city's elite could casually saunter and recreate, and also sites for official monuments and patriotic celebrations.[49] Based on its restrictive vision, the Oaxaca City government morphed the central areas of the city in order to move members of the popular classes farther into the capital's periphery.[50]

The 1897 regulations focused on proper conduct and movement in and around the gardens. The regulations sought to preserve elite tranquility by protecting flowers from harm and assured that "visitors on bicycles, horse back or [in] carriages ride" in the appropriate direction.[51] Government officials reinforced the elite status of the gardens by staging annual horticultural competitions and reserving the newly designed city spaces for scientific purposes.

In the announcement of the inaugural horticultural competition, Manuel Campos Galván and Rodolfo Lavie emphasized their civic duties in promoting the event, linking it to the broader theme of agriculture and to the progress of the nation: "Agriculture is not only a source of wealth, but also the maintainer of peace and a powerful agent of moralization and progress. To it [agriculture] we owe the formation and stability of societies. Its history is intimately linked to that of humanity; the state of civilization of nations is based upon her progress."[52] Participants in the competition hailed from the city's elite class. Politicians and mine owners such as Tiburcio Ramírez, Tomás Sánchez, Manuel Pereira Mejía, and Constantino Rickards exhibited their prize flowers, hoping to win local and national glory.

In addition to this patriotic usage, officials designed gardens for their scientific utility. Following the positivist prescriptions of the times, government administrators sought to order city space as they did society. City elites constructed municipal gardens as the showcase of their modernizing regime. Officials transformed nature as well as individuals according to their vision of modernity. The reconstruction of gardens served as a metaphor that captured the "new spirit [of scientific state simplification]. The gardener – perhaps a landscape architect specializing in formal gardens is the most appropriate parallel – takes a natural site and creates an entirely designed space of botanical order. . . . The garden is one of man's attempts to impose his own principles of order, utility, and beauty on nature."[53] In 1885 Luis Mier y Terán ordered the construction of a garden for the general hospital, in which medicinal plants and herbs were cultivated.[54] Starting in 1903 the Italian scholar-in-residence and director of the normal school, Cassiano Conzatti, began a series of petitions to the municipal government requesting a park in the Colonia Anglo-Americana in the shape of the state with plants representing each of the state's climatic regions. Again, however, elites disagreed over the specific implementation of developmental projects in the state capital. Despite Conzatti's persistence over the years as a city councilor, officials ultimately denied his request on the grounds that the project would exceed even the ample municipal budget for gardens and adornment.[55]

In 1890 the municipal government formed the new Commission on Avenues, Gardens, Public Adornment, and Carriages.[56] By 1892 the city had reconstructed within its limits eight gardens – each adorned with a statue depicting a heroic figure from the state's or country's official past. By 1909 planners constructed two additional gardens: El Hidalgo and El Bernardino Carbajal. Officials replaced the gardens' religious names with ones that emphasized the secular force of the Porfiriato. In so doing, elites fashioned an official history of Oaxaca and Mexico, mythologizing the past through a mix of Ancient Greek, Aztec, and Mexican Independence- and Reform-era leaders. Analyzing these aspects of the cityscape reveals the capital as a "complex but legible document that can tell us something about the values and aspirations of [its] rulers, designers, builders, owners, and inhabitants."[57] Gardens were once named for Catholic saints and symbols (Santa Rosa, Santa María de Guadalupe, El Rosario, La Merced, La Soledad). But starting in 1887 officials replaced the gardens' names with secular monikers such as La Alameda de León, El Benito Juárez, Nezahualcóyotl, Homero, Platón, Juan Peláez de Berrio, Sócrates, and Virgilio. As a harbinger of things to come, a decade earlier city planners had constructed a plaza named La Democracia on the ruins of the land of the former convent of La Merced.

Eager to echo the heroic designs of Mexico City's central avenue, the Paseo de la Reforma, Oaxaca City officials turned to architects from the country's capital to construct gardens and statues. In addition to consulting a gardener who had worked on Mexico City's Paseo, Oaxaca City officials contracted Ernesto Scheleske y Aguirre to work on several of the statues for Oaxaca's capital.[58] Scheleske received his training at the National Academy of Arts and worked in Mexico City until he became a teacher in the School of Industrial Arts and Trades of the State of Oaxaca in Oaxaca City.[59] In October 1893 the city commissioned him to sculpt eight statues.[60] Scheleske and other sculptors busied themselves throughout the Porfiriato erecting statues in the city's gardens. The capital counted four figures of Don Benito Juárez alone. Sculptors designed each statue in the city with a strong didactic and moral message. In addition to the primary figure, the artists inscribed recognizable dictums and symbols on the various sides of the monument. Similar to the sculptures along the Paseo de la Reforma in Mexico City, their Oaxacan equivalents were meant "to present living and important examples from [Mexico's] history to point out to future generations the names of heroes and patriots, that is, history artistically made into objects with a moral sense."[61] One of Benito Juárez, designed by Francisco Cosío and originally located in the city's central plaza, contained allegorical figures representing faith, justice, law, and reason. In the figure's left hand was a copy of the Reform laws of 1857. Officials also raised a monument to Miguel Hidalgo y Costilla, a Catholic priest and leader in the war of independence, in the garden bearing his name.[62]

In 1890 the Grand Circle of the Friends of General Díaz planned to raise funds for a lavish monument to their beloved president. Their design included incorporating marble pieces from "all over the country" into an octagonal structure ringed with images of seven of Díaz's generals and shields of each of the twenty-seven states and the territory of Baja California. Sections of the monument were to include a biography of Díaz and lists of his current cabinet members and secretaries.[63] This impressive figure that would have fused heroic references to the past and present was never constructed. Instead, the city opted for a simpler bust of the general designed by Scheleske and situated on the Porfirio Díaz Road, which ran through the city's center.

Individual elites also sought out the services of professional sculptors to adorn their homes. City elites hoped to help educate local artisans in the fine arts. In part to aid in this education, as state governor, Díaz opened the School of Industrial Arts and Trades on July 26, 1882. Students learned skills like drawing, clay modeling, and plaster casting. Affluent citizens of the city demanded the services of these newly trained artisans. Like others, Archbishop Gillow had his residence adorned with carvings and statues representing European antiquity.[64]

The city's gardens and their statues also served as spaces for official celebrations commemorating local and national heroes. Furthermore, as with the nation's capital, newly adorned parks, gardens, and avenues acted as showpieces not only for Mexicans but also, and most important, for foreign capitalists.[65] A key element in Cassiano Conzatti's proposal for a garden in the shape of the state was that it would impress the "numerous foreigners who visit us every day."[66] Oaxaca City officials sought to impress visitors in hopes of encouraging and retaining their business in the emergent mining industry. This aspect of the gardens fully justified the city's enormous expenditure in creating the Commission on Avenues, Gardens, Public Adornment, and Carriages.

Secular Architecture

Architecture seems to us the most impressive of arts and better than any other in which to paint the material and intellectual progress of a people.
— Gilberto Torres,
Periódico oficial del Estado de Oaxaca, May 16, 1889

In addition to gardens, government officials and city elites heralded the arrival of progress with examples of Porfirian architecture. After tearing down many religious vestiges of the colonial past, elites built new theaters, public buildings, and private mansions as monuments to the modern city. For city elites, modernity was not only circumscribed by the race, gender, and class of the city's inhabitants, but also by liberal anticlerical doctrines that viewed the church as an obstructionist force inhibiting progress. As the next chapter discusses, however, government officials also viewed the church as integral to the city's Porfirian transformation, especially in the realm of labor and the inculcation of a capitalist work ethic.

   The installation of electric lights, telephones, and water systems, along with the construction of new public and private buildings, ensured in the eyes of elites that the state capital was destined to become a modern city. Between January and September 1889, Gilberto Torres, editor of the state's official newspaper, *El periódico oficial del Estado de Oaxaca*, wrote a series of articles titled "The City of Oaxaca and Its Principal Buildings." In the series Torres detailed the history of many of the city's buildings, emphasizing what he deemed to be an important architectural shift away from church buildings to secular, European-style edifices:

   Around the beginning of the last century or at the end of the previous one, the appearance of the city must have been very unpleasant. Far from its cheerful presentation of today with its bright lighting, houses of modern construction, and navigable streets, the old city, unaware of the technology of pavement and tiling, was made up of dirt streets and poor quality houses without any more lighting than the lamps hung in the saints' recesses could provide. Among the small buildings, the convents and temples used to arise like colossuses weighing on the backs of the citizens, at all times imposing their wealth and power on the subjects below.[67]

As state governor, Díaz made sure that the capital of his native state received many of the latest furnishings Mexico City was developing at the time. During his tenure, Oaxaca City officials initiated plans to construct a network of electric lights, telephones, and water systems. In May 1884 Díaz returned to Oaxaca as Mexico's president to witness the inauguration of an initial network of electric lamps. Two engineers from the United States had traveled to the state capital to assist in the construction of the lighting system.[68] By 1894, of the 689 lamps placed in the city, most were located in and around the central plaza while the others illuminated the surrounding streets and buildings.[69] Peripheral areas remained in the dark. Eighteen years later, in 1912, citizens of El Marquesado complained that the lack of street lamps contributed to illicit behavior. The few lamps installed in the newly formed suburb had broken and the city refused to repair them.[70] By contrast, elite households and government buildings directly benefited from new telephone and water systems established in 1883.[71]

But it was the Porfirian architecture, and, more precisely, what it replaced, that most clearly revealed liberal elite designs for a modern city. Beginning with the 1856 Lerdo Law, which called for the privatization of corporate property belonging to the church and communal villages, city property became increasingly secularized. As the ample set of documents on the nationalization and confiscation of national lands in the General Archive of Mexico demonstrates, prior to and throughout the first decades of the Porfiriato, private individuals bought up city property once owned by the Catholic Church.[72] Staunch liberals like Gilberto Torres were quick to reject Oaxaca's ecclesiastical past in favor of its secular Porfirian present. In his series of articles, Torres repeatedly condemned the city's churches as "vulgar masses of stone" with "little artistic value." Torres did not hold back from attacking colonial-era governments as well, chiding them as "idle," "spoiled," and "sapping the vitality of the people with their preoccupation with the propagation of the Catholic faith and [other] useless contemplations and ceremonies more useless still."[73]

Written during the first half of the Porfiriato, Torres's articles do not take into account the many buildings that would be built over the subsequent years. Architectural growth in the city was so pronounced during the Porfiriato that architectural historian Carlos Lira argues that the common, present-day touristic designation of Oaxaca's capital as a "colonial" city is a misnomer. Lira points out that

many – if not most – of the buildings the present city and state governments celebrate as the essences of Oaxaca's beauty were in fact built during the Porfiriato
and employed novel architectural styles.[74] In addition to the numerous private
mansions built by foreign and national elites, the city government constructed
buildings like the Monte de Piedad (or state pawnshop, in 1882), the Institute of
Arts and Sciences (renovated in 1909), the Hospicio de la Vega (or city orphanage,
in 1896), the Porfirio Díaz School (1885), various market places, and the elaborate
Teatro-Casino Luis Mier y Terán (1909). These buildings and Torres's prolific writings attest to elite efforts to subdue the ecclesiastical past and "convert the old
Spanish city . . . into a modern urban center where the sweetness of its climate,
the fertility of its earth, and the sophistication of its sons rival the elegance of the
private homes and the majesty and beauty of the public buildings."[75]

Symbolic Spaces

Rituals

> The Porfirian holiday was an innovation of the regime, but it built on Mexico's
> long-standing practice of using celebrations as dramatic statements of the domi-
> nant culture. Porfirian ritual celebrations offer an indisputable expression of gov-
> ernance during the last quarter of the nineteenth century.
>   – William Beezley, "The Porfirian Smart Set
>   Anticipates Thorstein Veblen in Guadalajara," 1994

City elites and urban planners not only constructed new spaces as examples of
their Porfirian vision but also filled those same spaces with didactic and heroic
symbols of the new, modern Mexican state. Since colonial times Latin American
governments have used language and ceremony to legitimize their right to rule.[76]
Patriotic celebrations, street names, and city maps helped the various parts of
Oaxaca City to cohere into one imagined, modern whole and connected the state
capital's development with the formation of the nation-state. In their work on
English state formation, Phillip Corrigan and Derek Sayer argue that state power
works by continually recreating social identities through a process of cultural
revolution. They maintain that state formation is an ongoing process, a long-term
ritual of rule that delimits social, political, and cultural realms of acceptability.[77]
Similarly, Oaxaca's civic leaders mobilized and feted invented symbols of Oaxaca's
and Mexico's traditional past in order to reinforce their political power and assert
their secular and race-exclusive visions of Oaxaca's role in Mexico's modern state.
    Government rituals transformed municipal spaces such as gardens and plazas
into arenas of civic virtue[78] where city administrators constructed official histo-

ries of the past in order to forge a patriotic and modern citizenry for the future. Utilizing official rituals, Oaxacan elites mobilized heroes of the state's past to reinforce their liberal notions of modernity and to link local customs to national projects. Furthermore, in a population of mixed literacy, public rituals became didactic mediums for inculcating state-promoting messages. A clear separation was maintained between church and state in civic rituals. As with Porfirian-era architecture, elites consciously erased or subordinated the church's presence in public celebrations. As we will see, when Catholic festivals did occur, city and church elites integrated them into broader civic and national discourses.

Although celebrated throughout the Porfiriato, civic festivals grew in stature and number during the governorship of Emilio Pimentel (1902–11). Pimentel, the epitome of the *científico* politician, set Oaxaca's capital on a rapid pace of development encouraging foreign investment and urban renewal projects.[79] Among other events during the last decade of the Porfiriato, Pimentel and the municipal government commemorated Don Benito Juárez, Pimentel himself, and Mexico's independence from Spain, the anniversary of which coincidentally fell on Díaz's birthday, September 16.

On March 21, 1906, officials celebrated the one-hundredth anniversary of Benito Juárez's birth with the belated dedication of his statue atop the Cerro Fortín. To this day, the Juárez figure with his arm extended to the east "showing the way to the foreign usurper"[80] is a well-known symbol of the city. The program of festivities included a band-led parade through the city streets to the Fortín. At 12:30 p.m. students in every school of the city carried out civic ceremonies in honor of the Benemérito (distinguished one)—the quintessential liberal figure of nineteenth-century Mexico—and the Institute of Arts and Sciences held a literary festival. On the following day celebrants affixed commemorative plaques to the sides of the two houses in which Juárez had lived. The celebrations concluded in the evening as state and city politicians along with elite families watched while workers positioned a triumphal arch in the Paseo Juárez.[81] After the festivities Andrés Portillo wrote a commentary praising the event's size, precision, and seemingly high degree of civilian support:

> The act of celebrating the statue of the hero by the Governor of the state on the Cerro Fortín took place in front of a multitude of people that filled eight city blocks and the skirt of the hill on which this monument is located.
>
> The scholarly contest conducted by the Institute of [Arts and] Sciences was of equal merit to similar festivities in more erudite cities. And finally, the floral display along the entire Calzada Porfirio Díaz exceeded perhaps

the profusion of adornments the likes of which we have seen only in the Capital of the Republic.

The most notable fact of the parade, the most flattering and honorable note for the people of the city during the days in which the birthday of Don Benito Juárez was celebrated, was the enthusiasm and decorum of their behavior. The police were actively engaged in their jobs, but in a most peaceful manner because there was not one dissonant cry, not one person trampled, and not one person jailed because of the festivities.[82]

As is obvious from his commentary, Portillo was more interested in elevating Oaxaca City's position in the ranks of modern, orderly cities than in providing details of the celebration itself. His efforts represented the apotheosis of the Porfirian project to modernize the city. In subsequent years the city continued to celebrate Juárez's birth and also remembered his death. On the occasion of the thirty-fourth anniversary of the ex-president's death, the American colony presented a tricolor wreath to the city of Oaxaca, placing it on the statue in the Paseo Juárez. As with the gardens, civic rituals provided an opportunity for foreigners in the city to tie themselves to the elite's official vision of the capital.[83]

While the city government continued to organize festivals for its Reform-era hero in subsequent years, it also added, in a similarly ostentatious fashion, the celebration of Governor Pimentel's birthday.[84] The one-hundredth anniversary of Mexico's declaration of independence from Spain was celebrated in 1910 (independence was declared in 1810 and won formally eleven years later). Independence Day festivities throughout the Porfiriato attempted to connect the local to the national by extravagantly celebrating Díaz's birthday with banners in the colors of the nation's tricolored flag. The national event was also a chance to promote local capitalist enterprises and their owners. In 1907 the Cervecería de Oaxaca (Oaxaca Brewery) outfitted the parade's first float, which consisted of a giant Gloria beer bottle. Onlookers watched as "the enormous bottle caught the branches of a cypress tree in the Paseo Juárez, fell to the ground, and broke into pieces." Other floats enabled wealthy families to show off some of the city's few automobiles.[85]

Like its Mexico City counterpart, the centennial celebration in Oaxaca's capital was a grand and drawn-out affair. Lasting two full weeks between September 6 and 19, 1910, the centennial celebration allows us to witness how Oaxaca City's Porfirian residents imagined cultural representations of the nation and its history.[86] In Oaxaca City's case, elite planners in the Central Coordinating Committee of the Centennial additionally emphasized local variants of the official past, retelling the country's history through allegorical floats and speeches that proudly featured Oaxaca's cast of national leaders. As with the festivities for Benito Juárez, the committee recruited schoolchildren, with the military and political officials also key participants. In addition, the city's foreign community (North Americans, Spanish, German, French) collected over one thousand pesos to erect "triumphant arches" in three places along the Calle Progreso.

Unique to this event was the presence of workers in the parades. One whole day, September 15, was dedicated almost entirely to a parade of the city's workers' guilds and societies. In addition to feting Díaz's birth at the beginning of what would be the last full year of his reign, groups of workers paraded down city streets separated according to their specific trades. With the inclusion of workers in the parade, the committee attempted to inculcate workers with patriotism and civic duty.

More than anything, festival planners hoped that the celebration would encompass all strata of society, uniting them in one patriotic civic mass. On the main day of the event, organizers planned that "all of the city's inhabitants would join together at 4:00 p.m. at the Paseo Juárez where two bands of music play. The Central Coordinating Committee of the Centennial has extended a special invitation to all without distinction of class, age, or sex to walk to the Altar of the Patria at the second roundabout on Calzada Porfirio Díaz."[87]

As in most of the city's public celebrations, race became a central focus. The festivities on previous days also included static representations of Oaxaca's indigenous groups. Students from the Carmen Romero Rubio de Díaz School dressed up as Zapotecs, Mixtecs, Nahuas, and other native groups from the state, placing themselves on display in fixed racial categories at the Teatro-Casino Luis Mier y Terán.[88] Similarily, girls from the Colegio de Niñas "Triple Union," dressed as Indians from the state's fifteen distinct "races" and posed for photographs in the school's journal (fig. 1).

In the same way that public celebrations ignored Benito Juárez's Zapotec heritage, the students portrayed the distinct indigenous groups in a stylized and infantilized manner, highlighting their "simplicity" and thus supposed innocuousness. Celebrations represented Indians and Indianness as either charming relics of Oaxaca's past or as benign forces in a modern present and future. Officials in the Central Committee went to great lengths to construct a cohesive vision of a modern city uniting elites, workers, and indigenous groups under one patriotic umbrella of national glory.[89] Annual civic rituals like the centennial filled the city's spaces with symbolic, elite-generated meanings centered on notions of progress that tied the local to the national.

Later that same year, on December 15, Francisco Belmar, a philologist and judge on Mexico's Supreme Court, returned to his home state to help inaugurate the

LAS RAZAS EN EL E. DE OAX. —Cuadro plástico.—Colegio "Triple Unión."
19   EL CENTENARI

Figure 1. "The Races in the State of Oaxaca." El centenario:
Revista mensual ilustrada, January 31, 1911

Sociedad Indianista Oaxaqueña (Oaxacan Indianist Soceity), an organization that would aspire to "rescue" Indians from their "savage" existence.[90] It was to be a branch of the national organization that Belmar had helped establish earlier that year, whose main objective was "the practical study of the indigenous races of our country and most appropriate means of achieving the increase of their moral and material status."[91] A poem read by Professor Francisco Echeverría at the Sociedad's inauguration reveals the prevailing elite attitudes toward Indians in the face of "progress." According to the magazine coverage, the poem, "¡Pobre raza!" ("Poor Race!"), "very much impressed the audience and was recited with tenderness and garnered much applause." An excerpt from the poem read,

> Look at these sons of the noble race
> That sadly and in silence pass by
> They are no longer those feared warriors
> That fought with fury against the Iberians;
>
> They are no longer the same.
> Today they wander timidly

And they seem like strangers in their own land
All alone, very sad and without ideals.

Now is the time to show our humanity
With the poor Indians. They are our brothers.
Their humble appearance reveals bitterness
But their souls are white and pure.

Never is lost or useless the endeavor
To help the weak, give strength to the little one
And the Indian race needs that
In order to guide its steps along the path to progress.

According to the society, the Indians' "white and pure" souls would ultimately help officials "extirpate the vices of alcoholism and the laziness that grows among many of our colored races."[92]

Despite the intended coherent meaning in the elaborate preparation and display of elite celebrations, their impact on and reception by nonelites was not necessarily so simple and unified. Unfortunately, the sources we have concerning these official celebrations were entirely generated by the elite. One can assume only that the onlookers at the centennial celebration and other events interpreted the displays, parades, and speeches in multifarious ways.[93] Furthermore, many onlookers may have seen these celebrations simply as external rituals and rites and not have understood or chosen to ignore their nationalist implications.[94]

Maps and Signs

[Jorge Luis Borges] invites us to think of a map, or any interpretation, as an inexact model, which reveals not just its inevitable partiality as an incomplete representation but also its inescapable partiality as a design of power. As such, any representation must be evaluated by its uses and effects.
      − Fernando Coronil, "Smelling Like a Market," 1997

In addition to filling the year's calendar and city spaces with symbolic events of official pageantry, elites also abstracted the modern city through a series of municipal maps and symbolized it through the installation of new street signs. Oaxaca's urban planners utilized maps and street signs to impose their "design of power" and progress on the state capital. These abstractions reinforced the city as a legible document for elite surveillance and didacticism. The projects of mapping and surveying were integral to the formation of the modern Mexican

nation-state, giving space a fixed meaning and thus more effectively facilitating its commodification and regulation. Planners in other state capitals joined
their counterparts in Mexico City, initiating projects of urban regularization and
simplification throughout the Porfiriato.[95]

Of course cartographers had mapped the city of Oaxaca before the Díaz era,
but during the Porfiriato a profusion of mapmaking took place and maps began
to take on different meanings. In 1529 the first known map of the city was commissioned by Alonso García Bravo, a subordinate to Juan Peláez de Berrio of the
Real Audiencia of Mexico. A Capuchin monk, Francisco de Ajofrín, drew the next
extant cartographic representation of Oaxaca in 1763. Not until the end of the
Bourbon era in the late eighteenth century did more maps of the city appear. In
1795 the Viceroy of New Spain, the marquis of Branciforte, ordered the local in-
tendant, Antonio de Mora y Peysal, to simplify the layout of the colony's larger
cities. According to Branciforte, "The division of the populous cities into quarters or neighborhoods is an important point for the government, politics, and
laws, and is necessary for order and good administration of justice."[96] In subsequent years, maps of the capital faithfully detailed the rectilinear plan of the city.
In 1848, Antonio Conde Diebitech de Sabalkanski, an engineer working for then-
governor Benito Juárez, drew a densely detailed map of the city that would serve
as the basis for municipal maps of Oaxaca until the 1930s. As far as we know, starting in 1877, planners undertook the first of eight separate mapping projects of
the city.[97]

A map from 1903 printed by C. Vega in Mexico City titled "Topographic and
Commercial Map of the City of Oaxaca" stands out as an example of the elite
rendering of the modern city.[98] In addition to providing clear representations of
the city's streets, the map, locally distributed by the Julián S. Soto Book and Sta-
tionery Store, highlights key landmarks in the city: government buildings, markets, parks, and churches.[99] The first of the city's renderings to be privately commissioned, the 1903 map includes statistical notes on climate and geography and
highlights fifty-two of the city's businesses.[100] Representing only the city's commercial landmarks, the map is a simplification of its 1887 predecessor by engineer
I. P. Guzmán. It is meant to help local and foreign businesspeople as well as tourists locate the city's commercial establishments.[101] A summary of the city's history and photographs of businesses, people, and sites from the city's official history (such as Juárez's home and Díaz's birthplace converted into a school) makes
this map an exemplary text of the modern city.

If the centennial celebration of Mexico's independence from Spain represents
the epitome of elites' symbolic use of city spaces, then Andrés Portillo's magnum

opus, *Oaxaca en el centenario de la independencia nacional*, represents the culmination of the legible city. The work, an impressive attempt to gather and centralize statistical and anecdotal information on Oaxaca City, provides an excellent example of the highpoint of Oaxaca's Porfirian printing and mapping projects. Portillo published the volume in 1910 to coincide with Mexico's centennial celebration of the declaration of independence from Spain. *El centenario* is essentially an ultradetailed map of the city punctuated with statistics and excerpts from Oaxaca City's heroic past. It is fitting that the work opens with a quotation from the well-known German scientist and explorer Alexander von Humboldt praising the city's beauty and celebrating its Indian heritage. Following the introduction, Portillo and a collection of contributors assiduously dissect the city block by block into a legible aggregation of streets, buildings, and their proprietors, all with specified peso values. The fact that, by the end of Porfiriato, all the city's properties had been valued is indicative of the ultimate success the administration had in rationalizing the city's spaces. Specified property values also meant that the same government could more efficiently and profitably tax them. Furthermore, this success proves that the modernizing projects were more than just rhetorical flourishes; they had real social and economic consequences.[102] Portillo also contrasts the old city with the new, indicating the change in street names and increase in number of properties. Definitions and brief histories of the city street names with regional and national significance separate the maps, contributing to the volume's overall effect of reinserting Oaxaca City into the national narrative of progress.

The city council not only constructed new spaces and situated them in maps, it also renamed old spaces with "modern" names, as seen above with the reconstructed gardens. In 1883, the last year of Porfirio Díaz's governorship in the state, officials including then–city councilor, Emilio Pimentel, almost entirely renamed the city's streets, markets, and parks. Decades earlier, in the mid-nineteenth century, Benito Juárez oversaw the renaming of some of the city's streets. Names honoring heroes of the Independence such as Hidalgo, Morelos, and Bravo appeared for the first time. Throughout the mid-1800s street signs changed reflecting the change from conservative to liberal governments. It was not, however, until the Porfiriato that the municipal government undertook a comprehensive renaming project of all the streets, parks, and squares in the Emerald City. Replacing the old, colonial, and religious monikers, Porfirian city councilors labeled public spaces with new, secular nomenclature imbued with notions of "progress," names still in use today. Llano de Guadalupe and Perpetua became Progreso. Sangre de Cristo became Orden y Progreso. At the same time, city elites, hoping once again to reconcile their visions of tradition and modernity, strove to reinvent the city's history by adapting new names for public spaces. Focusing on the glorious postindependence past, politicians chose names that reflected their ideas of a strong, liberal nation. Indeed, a large aspect of constructing the modern city emerged from notions of nation building that would receive more attention following the Revolution. As such, Carmen Bajo became Porfirio Díaz, La Soledad became Morelos, and San Felipe became Independencia.[103] In 1903, a group of city councilors not entirely satisfied with the 1883 name changes proposed further alterations.[104] While proud of the historical significance of the new nomenclature, the councilors wanted to increase the city's legible, and hence modern, character by allowing only one name for an entire north-south or east-west avenue. The 1884 changes had included multiple names for one longitudinal and latitudinal street. Furthermore, the committee's chairman, writing for the group, noted that the strict regulation of house enumeration would allow officials to better manage the city. Their proposal is worth quoting at length:

> Without a doubt, once the transformation [of street names] is established along with a notion that culture is imparted by the change of [street] names from the colonial era—names without common sense, laughable and even ridiculous—the names that symbolize patriotism will exalt the notion of always ennobling and conserving in the mind the venerated names of the principal heroes of the country. Once the quantity of names is diminished and they are better arranged with the use of the ordinal numbers, the new street names will facilitate the important knowledge of the city's dwellings. It is important to applaud the improvement [that would be] realized by the benefits produced by simplification. Considering the current state of transition between the way of being traditional and the way of today, taking this to its highest level without removing the idea of patriotism, I think it will reach the summit of perfection.
>
> The city of Oaxaca de Juárez lends itself, like all modern cities, to using only one name for the streets running from one extremity to another, hence simplifying [their use] as much as possible and facilitating the study of houses and [their] inhabitants.[105]

The city council eagerly adopted these new titles for the city.

Urban planners designed cartographic and signage projects in the state capital to jog the inhabitants' memories of imagined traditions. The projects served as mnemonic devices of the city's official history, pointing toward ideals of progress and modernity.

Spaces of Discipline

As we have seen, projects to shape and fill Oaxaca City's public spaces took on an unprecedented vigor during the Porfiriato. For elites, the remaining task was to remove or at least relocate undesirable classes of people from the view of the city's *gente decente*. The institutionalization of a city police force, prison and asylum system, and hygiene regulations provided Oaxaca's government with additional mechanisms of rule over the city's popular classes. True to the liberal developmentalist ideology of the era, administrators equated issues of hygiene and vice with the incipience of Mexico's state formation. Porfirian elites identified "degenerate" populations throughout Mexico as elements deleterious to the nation's families and the country's well-being and progress.[106] Officials worked hard but unsuccessfully to stamp out what they determined were the capital's greatest threats to modernity: vagrants, alcohol, and prostitution.

Police

I am happy that today Mexico walks in hurried step along the path of material and intellectual progress in all of its branches and classes. Oaxaca, eminently liberal, is organizing its police in the same fashion as the most cultured and civilized nations of the world.

— Governor Porfirio Díaz,
message to Mexican Congress, September 17, 1882[107]

As governor of Oaxaca between 1881 and 1883, Porfirio Díaz initiated a series of projects in the capital city that he would later implement on a national scale as president.[108] Foremost on his agenda was modernizing his home city as part of a strategy to extend his rule throughout the country. To this end, in 1882 Díaz created a gendarmerie in the city named the Guardianes de Oaxaca as well as a company of state police (*rurales*); both units fell under the direct control of the jefe político.[109] Díaz solicited new recruits in the state's official newspaper and immediately called for the enumeration — and thus simplification — of the city's blocks in order to facilitate the organization of the new police force.[110] By that same year administrators had started to compile detailed statistics on crime in the capital.[111] Later in the Porfiriato the police force would get a new look when the city created a budget to formalize the gendarmerie's uniforms.[112] Throughout the Porfiriato, Díaz's liberal sympathizers formalized and rationalized local police and national military forces, often following aesthetic and administrative traditions from France and elsewhere in Europe.[113]

Prior to 1882, informal groups of men, often lantern lighters, acted as urban watchmen (*resguardos*).[114] In 1882 Díaz's Guardianes de Oaxaca was the city's first organized police force since the steady demilitarization of the state following decades of internecine warfare in the nineteenth century.[115] Police headquarters divided the city into four quarters, each in turn separated into four sections. About thirty auxiliaries and six officers manned each section. In 1889 there were 220 men on the force (including 48 trainees) and by 1902 the capital's gendarmerie swelled to 477 men.[116] In 1904, concerned that relatively well-paying employment in agriculture, mining, and industry discouraged men from serving as gendarmes, Governor Pimentel raised the salary for police auxiliaries (which had been the same since its inception in 1882) from fifty to seventy-five centavos per day. Pimentel also created a new mounted police force to serve the city and beyond.[117] Furthermore, the city government extended police powers to El Marquesado.

The capital's police force was part of an increasingly larger system of surveillance in the state run by the central district's jefe político, which included members of the rurales, the federal force. Díaz hoped to strengthen his centralized seat of power in Mexico City by continually fortifying his appointed local political bosses throughout the country with armed forces. This strategy eventually backfired around the country as the often decadent jefes increasingly were criticized by wary opponents of the Díaz regime.[118] The gendarmes, as will be discussed later, also caused city administrators some concern. Positioned by elites as ideal "instruments of social reform," gendarmes never amounted to the perfect long arm of the state or to the loyal representatives of the city's popular classes. Like their counterparts in Mexico City, members of the Emerald City's force served as "unintended intermediaries between policies and traditions, between institutions and communities, and . . . between criminals and victims."[119]

A new city prison built in 1898 helped the city's police force. The new prison was in fact the reconstructed former convent of Santa Catalina, which had been appropriated from the church in 1861 to serve as the city's first prison. In 1881 Governor Díaz passed legislation permitting a shoe company, N. Cuero y Compañía, to set up a workshop in the makeshift jail.[120] Prior to the opening of the renovated prison, editorials in city papers complained that the "deficient nature" of the prison in the former convent was responsible in part for the high rate of recidivism in the capital. One editorial called the prison "a medium for the propagation of crime" and argued that prisoners "needed to be made to work and to experience the rigors of isolation."[121] By the end of the Porfiriato prison officials had set up a precise temporal and spatial system in the city penitentiary. Men and women were separated, as were convicts guilty of different types of crimes (such as robbery, rape, and murder). Officials established a detailed time schedule for elementary school instruction and paid work (twelve centavos per day) as well as visiting hours. In 1909, 6,333 individuals of both sexes entered the prison and 5,614 left, leaving 719 in the city jail that year alone. The state government paid all expenses (including electric lighting) except for textbooks.[122]

This elaborate change in the capital's prison arrangements was not uncommon in turn-of-the-century Latin America. Positivist leaders in Mexico and elsewhere in the region looked to the study of penology and penal reforms as mainstays of their modern regimes. While secular education would shape the minds of future citizens, penitentiaries, according to Robert Buffington, would "isolate and (ideally) rehabilitate transgressors." A newly redeveloped penal system was, in the eyes of elites, essential for the formation of a civilized nation. Drawing on the management efficiency designs of British philosopher Jeremy Bentham, nineteenth-century Mexican politicians built on Bourbon-era ideas of criminal reform to shape a rationalized system of prisons throughout the country. During the Porfiriato the prison system was thoroughly reconstructed. Mexico City's penitentiary, opened in 1900, represented the zenith of the regime's projects of order and reason.[123] President Díaz and his coterie of positivist administrators believed that a reformed and rationally ordered penal system would eradicate crime from Mexican society. They perceived the penitentiary as the ideal space in which to inculcate a strong work ethic among prisoners and rehabilitate them from their vice-ridden pasts.[124]

The influence of these national and international penal reform movements found its way to Oaxaca's state capital. Oaxacan reformers, eager to keep undesirables off the streets of their modern city, filled the prison with what they determined were criminals and vagrants.

Social Hygiene

Without public hygiene there cannot be stable sanitary conditions, and without sanitary conditions there cannot be a complete and vigorous development of use to the population. There is not a social group in civilized countries that does not concern itself with an abundant water supply and proper sewage systems. It is therefore essential that the city of Oaxaca, which has existed for so long in lamentable disregard, seriously concern itself with making an effort for the generation of today and for those to come.

— Governor Emilio Pimentel, 1903

The increased attention paid to public hygiene by Porfirian officials like Governor Pimentel stemmed from both a life-and-death concern over the paltry sanitation conditions in the capital and from a desire to marshal the discourses of health and morality in order to maintain control over the city's public spaces. Addressing part of a larger concern over social cleansing and prophylaxis that included regulating the city's sex trade, government officials sought to cleanse the city of what they saw as its physical and moral contagions.

Since the colonial era officials had cited open sewers and the poor quantity and quality of water as the major contributors to high rates of morbidity and mortality in Oaxaca City.[125] Monthly Porfirian mortality statistics from the Central District and the city's cemetery records included details on the cause, age, and gender of the deceased in the state capital and surrounding towns and villages. Despite claims by the U.S. consular agent, Ezra Lawton, that by 1909 there was "very little sickness [in Oaxaca City], for the small attention paid to sanitary conditions,"[126] well over a thousand inhabitants died each year during the Porfiriato, over 80 percent due to water-born gastrointestinal diseases (*afecciones del tubo intestinal delgado y grueso*). Between 1878 and 1879 a small outbreak of smallpox killed close to seven hundred people. Infants under one year of age were most susceptible to the deadly stomach viruses.[127] Although not stated in the records, it is most likely that the lower classes in the city and surrounding towns, with poor sewage systems and reliant on communal and often untreated water sources, suffered the worst losses to disease and illness.[128]

Yet it was the moral implication of hygiene and sanitation that drew the greatest attention from government officials in Oaxaca City. In Mexico, moral reform measures gained prominence during the Bourbon period as elites utilized the "idiom of morality" to "spell out the cultural aspects of elite class membership as the *pueblo bajo*, unwilling or economically prevented from acquiring elite cultural accoutrements, became the social foil of the *gente culta*."[129] Morality campaigns continued throughout the nineteenth century as liberal leaders, drawing on the basic tenets of the Enlightenment, imagined the construction of a homogenized modern society. During the Porfiriato, Oaxacan officials, building on these traditions, linked issues of vice and hygiene to citizenship and state formation.[130] For city elites, insisting that the capital be "clean" meant that they could have access to peoples' lives and living spaces. Elites viewed disorder, vagrancy, and deviance as the principle causes of society's decline and worked to cleanse the city of them.[131] Officials employed the city's police force as an on-the-ground agent of detection, intervention, and discipline.

Studies of turn-of-the-century policing in Latin America have most often focused on the police's capacity to impose order.[132] In addition to "keeping the peace," city governments in Oaxaca and elsewhere in Mexico utilized police forces as crucial mechanisms to implement and enforce moral reform. Citing often unwarranted arrests of foreigners "visiting and doing business" in the state capital,

Adalberto Flores, the jefe político of the state's Central District, wrote the "Special Police Treatise for the Capital of the State of Oaxaca." The first thirty-five articles of the 1908 treatise focus on police responsibilities for maintaining hygienic conditions in the city. The majority of the remaining articles concern the behavior in and use of public spaces by the city's inhabitants. In Flores's treatise and in an early city police guide (1897) articles pay special attention to the issue of sanitation in private homes. Both documents emphasize the right of police to enter people's homes to inspect their "interior hygiene."[133]

In addition to granting them access to private spaces in the city, officials instructed police to root out vagrants occupying public spaces. From early in the Porfiriato, officials argued that beggars threatened the stability of democracy and progress. An article in the state's official paper warned that "it is without a doubt that today's mobs of begging children, tomorrow's men raised in idleness, will become gangs of thieves, revolutionaries, and constant enemies of peace and security. A little bit of vigilance now, a little bit of work to extirpate the bad, will bring immense benefits later for society."[134] Drawing on the segregationist scientific politics of the era, city elites linked class with morality in an attempt to separate themselves from the "lower" parts of society. Seeing social undesirables as a threat to upper-class decency, elites attempted to cleanse the streets of them.[135] An article in La unión titled "How to Destroy the Plague of Beggars" argued that, although the city had fewer vagrants than most cities (fewer than one hundred), the government should build an asylum for beggars.[136] Two years later, the editors of another paper, El correo del sur, complained that the city had been "invaded by beggars" who threatened the decency of visiting foreigners by following them and others into business establishments.[137] Theory became practice when the city government, following articles 848 and 849 of the state's penal code, instructed police to apprehend and imprison vagrants who were not "dedicated to an honest and lucrative occupation."[138] Like their counterparts in the state of Coahuila, police agents often deprived "individuals of their liberty" in order to appropriate their labor.[139] It was not until 1911 that government and Catholic Church officials joined forces to propose the construction of an asylum for beggars to serve in conjunction with the city's orphanage established almost forty years earlier.

Regulations

In a yet another effort to shape the Porfirian state capital into a modern urban center and reconfigure patterns of economic relationships and guidelines in order to foment capitalist development, city officials restructured and rationalized their own administrative system.[140] In 1872, in an attempt to standardize taxation, the

city developed a collective system of public taxes and regulations (Plan de Arbitrios). It was not until the mid-1880s, however, that city councilmen began to rigorously codify and regulate the different branches of the city's administration.
The city council instituted dozens of new regulations. Whereas the 1872 and later
1890 Plan de Arbitrios united various branches of administration (water, sanitation, transportation, etc.) into one broad system of regulation, the new regulations existed on their own and divided the city's administration into clearly defined categories. Between 1891 and 1908 the city council established twenty-eight
separate regulations ranging from regulations of cemeteries, brothels, and markets to water provisions, liquor stores, and the police force.[141] The rapid development of new regulations during Oaxaca City's late Porfiriato underscores elites'
persistent anxiety during this era of "order and progress." They hoped to control
the disorder inherent in the modernization they heralded.

The new regulations for the city's markets exemplify the council's project of
administrative rationalization. In August 1892, during the construction of the
new "Porfirio Díaz" market, the city council completed the first draft of the
"Regulation for the Collection of Market Taxes." The councilman in charge wrote
that there existed an "urgency to promulgate a regulation for the taxation of
the city's markets." The markets were, after all, the state capital's most lucrative
source of income, consistently accounting for over one quarter of the city government's total annual revenues. A rationalized system of regulation and taxation
was sure to bring in still more money.

After studying the existing market regulations from Mexico City, the Oaxaca
City council printed a poster indicating the new regulations. Unlike past "very
general rules" for local commerce, the new regulations were detailed and specific.
A newly formed Commission on Markets dictated procedure for the five city markets. A collector, four assistants, and ten custodians carried out the regulations,
collected taxes, and maintained order and hygiene in the respective markets. As
in other areas of Porfirian city governance, the Commission on Markets emphasized the establishment and enactment of the metric system to scientifically and
concisely measure and codify space, mass, and volume. In the documents no reference is made to how the newly rationalized measurements could also serve to
protect customers from an arbitrary weighing of goods and produce. The collector ensured that the size of each market stall complied with the new prescribed
dimensions. The 1894 amendment to the regulation states, "The area for stalls in
the 'Porfirio Díaz' market will consist of the following dimensions: one meter and
seventeen centimeters long by two meters wide."[142] On Independence Day, 1896,
Governor Martín González officially promulgated the new measurement system
in Oaxaca on behalf of President Díaz. Meters and kilograms replaced traditional

measurements of *varas* and *jarras*.[143] In the years following 1896, the system of weights and measures in Oaxaca City was routinely verified. By 1907 the government had established a Verification Office of Weights and Measures in the city. Violators of the new system could receive fines and up to a year in prison.

Emblematic of the prevailing tensions over Porfirian legislation, stall owners and salespeople did not always follow the regulations down to the last centimeter and gram. Wedded to self-defined measurements of space and goods, market workers continually complained of the city's attempt to relocate their stalls and to regulate their sales.[144] In the years after the implementation of the metric system, vendors continued to flout the city's regulations by selling their goods on the street away from officially sanctioned market spaces. When assessing newly arrived products in the city's markets, even officials continued, in some cases, to use older, imprecise methods of measurement.[145] Attempts to make the city more "legible" and in theory more efficient through new regulations often failed as city officials and marketers undermined the new system by continuing to use longstanding methods of measurement.

Conclusions

Elites asserted their notion of a dominant modernity by adjusting the spatial contours of the city along three different but intersecting lines. First, urban planners constructed spaces by building and rebuilding the capital's neighborhoods, streets, gardens, and secular architecture. Second, officials reinforced their segregationist ideals of social division by imbuing parks and streets with the strategic symbolic characteristics of rituals, maps, and signs. Finally, elites spaces of discipline with a strengthened police force, prison system, and administrative regulations that sought to uphold elite conceptions of social hygiene by removing unwanted members of the lower class from city streets.

By excluding the majority of the city's population, officials simply relegated the persistent social and economic inequalities of the capital farther to the margins. At the end of Porfiriato, elites had succeeded in modernizing the city's central areas and new suburbs through projects of beautification, hygiene, and spatial regulation, but only by deliberately ignoring the capital's growing underclass. Prostitution was yet another aspect of civic life that elites felt sullied the city's moral landscape. Unable to reconcile the moral and financial characteristics of the sex trade, the attempts by government officials to regulate the capital's "public women" floundered. Before examining the commercial sex trade, let us turn to the role institutionalized religion played in labor, morality campaigns, and education in the Porfirian state capital.

CHAPTER THREE

"A New Political Religious Order"
Church, State, and Workers

Capital cannot do without Labor, nor Labor without Capital. Mutual agreement results in the beauty of good order; while perpetual conflict necessarily produces confusion and savage barbarity. Now, in preventing such strife as this . . . the efficacy of Christian institutions is marvelous and manifold. First of all, there is no intermediary more powerful than Religion (whereof the Church is the interpreter and guardian) in drawing the rich and the working class together, by reminding each of its duties to the other, and especially of the obligations of justice. Thus Religion teaches the laborer and the artisan to carry out honestly and fairly all equitable agreements freely entered into; never to injure the property, nor to outrage the person, of an employer; never to resort to violence in defending their own cause, nor to engage in riot or disorder; and to have nothing to do with men of evil principles.

— Pope Leo XIII, *Rerum Novarum: On the Condition of the Working Classes*, 1891

Now that times have changed, a new era has begun, I hope, in the political religious order. From the conquest to the French intervention, the [Catholic] Church was politically active in Mexico. Under the present circumstances with the [Reform] laws in place, the Church does not have the political power it once had. In my opinion, it is time to establish a regime that allows the Church to follow the path of its counterpart in the United States. That is to say, completely unconcerned with politics and related matters.

— Archbishop Gillow of Oaxaca to President Porfirio Díaz, 1892

A series of anticlerical laws set in motion by Mexico's 1857 Constitution left Roman Catholic prelates and priests struggling to keep their religious faith alive within the walls of the country's churches and seminaries. Despite the state's attempts to weaken the church, Mexican society continued to be predominantly

[70]

Catholic throughout the Porfiriato. In fact, the moral teachings and social conventions of Catholicism continued to pervade and shape the daily lives of Mexicans. Oaxaca de Juárez exemplified the resurgence of Mexican Catholicism and the critical role it played in the formation of the state capital's encounter with modernity during the Porfiriato, even in the wake of the liberal reforms of the 1850s and 1860s. Including the fundamental contribution of the church and religion in a study of Mexico's modernizing processes challenges and complicates their past treatment as secondary and epiphenomenal stand-ins for more pressing matters.[1] Furthermore, it undoes notions that the process of modernity necessarily entails a teleological narrative of progress from religious to secular world views.[2] Oaxaca's Catholic Church contributed to the Porfirian capitalist project by attempting to cultivate productive and acquiescent laborers. The church hierarchy hoped that by instilling the city's workers with a combination of capitalist work ethic and Catholic morality they could achieve the double result of strengthening their membership base and allying themselves with the economic agenda of the Porfirian state. Like their secular, civic counterparts, church leaders worked to rationalize and make legible not only the city's workers (their parishioners) but also the church's leadership itself. The state capital's priests harnessed similar modern cultural elements examined in the previous chapter in order to affect these changes. Church officials practically and symbolically linked efforts to revitalize the church with Porfirian economic development by imbuing transformed city spaces with notions of progress and piety. Leaders like Archbishop Eulogio Gillow utilized public rituals, festivals, print media, and notions of thrift, recreation, and the purifying power of work in the hopes of cultivating devout and devote workers and fostering a culture of capitalism.

In Oaxaca City, the 1895 federal census recorded that, of the city's 32,437 inhabitants, 32,301 were practicing Catholics, 107 were Protestant, and the remaining handful identified themselves as "deists, free thinkers, and spiritualists."[3] Given the predominance of Catholics in the capital city, leaders and followers of the church needed to reconcile their conservative attitudes and practices with the newly developed projects of Díaz's government. The Porfirian history of Oaxaca City epitomizes these tensions between church and state and underscores the unique and influential relationship the president had with the political and religious life of his hometown.

The fact that Mexico was beginning to join an increasingly capitalist and industrialized world prompted Catholic leaders to take a stance on the labor and living conditions of the country's workers. Whereas anticlericalism characterized the liberal government's approach to modernization in the decades prior to the Porfiriato, Díaz directly involved the church in his designs of economic development. As such, the church played an integral role in Mexico's experience with capital and industrial intensification and social and cultural transformations at the turn of the century. In Oaxaca City, this role is most clearly expressed at the precarious intersection of religion, work, and state politics during the tenure of Oaxaca's archbishop, Eulogio Gillow, a friend and business partner of Porfirio Díaz. The notion of modernity in Oaxaca City included the seemingly incongruous roles of the church and the city's workers. Traditional historiography of the nineteenth century has long stressed the anticlericalism of Mexico's Porfirian era, assuming that the church and religion faded before the modernizing project. Yet in Oaxaca, the Mexican government and Catholic Church worked in tandem to construct a modern Mexico fueled by the labor of the country's workers. After years of anticlerical measures, the Porfirian process of reconciliation between church and state made the two institutions strange but complementary bedfellows. The liberalization of both institutions in a period of capitalist expansion depended on the exploitation of Mexican workers, and the relationship between Díaz and Gillow and Oaxaca City's workers typified this dynamic. In this era of rationalized city spaces and anticlerical regulations, the Catholic Church provided a vital base for the expression of religious faith and social services.[4]

The Church in the Reform Era

In 1855, after Benito Juárez and the leaders of the Revolution of Ayutla ousted Antonio López de Santa Anna from his long-held position as Mexico's conservative leader, they turned their attention to revitalizing the nation. A series of brutal civil wars and an imperialist invasion by the United States (1846–48) had sabotaged attempts to consolidate the nation after it won independence from Spain in 1821. Among other measures the leaders of Mexico's new government legislated in the 1857 constitution were several harsh reforms meant to curtail the power of the church. Since the colonial period, the leaders of the Catholic Church had closely allied themselves with conservative, centralist forces in the government. Juárez and his coterie of liberal politicians deemed the church's extensive properties, tithe collection, and political influence detrimental to the formation of the Mexican nation.

In the years before the 1857 constitution, the government passed two major anticlerical laws (leyes). The Ley Juárez (1855) abolished ecclesiastic and military fueros, which had exempted these institutions from trial in civil courts. The Ley Lerdo (1856) forbade groups (principally the church) from owning or administering property not used in everyday activities. This meant that the church could retain its churches, monasteries, and seminaries, but it had to divest itself of other types of urban and rural properties, whose proceeds it could keep. Both laws would be incorporated into the 1857 constitution. Following the War of the Reform – yet another bloody civil war dominated by ideological battles between liberals and conservatives (1858–61) – the Juárez government issued a series of decrees intensifying the separation of church and state and further subordinating the church to the Mexican government. The Juárez government nationalized church properties and retained the proceeds from further sales. Throughout the Reform era, church properties were confiscated at public auctions by the federal government and private individuals.[5] During this period, the federal government confiscated 1,102 church properties in Oaxaca City, almost 80 percent of the state's total.[6]

In 1857 President Ignacio Comfort signed two other statutes into law imposing further prohibitions on the church and secularizing ecclesiastical activities. In a radical break from over three centuries of church control, the registration of births, marriages, and deaths as well as the administration of cemeteries would now fall under civil jurisdiction. The Ley Iglesias (Church Law) required the church to administer the sacraments at reduced rates to a largely poor population.

While Mexico's northern neighbor fought a bloody civil war, French troops, after years of fighting, installed Napoleon III's puppet emperor, Maximilian of Hapsburg, on a throne in Mexico City (1864). The defeat of Benito Juárez and his armies provided government and church conservatives with a brief opportunity to regain some of the political ground that they had lost during the years of liberal reforms. Yet, the overthrow of the French army and Maximilian's execution only three years later sounded the death knell for the church. The partial recuperation of church control over its lands and rituals enjoyed during the French occupation government ended when Juárez reclaimed power in 1867. Conservative Catholics considered the years of the Restored Republic (1867–76) and the presidency of Sebastián Lerdo de Tejada (author of the Ley Lerdo, 1872–76) a "religious tyranny."[7]

Although Lerdo's successor, Porfirio Díaz, was a friend and supporter of the laws of the Reform, church leaders saw in him – as we will see – a chance to reconcile with the government. This reconciliation would come about in part, but not without enormous efforts by clergy and laypersons alike. On the eve of the Porfiriato, the Catholic Church was in disarray. It lacked economic and human resources and had lost many of its churches and institutional centers. It was not until 1871 that the government permitted Mexico's archbishop to return to his see in the nation's capital. Oaxaca did not fare any better. The state and its capital city devoted few resources to the ailing religious community. Until Gillow's arrival in 1887, closed seminaries and abandoned churches greatly hindered official church activities in the state capital. The city had only twenty-nine priests with ninety-eight in the entire diocese.[8] A comparison of city census records from the colonial and pre-Porfirian eras shows that the number of ecclesiastics as a percentage of the capital's total working population fell from 11.7 percent in 1792 to 1.2 percent in 1875.[9]

Reconciliation

During Porfiriato the Mexican Catholic Church experienced a revival. Although it would never regain its pre-Reform status, the church emerged from the years of Díaz's rule a much stronger and more influential institution. In Oaxaca, as elsewhere in the republic, church leaders like Gillow shifted their focus from emulation of the gospel in daily practice to social reform. In the state capital, leaders concentrated much of their reform efforts on the relationship with the capital's artisans. They hoped to confront what they saw as the detrimental effects of modernity by inculcating morality and ending vice and poverty among the popular classes.[10]

The Porfirian reconciliation between church and state emerged from a series of radical changes in the international and national church and government hierarchies. As the new head of the Catholic Church in 1878, Pope Leo XIII worked quickly to assuage relations between Rome and anticlerical governments in Europe and around the world. There has been a tendency in the historical literature to equate the late-nineteenth- and early-twentieth-century period of industrialization and state formation with secularization. On the contrary, this era, described as the period of "Neo-Christendom," witnessed an increase in the power of the Catholic Church around the world as bishops adopted a more flexible position vis-à-vis their government counterparts. Church leaders developed workers circles as a way to strengthen their ties with a growing workforce and to at once stave off the influence of socialism and preserve "Catholicism's ideological hegemony." In addition to in Mexico, the episcopacy in places like Brazil, Argentina, and Colombia regained privileges lost during the era of liberal reforms.[11] As Pamela Voekel has argued for the early independence period in Mexico, the revitalized Porfirian church needs to be reconsidered not as the government's handmaiden and a hindrance to modernization, but as integral to the processes of modernization on both ideological and material levels.[12] That is, especially in places such as Oaxaca City, church and government leaders worked to mutually advance each others' modernizing designs.

After successfully appealing to Chancellor Otto von Bismarck of Germany to improve relations with the Apostolic See, the Pope communicated to Díaz a similar request. Eager to benefit from a stabilized ecclesiastical institution, Díaz had already been acting to ameliorate interactions between church and state. In 1881 the president requested that Gillow marry him to Carmen Romero Rubio, a devout Catholic and daughter of Manuel Romero Rubio, Díaz's secretary of the interior. Although Gillow declined the honor, he convinced Mexico's archbishop, Pelagio Antonio de Labastida, to accept, thus joining Díaz with a conservative Catholic, supporter of Maximilian, and strong critic of the 1857 constitution. In fact, Díaz openly proclaimed himself a proud Catholic in his family; but, because of the Reform laws, he professed no religion as Mexico's head of state. Gillow also served as confessor to the first lady.

By the 1890s, the state-church reconciliation of the Porfiriato began to come to tangible and dramatic fruition. For example, in 1891, the Pope named Gillow archbishop of Antequera (the diocesan and colonial name for Oaxaca City) and published the papal encyclical *Rerum Novarum* (literally, "Of New Things"), which concerned the relationship of the world's working classes to emergent capitalist economies. As the Mexican Southern Railway made its way to Oaxaca in the following year, Mexico heralded its new liberal archbishop, Próspero María Alarcón, who replaced Antonio Labastida, a staunch monarchist. Then, on October 12, 1895, the church celebrated the coronation of the Virgin of Guadalupe, Mexico's patron saint and a powerful symbol of the country's fusion of indigenous and European religious traditions.[13]

The construction of nearly five thousand new churches, schools, and seminaries, as well as the creation of several new bishoprics, accompanied this succession of fundamental changes in Mexico's Catholic community. The country's official Catholic newspaper, *La voz de México*, which had previously spoken cautiously of the new economic and social policies of the Díaz government, now enthusiastically supported the president in his 1900 presidential reelection campaign. The paper lauded Díaz as a representative of "all that is serious, respectable, and honest in Mexican society." *La voz de la verdad*, Oaxaca's official Catholic paper and the voice of Gillow's diocese, similarly praised Díaz: "The presence of General Díaz at the head of our nation's government signifies peace, an indispensable and crucial factor without which the progress of Mexico, its indisputable advancement and prosperity, would quickly decline."[14]

Throughout the colonial and early independence periods, the Catholic Church had flourished in Oaxaca City. Ecclesiastical architecture dominated the capital, dotting most blocks with one of thirty-three churches. Gillow oversaw the rebuilding and revitalization of the physical and human infrastructure of his diocese. In an 1888 letter to Díaz, Gillow celebrated his early achievements as bishop:

I am pleased to tell you that in the short period that I have governed this diocese I have established the basis of a new regimen without any trouble from my priests, who each day show me more appreciation, respect, and affection. The majority of the church council supports me. Any belligerent priests have been removed from their parishes. I have received no further complaints [from their parishioners]. I am reforming the rules of the Catholic workers society in order that the workers always remain subject to ecclesiastical authority and refrain from all interference in [state] politics. I also have a clear understanding with the civil and military authorities.[15]

This letter and the many others like it between the two friends reveal the importance of their relationship, especially in the realm of reconciliation and development of the church, and the broad reach of Gillow into secular society. In order to maximize administrative efficiency, Gillow divided the city into three parishes, each with ten thousand inhabitants; appointed priests to the capital's seventeen remaining churches; and reorganized the diocesan seminary. He also managed to return some secularized property to church control and received permission for priests to wear their robes in public.[16] The latter concession provided a powerful symbol, increasing the visibility and presence of the church in daily life. By 1910 the number of churches in the state had risen to 1,340, a ratio of 774 inhabitants per church.[17]

Reconciliation between church and state on a municipal level reached its pinnacle in Oaxaca City with the celebration of the Virgin of Guadalupe and the coronation of Oaxaca's own patron saint, the Virgin of Solitude (la Virgen de la Soledad). Starting in 1896, Gillow linked the city's practicing Catholics to the nation's saint by arranging annual Virgin of Guadalupe celebrations in all of the city's parishes.[18] On the eve of Mexico's fourth national Catholic Congress, hosted by Gillow in 1909, the Vatican decreed that a colonial-era statue of the virgin be crowned as the Virgin of Solitude.[19] According to local newspapers, thousands of people attended the four-day event, including high-ranking ecclesiastical and civic officials.[20] Similar to the following year's centennial celebrations, the lavish events surrounding the virgin's coronation on January 18 by Gillow and a representative of Pope Pius IX symbolically linked the main event to notions of modernity and economic progress. On coronation day floats with costumed people staged tableaux vivants of Oaxaca's past, present, and future. Floats symbolizing commerce, Christian enlightenment, mining, and progress and industry paraded past throngs of onlookers. Together, all the floats clearly portrayed the city's Catholic and business communities on a common course of progress and civilization. Anticipating the theme of the Catholic Congress, several displays highlighted the evangelization of Oaxaca's indigenous inhabitants.[21] Members of Oaxaca's Catholic Workers Circle joined the show, where they rubbed elbows with a group of the city's prominent industrialists and children from the Zorrilla, Varela, Murgía, and Tejada families.[22] The following year "all classes of society" in the city repeated the celebration with nine days of pomp and circumstance.[23]

The Catholic Church had considerable power and reach throughout Mexico during the Porfiriato, lending symbolic coherence to most people's activities and functioning as an institution of social control. The principles and ethical norms of popular Catholicism that underlined the roles of respect and obedience were critical in the orientation of political action and social behavior. As such, the church served as a source for social identity and regional pride. In cities, neighborhood identities were associated with the church and its patron saint in manners that recalled the traditional guilds linked to the church. Catholic priests had tremendous influence in local events, politics, and public opinion. In addition, the religious hierarchy often maintained a strong rapport with the local urban elite.[24]

During the early years of Díaz's regime, under Archbishop Gillow's leadership, the institution of Catholicism in Oaxaca City experienced not just a renaissance of formal church structures but a resurgence of commitment from its faithful. Although the city's inhabitants had been expressing ambivalence toward the secularization of society and renewed commitment to Catholicism since the enactment of the Reform laws, outward displays of religious faith grew in frequency and intensity throughout the Porfirian era.[25]

In 1904 Oaxaqueños filled the streets of the capital to celebrate the visit of the pope's representative, Domingo Serafini. The author of an article in the official bulletin of the diocese proclaimed that he had "never seen in Oaxaca such spontaneous and universal enthusiasm as the population demonstrated on the afternoon [of Serafini's arrival]." Other articles reinforced that image. One proclaimed that "religious sentiment lives, filling with vigor the hearts of the great majority of the [church's] members. It is revealed on extraordinary occasions like the grand demonstrations of faith, of piety, of fervor during which one's heart cannot help but be inundated by ineffable comforts."[26]

Government officials wrote hundreds of impassioned letters to Gillow's predecessor, Bishop Vicente Fermín Márquez y Carrizosa, bemoaning their absence from the church and requesting absolution of sins committed in the name of the laws of the Reform. Indeed, an article in La voz de la verdad complained that the "ordinary family regimen of modern society" was to blame for the decline of Christian morality in the capital. The article went on to exclaim that families, losing their connection to Catholicism, needed to raise Christian children and not "simply procreate like animals."[27]

Scores of letters to the diocese from city inhabitants reveal the degree to which people thought about Catholicism and, more important, the extent of their concern for their own salvation. The handwritten letters, largely from lawyers and government officials, requested that the church accept a retraction of their oath to the anticlerical laws of the Reform. Thus, the official secular posture of the state had created a tension among government workers who wished to remain loyal to their Catholic roots. Luis G. Córdova and Manuel Mendoza, both civil servants, wrote to repent their "allegiance to the laws of the Reform" and to proclaim that "now as always my beliefs impassion me to live always in the bosom of the Church of Jesus Christ."[28]

Other state employees like Demetrio Sodi and Jesús A. Vásquez wanted to have their cake and eat it, too. Representatives of Oaxaca's state council and the city's mayor, respectively, each petitioned for a "license" from the church to work simultaneously for the state and pay their allegiance to the church. Sodi in particular hoped to avoid "the scandal that has resulted for other [government workers] with faith." In both cases the bishop granted their wish as long as they pledged they "would not attack the laws, finances, and rights of the church or its authorities."[29]

Other supplicants confessed that they had purchased church property auctioned according to the Lerdo Law. Juan Bautista claimed that he had been "ignorant of the business of disentailing and selling church buildings," and that he "had been tricked" by the government into purchasing a formerly church-owned house in 1872. Ten years later Bautista asked to sell it back to the diocese for what he had paid. In that same year Colonel Vicente Lozano wrote: "Wishing to ease my conscience as a Catholic, I admit to owning four houses that were the church's property but were disentailed due to the Reform laws. I took advantage of these laws, buying [the houses] at a [government] auction." After declaring the shame that he felt for his actions, Lozano asks that church leaders pay him only what they thought was fair for the four houses.[30]

What are we to make of this renenewed commitment to Catholicism among the capital's community? Certainly, the intensity and pervasiveness of people's reaffirmation to Catholicism underscore the importance of the church in the everyday lives of Mexicans during the Porfiriato. Furthermore, the rush by civil servants to repent their oaths of allegiance to liberal doctrines exposes challenges to the state's secular modernizing agenda.[31] Oaxaca state and capital employees could not simply relinquish their ties to the church in favor of a liberal government. Instead, they found ways to bridge their religious convictions and their civic duties.

The Díaz regime needed to find a way to to include the Catholic Church in its visions of modernity. How could the state mobilize the powers of the church to its own political and economic ends? For Oaxaca, the response came in the person of Archbishop Eulogio Gillow and his connection to the city's workers.

Gillow: The Porfirian Compromise

On November 18, 1887, Gillow entered Oaxaca City for the first time as its new bishop. In a symbolic gesture before his official reception, Gillow stood on the ruins of the San Juan de Dios Chapel (neglected during the decades of anticlerical governments) and proclaimed to an enthusiastic crowd of civic and ecclesiastical dignitaries his intention to restore the building. Listening among the other government officials in the audience, Miguel Castro, former governor of Oaxaca and a strong supporter of the Reform laws, must have taken notice of this historic moment of rapprochement between the government and the Catholic Church.

Born in 1841 to a wealthy industrialist and a member of the Spanish nobility, Eulogio Gregorio Gillow y Zavalza, Oaxaca's religious leader for most of the Porfiriato, embodied the era's trend of reconciliation between church and state.[32] Equally well versed in his economic and ecclesiastical commitments, Gillow was poised to benefit from and influence Díaz's modernizing agenda. Gillow biographer Manuel Esparza notes: "Without a doubt, what complicates the historical judgment of Archbishop Gillow is the fact that he was simultaneously a religious hierarch and a Porfirian landowner."[33]

In the decades before becoming Oaxaca's bishop, Gillow received an extensive education in business and religion. He began his business education at the early age of ten when he accompanied his father to London's first world exposition. At the exposition the elder Gillow hoped to promote his business, which was tied to the mechanization of Mexican agriculture. In his teens and twenties, Eulogio Gillow followed a distinguished path of university education. He attended academic institutions in Oxford, Paris, Bonn, and Salamanca, and finally earned his doctorate in law, political economics, and ecclesiastical diplomacy in Rome. Mexico's Catholic Church sent him as its representative to the Catholic Congress in Belgium in 1864. The Congress was one of three congresses convened by Belgium's Catholic authorities in an attempt to rally the church in the face of the country's anticlerical Liberal party. In 1866 Pope Pius IX named Gillow his privy chamberlain supernumerary (camarero secreto supernumerario) and then his domestic prelate in 1869. Gillow met Díaz in 1877 at Mexico's first regional exhibition of industrial agriculture. Gillow helped organize the event, which would later serve as a model for others throughout Mexico.[34] Eight years later President Manuel González (1880–84) sent Gillow as the representative of the Federal District to the New Orleans World Exposition of 1885. At the exposition Gillow worked closely with Díaz at the headquarters of Mexico's delegation.[35]

By the time Gillow took up his post in Oaxaca City, he had managed to forge strong relationships with Rome and Mexico City and to establish himself as a leader in the business and Catholic communities of Mexico. Gillow would draw on these qualities to restructure the ranks of Oaxaca's Catholic Church and its workers organizations and to improve relations with the city and state governments.[36]

Like his municipal government contemporaries, Gillow, as bishop and later archbishop (1891), radically restructured the church's infrastructure and administration. In addition to rebuilding and newly adorning many of the city's churches, Gillow made extensive pastoral visits (visitas pastorales) to the towns and villages of the state, during which he claimed to bestow the sacrament of confirmation on over six hundred thousand Oaxacans.[37] In his first decade as archbishop, Gillow expanded and rationalized the administration of the church. In 1901 he institutionalized regular meetings with the clergy of the diocese. Those in the city were to meet with him on the first and third Monday of every month to discuss church matters; those outside the city would meet with Gillow's state vicar (vicario foraneo). Additionally, Gillow required clergy to take an examination every five years in order to renew their registration in the capital.[38]

Gillow reinforced this administrative intensification with the publication of two church periodicals. In January 1896, after the archbishop installed printing presses in his newly created Sociedad Protectora de la Buena Prensa (Society for the Protection of Good Press), the editor, Lorenzo Mayoral, printed the first copy of the newspaper La voz de la verdad. As the state's official Catholic paper, it connected Oaxaca's Catholics with their international brethren in articles like "Bismarck and Catholicism" and "Baptisms in China"; it also provided information on church activities throughout the region and in the capital city. In addition to publishing daily news items, La voz de la verdad editorialized about the "immorality of the masses" and the "Yankeeization" of Mexico by Protestants and entrepreneurs from the United States. La voz also ran a weekly column titled "For Ladies," which prescribed "proper social conduct" for the city's female population.[39] Most important was the newspaper's support for Díaz and his policies. As noted above, La voz de la verdad, along with other Mexican Catholic presses, praised the Porfirian government's efforts to promote peace and prosperity in the country. With a correspondent in Mexico City by 1908, it claimed a weekly run of more than four thousand copies.

In March 1901 Gillow published the first edition of the *Boletín oficial: Revista eclesiástica de la provincia de Antequera* (Official Bulletin – Ecclesiastical Magazine of the Province of Antequera). The *Boletín* promoted the "uniformity of doctrine and the unity of religious and social action among the state's clergy."[40] As such, the publication served as a kind of trade journal for local clergy, emphasizing doctrinal and social renewal and clarity. In tandem, then, *La voz* and the *Boletín* highlighted Gillow's effort to modernize the church's infrastructure and to mediate church-state relations.

In addition to the rhetoric of the church's official publications, Gillow's relationship with the municipal and state governments was varied, but ultimately positive throughout the period. Despite the often confrontational official attitude of the government toward the Catholic Church and the restrictive Reform laws, Díaz, Oaxaca's state governors, and city officials maintained amicable, if not openly cordial relationships with Gillow and granted him concessions over property and church powers. Gillow's ties to General Martín González (1894–1902) and Emilio Pimentel (1902–11) represent the two, albeit moderate, extremes of relationship he had with the state's governors.

Despite vehement objection from some of his clergy, including his would-be successor, José Othón Núñez, Gillow maintained a friendly relationship with Governor González, on one occasion inviting the governor to celebrate Gillow's birthday. As he did on many matters, Gillow corresponded with Díaz following González's inauguration. The archbishop assured the president that church-state relations in Oaxaca would continue to contribute to the state's progress: "I had the honor of receiving the visit of the new Governor, Mr. Gen. D. Martín González, and the following day I was pleased to inform that I do not doubt that in this new period that is beginning I will have the fortune to preserve the best relations with the civic powers, and that united both of us have the intention, each in his own sphere of influence, to work for the progress and benefit of the state."[41]

In contrast, Gillow and Emilio Pimentel did not profess to be friends. In fact, they had officially met only once, when Pimentel arrived in the city to assume the governorship. Pimentel's close friend, Ramón Ramírez de Aguilar, the *jefe de hacienda* of the neighboring state of Puebla, lamented this lack of contact. He noted that with previous governors Gillow always had maintained a friendship and that Pimentel's predecessors had "never had reason to complain, because [Gillow] had always kept within his own sphere of power, never wanting to meddle in that of the government."[42] Pimentel blamed the distance between himself and the archbishop on a state tax levied on church properties. Apparently Gillow viewed the tax as an unfair fiscal imposition. Pimentel maintained that he had been just upholding the law. Nevertheless, despite this disagreement, Gillow and Pimentel continued to correspond on official matters and avoided confrontation.

Although the church expansion projects of the archbishop provoked criticism among members of the city's government, the two groups usually settled differences amicably. In one example of his ability to circumvent conflict, Gillow convinced the city to remove a tax on work done on the border of the cathedral's property. In June 1903 city officials attempted to enforce legislation that required a license for a worker constructing a tombstone near the cathedral's atrium. Gillow intervened and argued that, despite the government's assertion otherwise, the atrium was not a public space but belonged instead to the church, as guaranteed by Article 14 of the federal constitution. Municipal authorities agreed with Gillow's argument and released the worker from any licensing obligations.[43]

Gillow's unique educational and business background, along with his close personal ties to Díaz and other members of the federal government, made him an excellent intermediary between the state capital's church and government leaders. He would deftly utilize this unique position to transform the relationship between the city's artisans and the church.

Obreros Católicos and the New Capitalist Economy

Modern life is an incomprehensible activity. It is therefore necessary to search for all possible avenues in order to be able to function within it. Those who fall behind will only with difficulty be able to find their way again. . . . The worker and the artisan form the most important element of the modern era.
— Sociedad de Artesanos del Estado de Oaxaca
(Society of Artisans of the State of Oaxaca), 1908

In 1910 Mexico's wage-labor class reached 15 percent of the population. This was not the case in Oaxaca, where most of the state's laborers continued to work as rural peasants. For example, of the 11,605 textile workers in the state, only 570 worked in factories; the rest labored as individual producers in small cottage industries selling their wares at regional markets.[44] Independent artisans or proprietary producers dominated the capital city's worker population.[45] Despite the arrival of the Mexican Southern Railway and the development of the port at Salina Cruz, the predominance of indigenous artisans in the state impeded the development and expansion of regional markets. Unlike states in northern Mexico, industrial modernization in Oaxaca never flourished.[46] As a consequence, Gillow's relationship with workers in Oaxaca City would focus on people working in a variety of crafts as independent producers, jobs that had changed little since the colonial era.

Only a small percentage of the region's workforce labored in factories in the city and the Central Valley. Textile factories in San José and San Agustín in the districts of Etla and Xía in the Sierra Juárez, as well as beer, cigarette, and shoe factories in Oaxaca City, employed all told a mere 1,360 workers at their peak at the end of the nineteenth century and beginning of the twentieth.[47] Most laborers in the capital worked in small, independently owned shops with a handful of people, mostly close relatives. A comparison of municipal census records from 1875, 1895, and 1901 bears this out. Through those Porfirian years, little change occurred in the makeup of the city's artisan population. Positions included hat, tortilla, and candle makers; copper, iron, and brick workers; as well as street cleaners, day laborers, servants, water carriers, and tailors. Some new occupations emerged during the period, such as photographer and telegraph and railroad worker.[48]

Although Charles Arthur, the U.S. consular agent in Oaxaca City, was always quick to recommend the hardworking and inexpensive workers of the state, he neglected to mention to his foreign colleagues that Oaxacan laborers also worked under deplorable conditions.[49] Divina Providencia, a group of small business owners petitioning the city for a change in taxation regulations, described the state of the capital's workforce: "The workshops are in a grave state, almost to the point of complete deterioration. [This situation] worsens the already embarrassing condition of workers, who instead of receiving the protection they deserve from the authorities to guide them through the rough path of their daily needs, feel weakened and afraid, unable to provide the onerous contribution of daily bread to their families."[50]

In addition to sharing this difficult position as members of the workforce, women laborers were paid less than their male counterparts. Moreover, business owners permitted women to work in only a handful of trades: in addition to jobs as clothes washers and bakers, women worked in the capital's small hat, cigar, and match factories. Their wages most closely approximated those of men at La Sorpresa cigar factory. There they earned a daily wage of forty centavos to the men's fifty. In most other industries women received half of what their male coworkers were paid for the same amount of labor.[51] This gender inequality persisted throughout the state.[52] Women in the city's workforce also exemplified other trends in capitalist expansion. The introduction of women workers into small factories and the deskilling of labor were both examples of economic modernization beginning to appear throughout Mexico.[53]

Under government and church pressure, the city's labor unions found it difficult to organize this historically entrenched, highly differentiated workforce.[54] Instead, workers groups looked to the various mutual societies in the capital for social and financial support. In the last decades of the nineteenth century, mutual societies began to flourish throughout Mexico. They functioned largely as patronage organizations headed by elite politicians and entrepreneurs. They organized job training, basic education, recreational activities, and, occasionally, emergency funds for their members. The first society in Oaxaca, the Sociedad de Artesanos del Estado de Oaxaca (Society of Artisans of the State of Oaxaca), began in 1873 under the leadership of Francisco Vasconcelos, who later became municipal president.[55] The society claimed that it had formed to combat the degradation of artisanal work and the lack of formal education among laborers. Inspired by its national counterpart, the socialist Gran Círculo Obrero de México (Great Mexican Workers Circle, 1872), the Society of Artisans established a trade school and a newspaper for workers.[56] By the end of the Porfiriato, the society joined with the Antireelectionist Party of Benito Juárez Maza, son of the former president.[57]

Other mutual aid societies stayed clear of party politics. Leading a January meeting in 1910, José Zorrilla Tejada, Oaxaca City's preeminent politician and industrialist, decried the lack of enthusiasm and commitment exhibited by members of the sixteen-year-old Union and Mutual Protection Society of Employees. Zorrilla recounted the short history of the society, explaining that it had initially flourished with overflowing coffers and "hundreds" of members.[58]

Other workers associated themselves with individual *gremios*, or guilds, based on their specific trades. Water carriers, deliverymen, and domestic servants, for example, each formed a separate gremio. In fact, workers had no other options: the city required them to join guilds, submit their photographs to city registries, and adhere to municipal regulations. Membership obliged workers to contribute 10 percent of their monthly earnings to the guild and to follow a strict code of conduct. Administrators feared that without guidelines, workers and servants entering the homes of city elites would upset the already "precarious safety and tranquility" of the family. According to municipal administrators, regulations "guaranteed the moralization" of the city's workers.[59] Failure to comply with the regulations resulted in expulsion from the guild and hence joblessness. As I discuss in detail in chapter 5, the photographic registration and enumeration of the city's workers allowed the municipal government to reduce a diverse ethnic population to homogeneous and legible trades.[60] This rationalization of the popular classes enabled the state to control their location and behavior. The registries also provided a medium with which the government could reinforce its rigid class- and race-based notions of "modern" Oaxacan society.[61]

Despite the munificent assertions of education and financial support by gremios and mutual aid societies, they ultimately served the city government by preempting worker discontent and creating a system of discipline. The mutual society system forced workers hoping to gain concessions from authorities to rely on municipal leaders. Independent workers had little recourse or support. In one example from 1879, a group of hat makers petitioned the government for space in a city market to sell their wares. In their request, they claimed to be members of the Sociedad de Artesanos. Francisco Vasconcelos, the society president, quickly denied the group's declaration, attaching a list of current members as proof. The government rejected the hat makers' request, forcing them to sell on the street.[62] In another incident, a collection of twenty-nine independent meat sellers, all women, complained directly to the state governor, Martín González, that it was "unjust, intolerable, and even inhuman" that their weekly tax be raised from six to thirteen centavos. Furthermore, they claimed that tax collectors were abusive toward them and that the city government had acted improperly. "The people pay the municipal taxes," they wrote, "so that the city government can make their lives comfortable and safe, not so that their lives are sunk into desperation and flung into a state of voracious hunger." The councilman in charge of markets responded angrily, demanding that the women workers "maintain the principle of respect of authority, without which public morality is impossible." The state government agreed, arguing further that the women had exceeded their allotted spatial limits in the market.[63] Throughout the Porfiriato, municipal authorities either ignored or denied dozens of petitions by independent laborers looking to improve their working conditions and sell goods in city markets.[64]

Union activity in general lacked support and resources. In his letters to prospective North American businessmen, the U.S. consular agent, Charles Arthur, frequently penned statements such as "I find no evidence whatsoever of an impending strike or other trouble. . . . I personally believe that any trouble [of] that nature is very remote in this locality."[65] Toward the end of the Porfiriato, two strikes by textile workers in the neighboring Etla district were the exceptions that confirmed the rule. Disgruntled workers protested at the two factories owned by the Zorrilla and Trápaga families. In the capital itself, evidence of only one strike appears in the historical record from the Porfiriato. Only scant information on the strike is available. La voz de la verdad reported that in September 1910 mechanics and carpenters left their workshops and declared a strike for better wages. According to La voz, the workers hired a lawyer to settle the dispute and to negotiate for better wages from the shops' manager, Carlos Orchard.[66]

The Rerum Novarum and the Círculo Católico de Obreros de Oaxaca

The great mistake made in regard to [the hardship of the working class], is to take up with the notion that class is naturally hostile to class, and that the wealthy and the working men are intended by nature to live in mutual conflict. So irrational and so false is this view, that the direct contrary is the truth. Just as the symmetry of the human frame is the result of the suitable arrangement of the different parts of the body, so in a State is it ordained by nature that these two classes should dwell in harmony and agreement, so as to maintain the balance of the body politic. Each needs the other.

—Pope Leo XIII, *Rerum Novarum: On the Condition of the Working Classes*, 1891

In 1891 newspapers throughout Mexico published the encyclical of Pope Leo XIII, *Rerum Novarum: On the Condition of the Working Classes*.[67] Issued that same year, the encyclical emerged from the Vatican's concern over industrialization and new class relations. Church leaders feared that the forces of capitalism, devoid of Christian influence, would cause "chaos, greed, revolution, and great suffering among the masses." As such, the *Rerum Novarum* was as much an evaluation of the socioeconomic climate at the end of the nineteenth century as it was a prescription for social action.[68] Yet the Catholic Church, still reeling from the anticlerical reforms earlier in the century, realized that it could recover some of its lost power by aiding the state's developmentalist projects and establishing social programs for the working poor. In creating a "new political religious order," church leaders like Gillow augmented aspirations to political power with social action. However, this did not mean that church leaders removed themselves from state and national politics. On the contrary, ecclesiastical elites worked within the Porfirian system to gain concessions. The formation of Catholic workers circles aided reconciliation with the state and increased the institutional status of the church.

Unlike in Europe, where socialist movements had already taken hold, in Mexico, according to historian Manuel Ceballos, the *Rerum Novarum* "awoke the consciousness of Catholics to social problems."[69] During this period of rapid industrialization, Catholic workers circles sprouted up throughout Latin America. Circles formed in response to the *Rerum Novarum* in places like Buenos Aires and Bogotá, where the Jesuit-sponsored circle, in addition to providing a bank, school, and other social services, supplied a constituent base for the governing Conservative Party.[70]

Archbishop Gillow and Oaxaca's Catholics followed this larger regional trend. Gillow's most significant contribution to church-state reconciliation came with an intervention in the city's artisan community: his creation of the Círculo Cató-lico de Obreros de Oaxaca (Catholics Workers Circle of Oaxaca, CCOO) in 1906. The CCOO served as an institution where workers encountered the imbricated modernizing designs of both the Catholic Church and the Mexican government. Limited in their options and familiar with the long-standing existence of guilds and mutual aid societies, workers in Oaxaca City turned to the CCOO for finan-cial and social benefits. At the same time, however, the CCOO not only supported the city's artisan population, it also acted as a powerful organizational tool for the church (and city government) to educate and discipline that population. The Círculo emerged from a multinational effort by the Catholic Church and secular elites to become more involved in a growing industrialized world. In Mexico, as in other countries in Latin America, the church combined its commitment to the living and labor conditions of workers with its support of the government's de-velopmentalist projects.

In Oaxaca City, Gillow's Círculo Católico de Obreros de Oaxaca not only be-came the dominant labor organization but also epitomized the archbishop's in-termediary position between the social advocacy of the Catholic Church and the economic projects of the Mexican state.[71] The CCOO was also part of Gillow's larger effort to discipline and order the church's laity through new brotherhood organizations around the state and to cultivate fervent personal dedication to Catholicism and Rome's primacy.[72]

The impulse for a workers circle in Oaxaca City already existed prior to the founding of the CCOO. In 1885 church and secular elites in the state capital had founded a predecessor to the CCOO.[73] Like other workers circles from the era, the Sociedad de Obreros Católicos (Society of Catholic Workers) sought to "moral-ize workers" through Christian teachings and social and financial support. In its second year of operation the society united four other Catholic worker groups in the capital into a consortium. The society's board, headed by prominent officials like former and future governors Francisco Meixueiro and Miguel Bolaños Cacho, strengthened the influence of the state over the church and workers.[74]

The Sociedad de Obreros Católicos eventually gave way to Gillow's Círculo Católico de Obreros de Oaxaca. From its official creation on New Year's Day of 1906, the CCOO epitomized the paradoxical fusion of liberalism and Catholi-cism that marked the Porfiriato.[75] The CCOO's co-optation of municipal workers helped promote the state's agenda of economic modernization and prolonged elite control over the capital's workforce. On the opening night, hundreds of workers filled the theater in the Carmen Alto Convent, the headquarters of the Círculo. Jesús Acevedo, Juan Varela, Ramón Pardo, Federico Zorrilla, Wenceslao

García, Nicanor Cruz, and other members of the Emerald City's ruling elite also attended in support of the inauguration. These men and others received honorary membership in the Círculo and served on its board of directors.[76]

The CCOO quickly became the dominant labor organization in the capital. Workers and gremios had little alternative but to join the Círculo if they wanted any support. In its first year, membership in the CCOO exceeded one thousand workers, reaching a high of 1,781 in 1910. Workers joined the organization through their gremios. The Círculo represented twenty-eight of the capital's gremios, each with varying degrees of administrative organization. Some, like the carpenter, tailor, and shoemaker gremios supported their own board of directors within the CCOO.[77] Others with fewer numbers joined as part of a larger conglomeration of gremios. The 1907 regulations of the CCOO sought to promote the ideals of "God, Morality, Work, and Union," as its motto proclaimed. The regulations required that workers be at least fifteen years of age, professed Catholics, and of good standing in society. They also were obliged to attend meetings, carry out tasks, strictly adhere to religious teachings, attend festivals, avoid vice (gambling, drinking, and inappropriate reading material), and pay monthly dues.[78] Above all, the Círculo and its workers would remain "uninvolved in any form of politics."[79] This last stipulation was congruent with the general stance of the Catholic Church during the Porfiriato, which advocated political detachment as a way to gain concessions from the state. In reality, of course, the reverse was true. Although removed from official party politics, Gillow took great pains to maintain his influential relationship with local and national politicians.[80]

Failure to comply with the CCOO's regulations would result in penalties for the members involved. Depending on the severity of the infraction, penalties could include fines and expulsion. In return for their commitment to the Círculo, however, members enjoyed access to religious instruction for themselves and their families, some financial support in case of sickness and death, assistance from a prisoner advocate if needed, and the right to deposit money in the Círculo's savings account.

On the one hand, Gillow and the directors of the CCOO purported that these benefits would engender the "moralization" of the workers.[81] On the other hand, working together, church and government leaders sought to form disciplined and obedient workers who would support the expanding capitalist economy.[82] Therefore, the elite and middle-class focus on reforming the hygienic, moral, and educational standards of the city's workers was in fact an attempt to construct a modern work ethic.[83]

From the outset Archbishop Gillow spared no expense to make sure that his new organization supported a "moralizing" environment. Chapter 10 of the

CCOO's regulations mandated the construction of a recreation center, named "Festive Chapel."[84] Gillow spent 7,365 pesos on the center, a space free of "gambling and other vices" and filled instead with chess tables, ball games, and a reading room with books on religion, industry, arts, and economy. The center provided workers with access to dramatic productions, a choral society, a gymnasium with showers, and it also served as the clubhouse for sports teams, including the baseball team "Los Gillow." Federico Zavala, CCOO director and city councilman, hoping to curb the "degenerative" appetites of popular groups, held regular "anti-alcoholism" classes for workers and prisoners at the center and city jail. According to one newspaper, an average of four hundred workers attended the center on Sundays, the only day it was open (it was, of course, closed on workdays).[85] Literally connecting the center to the city's spatial modernizing projects, the Festive Chapel was also one of the first public buildings illuminated by electric light.[86]

Gillow also encouraged celebration and revelry among the CCOO's members, but, as with the recreation center, only in Círculo-sanctioned events and spaces. He hosted an annual fiesta for CCOO members and directors at his mansion in the neighboring town of San Felipe del Agua. The event was more spectacle than party. Like Carnival, it allowed workers one monitored day in the year to engage in activities otherwise prohibited. Accompanied by live music, streetcars and carriages transported workers and city elites alike to Gillow's home. There, nearly five hundred people feasted on barbecued meat and played sports. In an ironic disregard of official behavior, Gillow donated an entire cask of pulque "as a gift for his beloved workers."[87] As witnessed earlier, the Círculo often participated in municipal celebrations, joining parades down the capital's main streets. The CCOO's individual gremios would display brightly colored flags adorned with symbols of their trade as well as that of the CCOO.[88] Other gala events included annual festivals in honor of the Círculo's patron saints, the Virgin of Guadalupe and Saint Joseph. Government elites intended the parades to serve as symbols of the city's advancement, with all social classes united on the path of progress.

Saving Capital

In another attempt to moralize workers, the CCOO established a savings bank to encourage the "modern quality" of thrift among its members. Chapter 3 of the Círculo's regulations stipulated that a mutual aid savings bank be established for the benefit of workers. The requirement adhered to the pope's entreaty in the *Rerum Novarum*, encouraging workers to save some of their wages in the ultimate hope of purchasing and owning property. "Many excellent results will follow from this," the pope remarked. "Property will certainly become more equitably divided."[89] The directors of the CCOO had more modest aspirations. In order to combat the "slow but sure ruin" encouraged by the practice of usury in the capital, they actively promoted a volunteer savings program. Advocates for wage saving argued that workers poorly managed their money, often paying as much as 12 percent interest on loans. In times of a financial crisis, an editorial in La voz de la verdad claimed, working-class families were left with no other recourse but "begging and crime."[90] Gillow contributed five thousand pesos of his own money to the workers' bank. CCOO members could voluntarily submit weekly quotas of five, ten, or twenty centavos. Those depositing twenty centavos would receive one peso a day for two months in case of sickness. Members contributing five or ten centavos a week would receive twenty-five or fifty centavos, respectively, in case of debilitation.[91] By 1910 CCOO members had saved 1,528 pesos in the mutual aid bank.[92]

In 1907 a branch of the CCOO run out of the Iglesia de las Nieves started two specialized aid groups to promote savings. In the first group, the church started a mutual aid society for women workers called "The Needle." This branch society met every Sunday to "help women free themselves of usury."[93] The Workers Cooperative Society Union started that same year at the Iglesia de las Nieves, but it focused on exposing artisans to the alleged social and cultural sophistication of the middle class. The group established a store next to the church, a "cooperative society of consumers," where members could build credit by investing money to buy goods over time. In theory, the store, run by middle-class merchants, would benefit workers as they "saw that their (middle-class) partners were better dressed, fed, and housed than they were." A review of the cooperative society in the Oaxaca Herald noted that "although some workers would continue to succumb to the [habits of] vice on Sundays, they could still [because of the cooperative society] maintain their family in an honest and decent manner."[94]

While state governor more than two decades earlier, in 1882, Díaz had sought to aid the working poor by institutionalizing pawnshops in the city. Before the inauguration of the Monte de Piedad (literally, "mountain of piety"), the city's official pawnshop, dozens of unregulated pawnshops (casas de empeño) existed throughout the capital. Consistent with the modernizing trends of the era, Díaz attempted to control the casas by establishing regulations in 1881. Like all other new regulations in commercial areas of the capital, these rules required casa owners to pay regular taxes and obtain an annual license. Furthermore, an appointed municipal "expert" visited the pawnshops weekly in order to authenticate the prices of items for sale.[95] The official pawnshops also helped channel funds to municipal coffers. By 1903 the four branches of the Monte de Piedad together earned over eleven thousand pesos for the city.[96]

Oaxacan leaders also hoped to develop a kind of fiscal morality among artisans and workers in order to foster a "culture of capitalism."[97] Thus their attempts to improve the financial status of the city artisans — mutual aid savings banks and state-run pawnshops — also served a crucial interest of the state. In promoting the long-term benefits of saving and credit, these institutions prepared workers to be consumers, vital players in a growing capitalist economy. Although the low wages of Mexican workers prevented them from being a real economic force in the country, it is clear that the state and the Catholic Church had more than thrift in mind when establishing these financial institutions. In his work on nineteenth-century Bogotá, David Sowell points out that in addition to providing much needed funds for the city, savings banks also served to "instill 'progressive' thinking among the populace, which some leaders thought might help the region keep pace with other nations of the Atlantic community."

Government and privately run pawnshops in Oaxaca City must be seen in the larger history of popular credit in Latin America. In 1775 the Spanish Crown opened the first public pawnshop in Mexico City. This Monte de Piedad would be the first of the government's many failed attempts to displace private lending establishments usually located in small stores (pulperías) and cantinas. Smaller, privately owned establishments proved resilient in a demanding market. During the Porfiriato, in addition to Oaxaca City, the federal government sponsored new branches of the Monte de Piedad in Puebla and San Luis Potosí. Pawnshops provide a lens through which to view the intersection of material culture and popular credit. They were spaces where private materials from the domestic lives of men and especially women (the majority of pawnshop clients) became public commodities. Furthermore the kinds of objects pawned (clothes, luxury items, jewels) revealed the economic status of clients. As the middle class grew in Mexico, transactions involving luxury items increased.[98]

Private and state-run banks also appeared during the Porfiriato as demand increased for credit from growing domestic and foreign industry. Oaxaca City's first bank, a branch of the Banco Nacional de México, opened its doors for business in 1888.[99] Just after the turn of the century, two others, the Banco de Oaxaca and the United States Banking Company, established branches in the city. These three banks, however, served the city's moneyed classes and did little to support thrift and other forms of fiscal morality among artisans and workers.

The Purifying Power of Work

The ccoo encouraged a "proper" work ethic among its members by presenting prizes to those gremios with the best records of attendance and good conduct.

Editorials in the CCOO's official newspaper, *La voz de la verdad*, condemned the sins of truancy and tardiness. In reference to the spontaneously celebrated holiday, "San Lunes" (Saint Monday), one editorial reminded workers of the virtue of fulfilling their duty:

> Duty, regardless of its nature—be it spiritual or temporal—is sacred, and for that reason demands completion. What you call a promise or an obligation, referring either to attendance at the workshop or to the submission of projects on determined days, that is what duty consists of. Among you, unfortunately, one notices a great deficiency in the completion of duties, in the realm of both attendance and completion of tasks. Saint Monday is one of the worst enemies of the worker because it reduces a day of work, of labor, to a day of idleness, dissipation, drunkenness, and crime! Yes, because you have missed a day of work, work that honors, dignifies, and purifies the moral virtues of the individual. Missing work makes your family suffer privations, if not complete misery, and it poisons the organism with alcohol.[100]

The editorial continues to list great men of Latin American and world history—Simón Bolívar, Miguel Hidalgo, George Washington, and Louis Pasteur (the gender bias was, no doubt, intentional)—as examples of those who, by fulfilling their duties, have done "great things in the eyes of God and humanity." Other editorials construct a similarly rigid dichotomy between the good of the workshop and the evil of the tavern.[101] The notion of work as purification of the soul stemmed, according to an officer of the CCOO, Trinidad Sánchez Santos, from the biblical story of Jesus as the worker who brought the world to its feet. In his speech before the CCOO's third anniversary celebration, Sánchez was "breathless" at the "brutal ignorance" in which most working-class people lived. "What then," he asked, "is the duty of the Catholic worker in such dire circumstances? I do not hesitate to declare it: the struggle. But not the struggle against the legitimate interests of capital, which have sacred rights, but the struggle against error that is precipitating the working world into incalculably profound abysses."[102] Furthermore, argued *La voz de la verdad*, workers needed to be vigilant against the "tyrannical" influences of non-Christian unions like those in Germany and France. The paper warned CCOO members that bosses in these unions would start strikes without a care for the workers, and then pocket the benefits for themselves.[103]

Yet, despite the exhortation of Sánchez and others that workers harmoniously labor for the glory of capitalism, truancy and other work-related "vices" continued to plague elites determined to develop the state capital economically. Workshop leaders complained to local newspapers that their workers were dishonest and arrived late.[104] As with workers in the city's commercial sex trade, popular groups often thwarted elite attempts to shape and regulate their lives.

Gillow's success at promulgating Social Catholicism and preempting worker unrest in the capital fell short in the surrounding districts. Despite his proposal that branches of the CCOO be opened in the textile factories mentioned above, workers, unhappy with the deplorable conditions and the imposition of a quota for religious festivals, went on strike. Gillow would later blame the workers' radicalism on the "evils of socialism, which influence the students and workers of diverse nations and disturb the social order and the tranquility of families."[105] The Vista Hermosa factory in San Agustín Etla witnessed the most unrest. In 1907 editors of La unión chided the workers for proclaiming their allegiance to "our compatriots of Río Blanco," which the newspapers alleged to be their only reason for striking.[106] More, of course, had been at stake. The previous year had seen the bloodiest days of labor unrest in the Porfiriato. In one of many incidents, textile workers in Río Blanco, Veracruz, burned down the company's store, which they saw as a symbol of their poor treatment and low wages. Federal troops sent by Díaz resolved the strike by firing into a crowd of protestors.[107] Workers in Oaxaca, forced into mutual societies by an absence of options and threatened by violence from the state, lacked the support to form unions. In 1912 President Francisco Madero received a series of reports indicating that only two unions existed in Oaxaca's twenty-six districts. All other listed labor organizations were legally sanctioned mutual aid societies.[108] Significant union activity in the state would not appear until the 1920s with the start of organizations like the Confederation of Socialist Leagues of Oaxaca (Confederacion de partidos socialistas de Oaxaca, CPSO).[109]

Sealing the Deal: The Fourth Catholic Congress

The conclusions reached by Archbishop Gillow and other local church leaders at the Fourth Catholic Congress held in Oaxaca City in January 1909 signaled the apex of church support for the Porfirian goals of economic development. During the Mexican Revolution (1910–20) church-state relations would once again fall into disrepair. Yet this congress, the last one of the Porfiriato, demonstrated the extent of the Catholic Church's resurgence during Díaz's reign. The previous three conferences, held in Puebla (1903), Morelia (1904), and Guadalajara (1906), had all focused their agendas on the development of Social Catholic action. The conferences marked the solidification of a new current of Social Catholicism in Mexico.

Earlier in the Porfiriato, Catholic-supported labor organizations had developed in principal cities throughout Mexico.[110]

In addition to promoting the continuation of Social Catholic action in Mexico, the ostensible focus for the Oaxaca City congress was the "Indian problem." As in Mexico's other southern states (e.g., Chiapas and Yucatán), indigenous groups dominated Oaxaca's population. Church and state leaders searched for ways to transform this "backward, ignorant, vice-ridden, and unhygienic" population into productive workers and citizens.[111]

Yet the real focus of the congress, unlike the previous three, was on how best to mobilize the resources of the church in support of the economic projects of the Díaz government. Whereas the preceding conference in Guadalajara had emphasized improving workers' wages and living conditions, the Oaxaca gathering instead sought to reinforce the domination of landowners and industrialists. Conference participants, predominantly lay people, including government representatives, published the conclusions of the conference, contained in 177 separate articles.[112] The conference report only nominally addressed issues of improving worker wages (Articles 69 and 146). In a reversal of previous conference decisions, the report promoted company stores (tiendas de raya) as beneficial to both manager and worker and encouraged owners to make a profit from their sales (Articles 81–83). Other issues that marked changes in direction from previous conferences included new forms of punishment for workers and increasing concessions to employers and landowners (Articles 25, 26, 28, 91).[113] "These and other conclusions," writes Manuel Ceballos, "give the impression that the Oaxaca congress was attempting to establish and fortify the Porfirian order as the necessary norm."[114]

"Yankeeization" and the Protestant Church

Despite constitutional amendments decreeing the contrary, Catholic leaders made sure their religion remained dominant at any cost. The growth of Protestantism in Mexico threatened that religious hegemony for the first time at the end of the nineteenth century. A series of historical events in the late nineteenth century created a propitious environment for the first major wave of Protestant missionaries in Mexico. The end of the U.S. Civil War (1860–65) and an increasingly stable environment in Mexico encouraged American missionaries to spread their word to the south. The triumph of liberalism and the proclamation of the 1857 Constitution and the laws of the Reform helped pave the way for religious tolerance in Mexico. Liberal leaders in the country felt that the anti-Catholic stance of Protestants would support the separation between church and state and encourage North American investment.[115] Despite these trends, Oaxaca and its capital city remained staunchly Catholic. Catholic opposition to Protestantism in the state underscored the dominance of Gillow's church in Oaxaca City and suggested the ambivalence many Mexicans felt about the infusion of North American capital.

In 1872, Oaxacans witnessed the arrival of Methodist missionaries led by John Wesley Buttler of the Episcopalian Methodist Church of the South. By the end of the Porfiriato, the American colony in Oaxaca City had established a small congregation and built a church near the center of town.[116] Despite an enthusiastic reception of North Americans and their business, Oaxacans turned a cold shoulder to the state's fledgling and inchoate Protestant community. In 1907 Victoriano D. Báez, a historian and the capital's most outspoken Protestant minister, complained to the Pimentel administration of religious persecution in towns throughout the Central Valley. In one incident Báez protested on behalf of the Protestant community in the town of Santo Domingo Nuxaa in the district of Nochixtlán. The local government had closed down the Methodist temple and demanded that the congregation publicly renounce its beliefs. Officials had broken religious objects, thrown members of the Methodist church in jail on trumped up charges, and forced others to serve in the army. One congregant was denied a burial plot for his dead son in the municipal cemetery. In a typical response, the Pimentel government ignored the charges, leaving the municipality to work out its differences, no doubt in favor of the Catholic majority.[117]

The Catholic press lambasted the city's Protestants and their one newspaper, *La bandera del evangelio*. Articles in newspapers like *La unión*, *La voz de la verdad*, and *La hoja del pueblo* labeled Protestants and Americans as the "devil" and as "Yankee evangelizers." One article was particularly aggressive:

> The object of their plan is clearly criminal: to divide the Mexicans, including their beliefs, in order to render them debilitated at the hour of struggle. For this reason, the Protestant North Americans, who come here to preach their errors, are truly *pernicious foreigners*. It is pernicious to divide the Mexican people, to come to undermine the foundation of our national unity, to sow new elements of transcendental discord, and to convert the Republic into an embittered country. For this reason it is meritorious to attack Protestantism, not only in the eyes of [the Catholic] Religion, but also in the eyes of the Nation.[118]

The victory of the United States in the Spanish-American War increased the fear of "Yankeeization" in Oaxaca.[119] Earlier in the Porfiriato, the editors of *La hoja del pueblo* went so far as to issue rules of conduct for the city's Catholics. The list of rules focused on the "illegality" of reading or collecting Protestant literature, owning a Protestant Bible, or attending services at the capital's evangelical temple.[120]

Protestant support of antireelectionist forces also concerned Oaxaca's pro-Díaz Catholics. Victoriano Báez and Angel Barrios, a Oaxacan engineer, were among the few to welcome Díaz's would-be presidential successor, Francisco Madero, to the state capital in 1909.[121] The outbreak of the Mexican Revolution in 1910 further exacerbated the fears of the Catholic Church, which blamed North Americans and Protestants for the growing instability.[122]

Conclusion

The Revolution overthrew Díaz in 1911 and initiated the decline of the Catholic Church of Oaxaca's close relationship with the federal government. In 1914, three years after President Díaz fled Mexico for Europe, Archbishop Gillow escaped to the United States fearing persecution by the Revolution's constitutionalist "first chief," Venustiano Carranza. Gillow had performed the marriage ceremony for the son of Carranza's enemy, General Victoriano Huerta.[123] In 1921 Gillow returned and attempted without success to rescue a financially dilapidated diocese. When he died the following year, the city's workers had switched their allegiance from the defunct CCOO to secular mutual aid societies and had, amid a less restrictive institutional and governmental climate, started to join the city's first unions.[124]

Limited in their alternatives, Oaxaca City's workers had turned to the Círculo Católico de Obreros de Oaxaca for much needed social and financial support during the late Porfiriato. Unlike unions, however, the Círculo did not seek to improve the low wages or harsh labor conditions of its members. Instead, the CCOO facilitated Archbishop Gillow's pact with Porfirio Díaz to discipline and inculcate "proper behavior" in the city's workers, behavior that included cultivating a culture of capitalism.

Gillow's efforts to reform and rationalize Oaxaca's Catholic Church in conjunction with and in support of Díaz's developmentalist plans reveal the fundamental role played by the state's main religious institution in the Porfirian project to modernize Mexico's workers. Furthermore, the case of Oaxaca's Porfirian Catholic Church provides a clear example of the religious dimension of the construction of modernity.

The leaders of Oaxaca's Catholic Church concerned themselves not only with the integration of the city's artisans into Mexico's expanding capitalist economy,

but also with their protection from urban vice. Protestantism, alcohol, and ignorance ranked high on the church's list of corrupting social influences. Higher still,
however, was prostitution. In their modernizing initiatives, Catholics and municipal officials alike would struggle and be forced to accommodate female prostitutes in order to regulate the Emerald City's commercial sex trade.

CHAPTER FOUR

"A Necessary Evil"
Regulating Public Space and Public Women

> A recurrent pattern emerges: the "top" attempts to reject and eliminate the "bottom" for reasons of prestige and status, only to discover, not only that it is in some way frequently dependent upon that low-Other . . . , but also that the top *includes* that low symbolically, as a primary eroticized constituent of its own fantasy life. . . . It is for this reason that what is *socially* peripheral is so frequently *symbolically* central.
>
> — Stallybrass and White, *The Politics and Poetics of Transgression*, 1986

On July 8, 1893, Joaquina G. submitted the first of five petitions to the Oaxaca City council (*ayuntamiento municipal*) as the *matrona* or madam of a second-class brothel in the tenth block of Avenida Hidalgo. Over the course of more than a year she would claim that government officials had violated her constitutional rights and had harassed the sex workers under her care.[1] She argued that the municipal government was attempting unfairly to move the location of her brothel out of an officially designated "red zone" that the government had established earlier that year. She told the council that the charges accusing her of being overdue on her monthly taxes were unjust. According to her, she had always complied with the increasingly rigorous and detailed regulations of the Comisión de Sanidad y Prostitución (Commission on Public Health and Prostitution). She and the prostitutes working for her had paid all their fees, submitted themselves to the weekly medical examinations, and turned in the required photographs and descriptions of themselves to the city secretary. Yet Joaquina had been lying. She had been late on payments before and her brothel was situated in an unsanctioned public space. Nevertheless, over a year later, on October 20, 1894, the city council granted Señora G. an extension on her debt payments and allowed her to move into a new place of business.[2]

Joaquina's story illustrates the tension that existed between city administrators, madams, and sex workers in Oaxaca City during the Porfiriato. City elites and workers in the commercial sex trade continually negotiated their positions in and hence mutually constituted and defined the discourses and practices of tradition and modernity. Like other urban centers around the world that were moderniz-ing during the late nineteenth century, Oaxaca City strove to forge new paths of "progress" and "civilization," and the sex trade was an important part of that pro-cess.[3] In an attempt to craft a hegemonic and homogeneous form of modernity, elites positioned the prostitute's body and actions along excluded and intersect-ing racial, class, gendered, sexualized, and spatial lines. In defining modernity by what it was not, the capital's elites simultaneously constructed as "traditional" those elements of society judged to be obstacles to progress.

Sex workers did not simply react to the regulatory measures of the city gov-ernment. Instead, by contesting official policies and mobilizing liberal discourses and methods of surveillance (such as photographs), the women workers played an integral, albeit subordinate, part in the construction of the city's commercial sex trade.[4] As such, these marginalized individuals not only became central historical agents, but they also revealed the inherent weakness of dominant discourses and practices.[5]

Between 1892 and 1907, Oaxaca City underwent an economic boom based largely on export mining production but also on the commercial sex trade. Hun-dreds of sex workers from the surrounding indigenous villages and from around the country and the world plied their trade in the state capital. An abundant and diverse set of documents in the city's archives attest to the broad impact the female sex trade had on the capital during the Porfiriato.[6] This chapter focuses on the period from 1885, when the regulations of prostitution first appeared, to 1911, when the Díaz regime fell and the city's regulated sex trade suffered a rapid de-cline. We will pay particular attention to the state's attempts to regulate and con-trol the sex trade in the city by defining the limits of morality and public space.

The city's governing elite took great pains to define the roles of all the city's women by regulating the commercial sex trade in the state capital and by con-trolling the spread of what they perceived as vice into public spaces. At the same time politicians recognized that prostitution "was necessary"[7] and constantly de-bated the degree of control and limitations they could impose on the sex workers' bodies and the spaces they occupied. In fact, dating back at least to Mexico's Bour-bon period, elites had organized campaigns of social control as a way to assert their power over and distinguish themselves from a growing urban underclass. Bourbon-era elites in Mexico City inscribed specific meanings in the bodies of the lower classes (reinforced by systems of surveillance and punishment) to delimit social and spatial boundaries along lines of political power.[8] In Porfirian Oaxaca

City, sex workers and elites contested the meanings, locations, and relative power of the female body. The body became a powerful symbol of the unresolved tension between tradition and modernity as city inhabitants redefined it as an integral aspect of the construction of gender, class, the family, and the nation.[9] As we will see, the prostitute's body and its location both in city spaces and in specific formulations of tradition and modernity played fundamental roles in how elites and sex workers constructed and contested public and private spaces in the city.

Although contradicting their expressed exclusivist definitions of modernity, elites (begrudgingly and indirectly) deemed sex workers a vital aspect of the progress and civilization of their Porfirian city. Elites relied on sex workers both to contribute through taxation much needed funds to municipal coffers and to maintain what elites believed was domestic tranquility by taming the lascivious desires of men. At the same time, sex workers struggled to position themselves within the discourse and practice of the city's Porfirian development. Augmenting the examination of religion and the church in the lives of the capital's workers, our understanding of the development of modernity in Porfirian Oaxaca necessarily changes when viewed through the lens of the city's commercial sex trade. Sex workers, actively negotiating the government's regulatory practices, forced Porfirian elites to reconsider their notions of social control and discipline. Workers in the commercial sex trade appropriated and rearticulated rigid codes of elite behavior, appearance, and social status for their own benefit. The histories of indigenous and nonindigenous sex workers in Oaxaca City underscore the multiple and intersecting characteristics of Porfirian modernity. The experiences of sex workers like Joaquina G. shed light on the changing practices of and attitudes toward women, work, urbanization, private and public spaces, and citizenship in Porfirian Mexico.

Elites and commoners developed projects of modernity not only in and through the gendered body of the prostitute but in and through her racialized, gendered body.[10] Notably absent in studies of Latin American prostitution that favor analyses of gender, race played a critical role in the way Oaxacan sex workers could imagine themselves (and be imagined) as respectable women.[11] In order to understand the sex trade in Porfirian Oaxaca, an analysis of the construction of race must be included, since race was critical in the identity formation and regulation of sex workers. Throughout the Porfiriato, elites and prostitutes constructed normative and deviant characteristics of race and incorporated them with similarly constructed notions of gender, sexuality, and nationality.

Since the 1980s scholarly work on prostitution has moved away from viewing sex workers as "pornographic" and has begun to seriously consider prostitutes both in the larger context of expanding nation-states and modernity in the late nineteenth century.[12] The literature on prostitution has turned to see these women as working members of a growing urban underclass, and this focus has illuminated the roles of gender, sexuality, and the family in society. Instead of reducing the sex trade to issues of gender and sexuality, recent studies have sought to expand the understanding of culture and power within and alongside the more "traditional" analytical structure of political economy.[13]

I divide my study of the city's sex trade into two chapters. In this chapter I explore the reciprocally constructed relationship between the city government and sex workers in defining and regulating the commercial sex trade. Elite discussion and reinforcement of codes of gender and sexuality involved both women and men. Although never explicitly stated, the regulation of female prostitutes indirectly involved a close inspection of male sexuality. As a crucial part of gender's construction, the formation of masculinity in Porfirian Oaxaca helped to shape the broader discourses and practices around the role of women and the family in society. Integrating Western European and North American ideas of progress into the Porfirian-Mexican context, officials attempted to modernize the city's inhabitants, administrative infrastructure, and city space.

The fragmented modernity of the Oaxacan state capital grew out of the intersection of class, ethnicity, gender and sexuality, and perceptions of progress and civilization. Although out of analytical necessity I discuss these characteristics individually, to varying degrees they all acted in concert. The resulting cultural and political potpourri gives us insight into how histories from "above" and from "below" can be integrated to reveal nuanced and multifaceted interpretations of the past.

Science and Prostitution in Nineteenth-Century Mexico

Sex work of course predated the Porfiriato. Porfirian references to the "continuing problem" of prostitution in Oaxaca City indicate that the sex trade in an unregulated form had been in existence at least since the colonial era.[14] In Mexico City, officials had long since regulated the sex trade when the French occupation government legislated the *Reglamento para el Ejercicio de la Prostitución* (Regulations for the Practice of Prostitution) in 1865.[15] It was not until the late nineteenth century, however, that a burgeoning medico-legal administrative structure began to redefine prostitution and the female body. The authoritarian attempts of the Porfirian regime to redesign the urban built environment further marked the era as unique in Mexico's history. It is at this historical juncture that positivist institutions and individuals in Mexico began to formulate scientific discourses on the position of women, prostitutes, and additional "others" in society. Methodologies from social anthropology, criminology, statistics, physiognomy, phrenology, and other "hard" sciences aided in the construction of social deviants like the *mujeres públicas*.[16] Elites constructed a hierarchical medicalization of the body that endowed some people with more (bio-) power than others. The Foucauldian notion of bio-power brings the locus of state and society interaction to its most fundamental level: the body. The categorical differentiation of bodies in society created "concrete mechanisms and practices through which power [was] exercised."[17] By designating certain bodies (e.g., prostitutes) as degenerate, scientists and criminologists developed a rational justification for stigmatizing and separating them from the rest of "decent" society. This social construction of somatic meaning was reinforced by ample artistic and literary representations of prostitution in the Díaz era. Narratives concerning the lives of prostitutes, such as Federico Gamboa's *Santa*, and regular newspaper columns showcased the sensual and emotional aspects, the pleasures and pains experienced by these women's bodies, those of their clients, and of broader society.[18]

The Porfirian social hygienist Luis Lara y Pardo utilized the criminological approach to the body in his *La prostitución en México* (1908). He argued that poverty, joblessness, abandonment, and depression were merely incidental causes of prostitution. The "fundamental" cause was, according to him, "psychological and social inferiority."[19] Lara y Pardo's theories were part of the prevailing belief in Mexico that prostitution was a disease, inherited from the previous generation's "pathological" condition. Like other contemporary social theorists, Lara y Pardo characterized female prostitutes as passive subjects bereft of free will. While his views are more an indication of his own stereotypes of popular class degeneracy than the real practice of the women workers, his study remains a useful (although problematic) guide to the history of Porfirian-era prostitution.[20]

La prostitución en México stands alongside similar medical-legal and criminological texts of late-nineteenth-century Mexico.[21] Debates over prostitution and criminality, inspired by thinkers like the Italian positivist criminologist Cesare Lombroso (1836–1909), emerged in conferences and academic journals throughout Europe and the United States.[22] Latin America's ruling elites eagerly embraced the eclectic and often problematic research of Lombroso and his disciples because it provided a unified and persuasive justification for rationalizing and controlling the decentralized, regionalized populations that characterized nineteenth-century Latin America.[23] Echoing this type of scientific thinking, government officials in Mexico City and later Oaxaca City adopted the original French prostitution regulations from the mid-1860s in slightly modified form throughout the Porfiriato and beyond.[24]

The Oaxacan press printed articles on criminality and deviance. In an article representative of the prevailing view toward criminality in the city, an author from the *Diario oficial del Estado de Oaxaca* cites Lombroso, explaining the hereditary nature of deviance: "Unsuitable beings, not only obstruct, they damage. Lombroso says that an instant of pleasure between two drunkards can provide the origin of many generations of prostitutes, vagrants, and neuropaths." [25]

Law student Miguel Calderón's professional thesis at the Instituto de Ciencias y Artes del Estado de Oaxaca (Institute of Science and Art of the State of Oaxaca) draws on theorists like Lombroso and Lamarck to discuss the racial and hereditary origins of crime and suggest avenues for its investigation in the state of Oaxaca. His work *El crimen según las leyes naturales* (Crime According to the Natural Laws) explains that criminals "lack the reason" to distinguish between good and evil. After citing several racially inspired anthropological studies of criminal activities of "negros" in "less civilized" countries such as Australia and the regions of the Nile River valley, Calderón argues that the number of crimes and criminals in a country are in inverse proportion to its level of progress. Thus, the fewer the crimes the higher the level of a country's civilization. According to Calderón, what was needed in civilized countries (*naciones cultas*) like Mexico was the further development of regulations, penal codes, and laws in order to "defeat the attacks of the weak, be they ignorant, demented, or merely social parasites." [26] Criminological definitions of deviance and civilization depended in large part on normative constructions of gender, sexuality, and race.

"The Seeds of All Great Deeds":
Gender and Sexuality in Porfirian Oaxaca

> The domestic household is the source of all social virtues and in it the seeds of all great and heroic deeds are guarded as if it were a sanctuary. Each private home must be a reflection of society's home; the states [of Mexico] are worth neither more nor less than the sum of all the families of which they are comprised.
> — *La voz de la verdad*, "Para las damas" (For Ladies) — Oaxaca City, 1910

Attempts to define and regulate female bodies were not limited to sex workers. Officials defined prostitutes as the city's deviant and degenerate population, in stark contrast to normative constructs of respectable ladies of a polite and civilized society. In order to construct a prosperous and modern nation out of the fractious, internecine conflicts of the nineteenth century, Mexican elites imagined a nation built on the virtuous foundation of the family. Women lay at the base of that foundation, both supporting it and oppressed by its weight. [27] Elite promotion of domestic and family discourses facilitated not only a means of social control but also a way in which elites could define their dominant gender- and sexuality-specific form of modernity. According to historian William French, Porfirian social reformers "advocated a . . . cult of female domesticity in which they carefully prescribed women's role: women were to serve as properly educated mothers and guardian angels of the home. While they insisted that women's 'natural' place was in the home, by contrast the prostitute reigned as a particularly cogent symbol of Mexico's dangerous classes."[28] The term *mujeres públicas*, or public women, often utilized in the press and in Oaxacan state-generated documents to describe female sex workers, reveals elite and government attitudes toward prostitutes and their position in public space. In general, members of all classes prescribed the opposite of the term: women were to remain private and reserved, to be seen in public only when escorted by a male of "decent character." While at the center of the paramount institution of the family, women were also seen as a threat to its decency and as temptresses for unsuspecting men. It was the role of men in the society, then, to protect the woman from herself and thus ensure the integrity of the family.[29] The almost complete absence of men in the documents concerning prostitution in Oaxaca City is therefore not surprising; women needed to be regulated, not men. Men were referred to only in passing as "los concurrentes," the clients or those in attendance. The governing elite perceived prostitution as a "necessary evil" to maintain social morality and to safeguard honorable women and decent families.

A study of the city's newspapers and criminal records reveals the perceptions of elites and commoners alike of gender and sexuality and helps to explain the motivations underlying the regulation of public women. Like many of the city's newspapers, La voz de la verdad, the authoritative Catholic paper founded by Archbishop Gillow, ran a weekly column titled "Para las damas" in which the paper pronounced the "proper" customs, duties, and obligations of the Oaxacan woman. A woman, according to La voz de la verdad, needed to cultivate social virtue not through a demonstration of her intellect (which was not at all necessary for a woman to possess) but through a display of her "modesty as a single woman, tenderness as a wife, and through her daintiness and religiosity as a woman." Furthermore, a woman needed to appreciate the "key to securing her influence" in society: beauty. While physical beauty was important, the most crucial factor of womanhood was the attainment of *moral* beauty, or perfection.[30] Women were often deemed as the means to a greater end. As mothers, women created stability in the home and, by extension, the nation. They were, according to another of the city's newspapers, La libertad, the generative force of the nation. In giving birth to leaders such as Benito Juárez and Porfirio Díaz, women were seen to promote the country's greatness. In the words of La libertad, "The Oaxacan woman has always been distinguished by her uncommon virtues whose moral value is eloquently proven by the great number of illustrious men who honor Oaxaca."[31]

In addition to pronouncements concerning the behavior of women in Oaxacan society, city publications announced events promoting a respectable, upper-class female image.[32] Newspapers showcased the events for women held by elite social clubs. One paper, El eco mercantil, ran its own beauty contest. Only women from elite families like the Díaz Ordazes, Meixueiros, and the Larrañagas participated. City inhabitants cast over two thousand votes and the winner received a painting symbolizing the beauty of the champion.[33]

Records in the city's criminal files reveal broad societal attitudes and practices not only toward women but also toward sexuality and its officially designated location in city space. According to officials, the sexuality of the city's inhabitants (except, of course, of prostitutes) was ideally to be ensconced within the private, domestic sphere. Latin American urban elites had long been making great efforts to construct the home as a distinct and separate space from the public city streets. While elites deemed the house as the bastion of social order and propriety, the street was dirty, unruly, and unpredictable. The physical spaces of the house and street served as cultural markers for distinguishing and designating so-called proper social practices.[34]

In Oaxaca City, lawmakers quickly punished overt displays of sexual desire and activity by men and women. Police immediately apprehended lovers caught with "their pants down" in public spaces. City officials filed the cases of sexual acts in public spaces under the rubric *faltas contra la moralidad pública o buenas costumbres* (violations against public morality or good manners). In one case, at 8:00 p.m. on October 11, 1882, police caught Juana G. and Teodoro V. "in an extremely unpleasant position that violated public morality" in the corridors of the city market. Juana, a washerwoman from the city, and Teodoro, a hat maker from the neighboring village of El Marquesado, admitted they were lovers but argued that they simply had been eating dinner when the policeman arrested them. As with other similar cases, police released Juana and Teodoro for lack of evidence. There were no other witnesses to corroborate the officer's story.[35] The common occurrence of this type of intervention pitting law officers against public lovers underscores the importance city officials placed on prohibiting these "private" acts in public spaces.[36] Furthermore, there is a pronounced class element in these types of proceedings. Arrests uniformly involved only the city's workers. In addition to policing sexuality, officials used this type of arbitrary intervention to intimidate the city's poor. Significantly, more often than not, as in the incident with Juana and Teodoro, judges dismissed the cases for lack of proper evidence.[37]

Records of prosecution of and discourse on male homosexuality in the state

capital, while limited, provide further insight into officially prescribed gender roles and, in particular, into the construction of masculinity in Porfirian
Oaxaca.[38] Mexican criminologists equated sexually "deviant" acts with crime.[39]
Men caught in sexual acts with one another were summarily forced to undergo
a detailed and no doubt humiliating physical examination to determine proof of
anal penetration (the only utilized indicator of male homosexual activity) and, if
found "guilty," were incarcerated. Although most accounts of homosexual sex in
the city come from the city prison, one incident transpired in the most sacred of
public spaces.[40] Police surprised José Luz Valencia, a pulque maker from the city,
and Rafael Castellanos, a laborer from Nochixtlán, with their legs entwined in a
"scandalous act" in the portico of the city's cathedral. After the mandatory physical in which "recent signs of pederasty were found," the judge in charge still argued that not enough evidence had been presented against them and released
them from custody.[41] In the homophobic culture of Porfirian Mexico, homosexual
practice threatened elite's rigid notions of masculinity and, like the activities of
"public" women, jeopardized the perceived stability of the family.

An incident of *estupro*, in this case the rape of a minor, further serves to underscore the construction of gender in the city and specifically how notions of
masculinity and femininity were constructed simultaneously and against one another. According to some neighbors who witnessed the incident, on a spring afternoon in 1876, Zeferina G. had been out fetching water when Antonio Z. "grabbed
her hand and pulled her into his patio exclaiming, 'just be quiet for a second.'"
Zeferina's mother caught him in the act and with a punch to the face (*moquete*)
sent Antonio running. According to the alleged aggressor, a fourteen-year-old
shoemaker, the girl had chided him for being "afraid to leave his house," called
him a *puto* (the derogatory form for homosexual and the masculine version of
puta, or whore), and invited him into her room. Shamed into compliance, he entered her house. Zeferina's derogatory remark is instructive because it reinforces
the feminized status of private, domestic spaces. Furthermore, the expletive *puto*
– in reference to a domesticated male – marks the difference between prescribed
notions of masculinity and femininity in Porfirian society.[42] Men who refuse to
engage in public life on the streets are feminized and branded as homosexuals.
Women, in turn, must remain cloistered in their homes or risk, as the judge in
this case points out, estupro.[43] Placed in their social and legal historical context of
Porfirian Oaxaca City, these incidents of homosexual activity and estupro clearly
demonstrate how constructions of gender and sexuality order social practice. Furthermore, as R. W. Connell points out, "gender is not fixed in advance of social
interaction, but is constructed in interaction."[44]

Prostitution, the most public display of the "dangerous" roles of gender and sexuality in the city, forced officials and urban reformers to confront the ways femininity and masculinity inflected their notions of modernity. Through their overt and sometimes ostentatious displays of "perverse" sexuality, prostitutes threatened elite conceptions of gender and family, conceptions at the foundation of Porfirian modernity. The rapid growth of prostitution in Oaxaca City in the early Porfiriato made these issues impossible to ignore.

Race and the Growth of the Sex Trade in Oaxaca City

During the Porfiriato, women migrated to Oaxaca City by the hundreds and many eventually worked as prostitutes. The dramatic increase in prostitution in the late nineteenth century was not exclusive to large, industrial cities. As the example of Guatemala City at the turn of the century demonstrates, sex workers also increasingly plied their trade in agricultural and mining export societies. The case of Porfirian Oaxaca City further proves this point. The arrival of the Ferrocarril del Sur (Mexican Southern Railway) in 1892 and the subsequent mining boom – with its accompanying supply of men – facilitated a period of economic expansion that, along with the continued disentailment of indigenous property, created a propitious climate for the institutionalization of commercial sex.[45] In this context, the important symbiotic racial relationship between the city and its indigenous hinterland also become more evident.

In addition to the secularization of church properties, Reform-era laws also demanded the subdivision of indigenous communal lands (including *ejido* and forest land) for sale to foreign and domestic individuals and corporations. Although villagers in Oaxaca, unlike Mexico's northern states, retained much of their land as common pasture (ejido), the government commodified a considerable amount of it, especially in the Central Valley, for the state's growing capitalist economy.[46] As a result, increasing numbers of villagers from the surrounding indigenous countryside migrated to the capital in the search of work during the Porfiriato.

These indigenous villagers, however, are all but absent from the city census records of the era. City officials, determined to make legible only a specific demographic, effectively erased the "traditional" indigenous population of Oaxaca City in order to present a predominantly white and mestizo and hence "modern" city. The records conflated the capital's diverse ethnic population into the ambivalent racial categories of "blanca," "mixta," or "negra" (white, mixed, or black); the categories of "india" or "indígena" did not appear. Very few inhabitants appear as "negra," with the single largest concentration (eighteen men) living in the infantry barracks next to the Santuario de la Soledad north of the city's central square.

Comparing the census records to the city's photographic trade registries—an annotated photographic catalog of the city's workers—further reveals the arbitrary nature of racial categorization by elites in the city. The census and the trade registries amounted to the two official indexes of race and ethnicity produced by city elites. Although the trade registries do not utilize the category "raza," they do include the entry of (skin) "color." In these demographic records there appears to be no correlation among skin color, ethnicity, and place of origin. The "color" of the male and female (prostitute) workers is listed as either "trigueño" (wheat colored), "moreno" (brown), or "rosado" (rosy); the category "negro" does not appear. When compared to the photographic images themselves, these phenotypical markers seem arbitrarily selected. In other words, the only consistent index of race in the city's demographic records is the absence of "indio." [47]

Like subsequent records during the Porfiriato, the 1895 federal census erroneously registered only 22 Zapotec speakers (listed as "mixta") out of a population of 32,437 people. [48] Earlier city censuses indicated both birthplace and place of origin (i.e., last place inhabited prior to the capital) for Oaxaca City residents. The inclusion of Zapotec and Mixtec towns and villages such as Ejutla, Etla, Ixtlán, Tlaxiaco, and Nochixtlán as places of origin clearly demonstrates that the state capital received an influx of indigenous villagers. [49]

The absence of Zapotec and other indigenous language speakers (e.g., Mixtec) is less an indication of the percentage of the capital's indigenous population—a fact impossible to know with certainty—than it is of Porfirian attitudes toward race and ethnicity. Porfirian social theorists like Oaxaca's own Miguel Calderón (see above) wrote volumes examining the racial contours of Mexican modernity. [50] Their goal, however, was to explain how the "traditional" Indian inhabitants of Mexico obstructed the country's path to progress and civilization. [51] Eric Van Young demonstrates that elite Porfirian visions of Indian degeneracy hearken back to the colonial period and underscore a continuity in Mexico's cultural history.

> The multivocality of the concept "Indian" is turned at one and the same time to nation- or state-building, to the invention of tradition, and to the construction of an imagined community, while it is also employed to squash resistance to the state's project and destroy a real community. Through this appropriation of Indianness the Porfirian state may be seen as a kind of ideological vampire, sucking the life from real people to ensure its own immortality and mummifying the past to control the present and guarantee the future. [52]

Within this race-exclusive notion of modernity it comes as no surprise that the term *indígena* was erased from the capital's historical record. Porfirian discourses of modernity incorporated Oaxaca's rural elements into a simplified racial taxonomy that excluded Indians.[53] City and state official presented the capital as a white and mestizo city, incorporating and legitimizing only the "heroic" Indians of the colonial era into their discourse of modernity (see chap. 2). One official celebrated the supposed obliteration of Zapotec culture and its subsequent assimilation into dominant society: "The inhabitants of this city belong to the Zapotec race, whose language now has been lost completely; as such, all of them speak the beautiful language of Cervantes."[54]

This erasure of *Indian* as a racial category in the capital is made all the more evident by its ambiguous existence in census records for neighboring villages. The predominantly Zapotec village of Jalatlaco includes the category "indígena" in its census report but inserts all of its 668 inhabitants into the categories of "blanca," "negra," or "mixta." Similarly the adjacent town of El Marquesado, later incorporated into the city, lists the "raza" of all of its 1870 inhabitants as "mestizo."[55] As with the photographic registries discussed in chapter 5, government officials utilized the census to simplify a highly differentiated population into legible, modern units. This statistically coherent demographic representation was part and parcel of a race-exclusive modernity that conceptualized "white/mestizo" as "modern" and "Indian" as "traditional."

There is a direct connection between the increasing arrival of indigenous domestic workers and the growth of the sex trade in Oaxaca City.[56] Prostitution registries and records of personal requests to retire from the sex trade indicate that the women frequently moved in and out of work as domestic servants, and, in the process, women became part of the growing urban labor class.[57] A comparison of city census records from 1875, 1887, and 1890 demonstrates the substantial change in the number and percentage of domestic servants (*domésticos*) in the city.[58] The 1875 census, a contributors list for the state's poll tax (*capitación*), records the name, address, occupation, and, in some cases, origins of the city's adult males (i.e., those over sixteen years old). Although this census omits data on women and youth workers, it provides a rough indication of the number of workers in the city during the early Porfiriato. The census lists 165 male domestic workers laboring in Oaxaca City in 1875. The 1887 and 1890 censuses are also incomplete; although they contain detailed household information that includes women and children, some areas of the city are not covered. Nevertheless, it is clear from a comparison of these sets of census data that the number, percentage per household, and diffusion of domestic workers increased in the city during

the early Porfiriato. In the 1875 record, domésticos lived and worked in the affluent homes within a two-block radius around the zócalo. By 1890 and the beginning of the state's mining boom, the record shows that upper-, professional-class
Oaxacans who lived within an expanded four block radius of the zócalo employed
domestic servants, almost all of whom came from the surrounding indigenous
pueblos. By the early 1890s the demand for domestic labor had increased. Furthermore, the servants comprised on average 35 percent of the centralized household
in the 1890 census. For example, on average, houses in the city center registered
with ten people would include three to five domésticos. In each data set, as one
moved farther away from the center, the number and percentage of servants dramatically decreased. In dwellings more than five blocks away from the zócalo,
where the number of workers increased, domestic servants effectively ceased to
appear in the census records.

In her study of social reform in postrevolutionary Mexico City, Katherine Bliss
offers another possible rationale for entering the city's commercial sex trade. She
argues that prostitution was "a common route of urban assimilation, quickly ab-
sorbing women who moved into the urban world of free time, expendable cash
and freedom from moralistic family structures."[59] Although this reasoning likely
pertains more to primate urban areas like Mexico City, it does point to a critical
factor in the experience of many of Oaxaca City's prostitutes: as for other new arrivals from the surrounding rural areas, their work in the capital city was their
first prolonged and concentrated encounter with modernity.

Regardless of the factors pulling or pushing women into the sex trade, a dramatic increase in the number of registered prostitutes occurred between 1890
and 1907.[60] In 1890 only twenty-seven women registered as prostitutes. By 1892
their numbers had increased eightfold to 218, and between 1901 and 1909 an average of 137 prostitutes registered per year. A comparison with Guatemala City
underscores the rapid increase in sex workers in Oaxaca's capital. In the 1880s,
Guatemala City, with a population of fifty-eight thousand, had a total of twelve
brothels and forty to fifty sex workers (an average ratio of one sex worker to every
thirteen hundred inhabitants); Oaxaca City, with a population of less than thirty
thousand in 1892 – the year of the arrival of the Ferrocarril del Sur – had thirty different brothels and more than one prostitute for every 150 inhabitants.[61] The commercial sex trade grew so prolifically that in 1907, a year before the city of Oaxaca
annexed El Marquesado, that village issued its own set of prostitution regulations. Based on Oaxaca City's regulations from 1905, they reflected the relatively
smaller size of El Marquesado's sex trade.[62]

Starting in 1907, the year of a worldwide financial crisis that affected the state's
mining industry, the number of registered sex workers began to decline dramati-

Table 2. Number of Registered Sex Workers

Year	Number[a]		Year	Number[a]
1890	27		1903	99
1892	218		1906	169[b]
1901	93[b]		1911	45[b]

Source: AHMO, Orden 03, Grupo documental Secretaría Municipal, Registros de prostitución, 1890, 1892, 1901–3, 1903, 1905–09, 1909–16.

[a] Numbers of *new* sex workers. Women did not reregister each year. Figures do not include the number of fugitive or clandestine (*prófuga* or *clandestine*) prostitutes in the city during the years indicated.

[b] Numbers are averages taken over several years, up to and including the year indicated.

cally.[63] By 1911 an average of only forty-five women registered per year as prostitutes in the city registries (table 2).

In response to the increasing number of sex workers in the state capital, city officials enacted a new series of prostitution regulations.

Regulating Public Space and Public Women

In the emergence of the modern discourse on sexuality of late nineteenth-century Mexico, capturing, dissecting, embracing and limiting the body of the prostitute played a pivotal role in making sense and extracting truth of modernity itself.
— Cristina Rivera-Garza, "Masters of the Streets," 1995

In June 1908 the Catholic newspaper, La voz de la verdad, ran a series of editorials urging the city to reform its prostitution regulations. According to the author, Article 4 ("Of the Obligations of Public Women") of the 1905 regulations desperately needed to be altered. The author focused on the demoralizing and socially dangerous presence of sex workers in the city's public spaces. "The mere presence of public women," he wrote, "offends the morality of society because when presenting themselves in streets or other places they frequent, they display the idea of equality, of no distinction between the honorable lady, her chaste daughter, and the prostitute who sells her disgusting services to anyone."[64] The author admonished the city government for its lack of control over the sex trade. In order to protect the (passive and unsuspecting!) men and impressionable children from the "seductions that the prostitutes exercise . . . as they pass in open carriages and even walk through the *center* [author's emphasis] of the city," he implored the city council to tighten restrictions and increase the number of watchmen.[65] La voz de la verdad's article points to many of the unresolved issues urban officials

confronted when attempting to regulate the city's commercial sex trade. The.ap-
pearance of "dangerous" women in public spaces seemed perverse to elite notions
of the Porfirian city. The article further demonstrates that regulations continued
to flounder even in 1908, twenty-three years after the city had issued its first set
of regulations and at a time when the levels of prostitution in the state capital had begun to decline precipitously. Throughout this period, city officials remained ambivalent toward the regulation of the commercial sex trade.[66] In her
study of Mexico City, Rivera-Garza argues that scholars have viewed the "failure"
of the regulation of prostitution in Mexico in one of two ways: as sabotaged either
by the government's overly literal adaptation of the regulations imposed by the
French in the mid-nineteenth century or by the "double standards and contradictions of the regulation itself." Rivera-Garza points out that these two approaches
neglect "the significance of local conditions and the active agency of prostitutes
themselves in the constant inefficiency and eventual collapse of the regulatory
system."[67] Furthermore, I argue, it is difficult to discuss the "failure" of prostitution regulations in Oaxaca City when government officials never entirely wanted
them to succeed. City officials, caught between condemning the apparently per-
nicious effects of prostitution and promoting it because of its alleged ability to
stem the licentious activities of honorable family men and bring needed funds
to the city administration, wavered in their legislation of the sex trade. Corrupt
officials also hampered efforts to promote a "decent" urban atmosphere for the
civilized family.

    During the Porfiriato, the Comisión de Sanidad Pública (Commission on Pub-
lic Health) regulated the sex trade as part of a larger effort to maintain hygiene
in Oaxaca City.[68] The municipal government introduced new programs ranging
from infant inoculations to environmental cleanups in city streets and leather
tanning factories.[69] The budget for public sanitation (limpieza pública) grew from
1,800 pesos in 1884 to 3,520 pesos in 1893, and to 6,020 pesos in 1905.[70]

    The first regulations of prostitution in Oaxaca City, enacted in 1885, emerged
in response to the growth of the sex trade in the city within the broader nineteenth-century context of state practices and discourses of positioning, regulating, and commodifying the sex worker's body. Regulations of prostitution were
the city government's attempt to script its official version of modernity by regulating the gender and sexuality of sex workers. By imposing strict limitations
on the location and behavior of women's bodies, elites designated a social and
cultural boundary between themselves as moderns and the "others" of society.
A demand that prostitutes be regulated first appears in city council debates on
March 24, 1882. City Councilor José Espinoza's plea for hygiene and moral reform depicts the unregulated sex workers as evil promoters of venereal disease.

Espinoza described the women as threats to the decency of the family and called for the immediate regulation, surveillance, and taxation of the women workers.[71] When the municipal government formalized Espinoza's suggestions in the 1885 *Reglamento de mugeres [sic] públicas* (Regulations of Public Women), it initiated decades of official debate over the role of a commercialized sex trade in the state capital. It also transformed a once arbitrarily regulated activity into a codified and commercialized legal business.[72] In the process, the Oaxaca City government officially inscribed sex workers in the developing discourse and practice of Porfirian modernity.

Starting in 1885, the regulations of prostitution in Oaxaca City began to circumscribe clearly the urban spaces in which sex workers could legally ply their trade. The regulations of 1894 and after devoted three sections to delineating the appearance, behavior, and location of "public women" in the city. In addition to designating areas for the city's sex trade, the 1894 regulations precisely defined the character and deportment of the sex worker herself. A "muger pública" was a woman who "practice[d] the dishonest and public trafficking of her body either in order to earn money or for any other motive. [She was] a woman who live[d] in a brothel or house of prostitution."[73]

Moreover, the regulations emphasized that prostitutes were to be above the age of puberty, register (without speaking in obscenities) with the Commission on Public Health, undergo regular medical examinations, and pay a monthly tax to the municipal treasurer. The regulations required madams to locate in first-, second-, or third-class brothels, run a respectable business, be female and at least thirty-five years of age (if they were under forty-five they were also considered prostitutes and had to follow the same regulations as other prostitutes), prohibit gambling, and pay extra monthly fees if they sold alcohol and allowed dancing. Two councilmen appointed by the municipal president, who were in charge of the Commission on Public Health and its corresponding branch of prostitution, administered the commercial sex industry as a whole. In turn these city officials named two doctors of public health (*médicos de sanidad*, also professors in the Instituto de Ciencias y Artes) and watchmen (*vigilantes*) to monitor the practice of prostitution in the city and conduct weekly medical examinations.[74] Finally, an elaborate system of dues and penalties was set in place as a further measure of control and to finance the operation of the governing agency.

Oaxaca City administrators responded to the rapid influx of mujeres públicas by revising the existing regulations on prostitution. On September 5, 1894, the city council posted a broadside containing the most recent version of the regulations. Officials had altered them several times in the nine years since their original enactment in 1885.[75] This most recent version included important changes resulting from the accelerated growth of prostitution in the city since 1892. Two changes underscored the fundamental tensions in the regulatory system. First, city officials who saw the potentially lucrative nature of the trade, restructured the system by harnessing the schedule of fines and taxes to make prostitution a key source of income for the city. Prostitution became a business; vice paid. Second, officials who viewed prostitution as a social contagion sought to move sex workers from the city's wealthier central neighborhoods to peripheral areas. While government administrators moved the sex trade out of sight of the city's elites, it was certainly not out of mind. The economic benefit of the trade weighed heavily against its perceived social and cultural costs.

The Political Economy of Vice

By 1894 government officials had turned the sex trade into a profitable business.[76] Prior to that year the regulations of prostitution included only cursory references to monthly fees and fines sex workers were required to pay to government coffers. The 1885 and 1892 regulations stipulated that prostitutes pay a low monthly quota of one or two pesos and madams five or ten pesos depending on whether they worked in second- or first-class brothels. These earlier regulations legislated fines for errant prostitutes and madams requiring them to pay—depending on the severity of their transgression—from one to fifty pesos and/or serve from one to thirty days in prison. Officials considered missing medical examinations, soliciting adolescents, and committing public scandals the most severe of illicit behavior.[77] Responding to the rapid growth of the city's sex trade, officials essentially reversed this structure in the 1894 and 1905 regulations in order to increase the flow of money to city budgets. The 1894 regulations included an entirely new section on "taxation and payment of quotas" in which officials added an additional third class of brothel and charged a fee for serving alcohol and holding dances. Administrators doubled monthly fees for prostitutes and madams and, by including additional taxable categories, established a new base for municipal income. While taxes increased, fines decreased in order to encourage the proliferation of this "vice-ridden" and lucrative industry. The maximum financial penalty was reduced to twenty pesos and the maximum jail time to twenty days. The inclusion of fees for alcohol and entertainment signaled the city's acknowledgment that "vice" paid; the services of prostitution and entertainment and the sale of alcohol brought funds to the city.[78] Female cantina and pulquería owners dominated the city's liquor trade, reinforcing both elites' gendered notions of vice and their reliance on women to ease the capital's social and financial burdens.[79]

A harbinger of things to come in the following year, the 1893 city budget included for the first time a line item on brothel income and expenses. That year's salaries for the doctor of public health, a nurse, and watchmen nearly absorbed the revenue gained from brothel taxes. But by 1904, brothels, together with the other "vice-ridden" businesses of bars and cantinas, brought more income to the city than any other taxable area except for the city's markets, federal subsidies, and cemetery, livestock, and transport taxes.[80]

The 1905 regulations more than doubled monthly brothel taxes and added new levies on independent sex workers and hotels catering to the sex trade. Understanding that the more a prostitute worked the more she had to pay the city in taxes, administrators reduced fines and the maximum jail time to two weeks. In 1906, city officials taxed brothels selling liquor according to their class. First-class brothels paid one hundred pesos per month to sell liquor, second-class brothels, seventy pesos, and third-class brothels, twenty pesos.[81] The fact that at different times over thirty brothels operated in the city meant a steady source of income to the city coffers.

Government officials had turned a system meant primarily to regulate the city's sex trade into one that also increased municipal income. The political economy of the trade was at the heart of administrators' ambivalent efforts at regulating the lives of prostitutes and madams. Pulled between cleansing the city of "vice" and relying on that vice financially, city elites continually vacillated in their approach to controlling the sex trade.

The Moral Geography of Vice

While officials sought to maximize their profits from prostitution, they also strove to protect their notion of modernity by isolating the activity to specific spaces in the city. Responding to the increase in the sex trade after 1892, city councilors quickly moved to demarcate precisely where the trade could operate, constructing what Philip Howell, following Alain Corbin, has called "prostitutional space."[82] The regulations prohibited prostitutes from working in the more affluent central areas of the city. In May 1893, the mayor (presidente municipal), Eduardo Ramírez, proposed changes to Articles 5 and 13 of the 1892 regulations. Ramírez wanted to replace part of Article 5 that prohibited prostitutes from "appearing in public areas, walking in groups greater than two, and wearing indecent clothing" with a more restrictive article from the city's police regulations.[83] Other city councilmen argued that this change to the regulations was an "attack on the principles of individual liberty"[84] and voted against the proposal, showing a limit to the government's willingness to control the rights of the prostitutes. As we will see in chapter 5, sex workers would appropriate the terms of individual liberty to win concessions from the city government. The councilmen, however, enthusiastically agreed to Ramírez's changes to Article 13 of the regulations. These amendments demanded that, for the good of "public morality," brothels must locate in the "last two blocks of the city" and away from any schools, public facilities, or churches. The 1894 regulations excluded brothels from "central areas" in the city. Ramírez clarified this vague wording by including a detailed map of the city. A square drawn in red ink around the center of the city highlighted area within which brothels could not legally be situated (note the darker line in this black and white reproduction, map 4). The resolution, immediately passed, forced madams to relocate outside the "red zone" within two months of the amendment's publication or face a fine equivalent to two months' taxes. By 1901 twelve of the city's thirty-two brothels were still located inside the designated red zone. Maximiana G., Paula A., Francisca G., and other madams of second- and third-class brothels established their businesses mainly in the western half of the city within the six blocks to the south of the church of La Soledad. Madams of first-class brothels such as Adelaida D., Elena S., and Joaquina G. set up business across town in the blocks just to the east of the army barracks and the church of Santo Domingo.[85]

In their endeavors to control the location and practice of commercial sex, city officials were attempting to establish what William French calls a "moral geography of vice," or what Edward Soja, paraphrasing spatial feminists, calls a "veiled cartography of power and exploitation." Soja argues that "the social production of cityspace and the institutionalized citybuilding processes that drive it [are] contested terrain, filled with new spaces and places of community, resistance, and critique."[86] As we will see in chapter 5, sex workers and madams, deploying the liberal discourses of the day, fought with city officials over the placement of their businesses in the city.

As we saw in the case of Joaquina G. at the beginning of this chapter, city officials often argued among themselves about how to regulate where prostitutes could and could not practice their trade. A case in point comes from a proposition made by council member Francisco Ramírez in May 1893. Frustrated by the increasing number of prostitutes in the city, Ramírez proposed to raise monthly taxes so high that the brothels would all eventually have to close: "Our society is understandably alarmed by the disastrous increase of prostitution that is taking place in this city. The public [la voz pública] affirms that the new houses that are being established are exploiting, in the most scandalous of ways, the men that enter them. In order to avoid these evils in some future time it is necessary to secure the closure of the houses in question through heavy taxation."[87]

While the city council agreed to raise the taxes on brothels, it did so gradu-

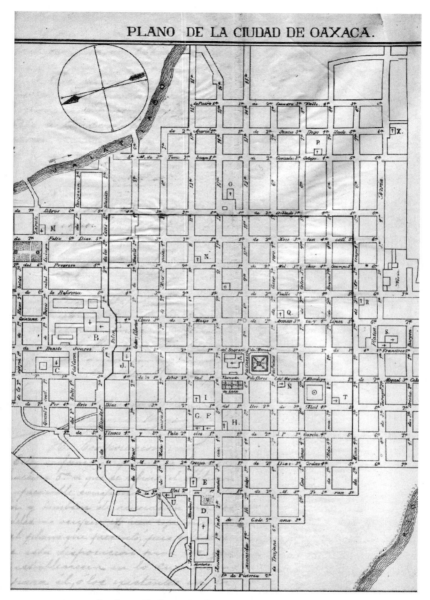

Map 4. "Red Zone" of Prostitution. AHMO, 1894, unnumbered file

ally, waiting until 1905 to implement some of Councilman Ramírez's changes.[88] Furthermore, the council, spearheaded by Laureano Ojeda, firmly refused to close down the houses, arguing that despite their depravity, they were a necessity.[89] Torn between extirpating sexual vice from the streets, reaping the financial benefits of the trade, and believing that they "needed" sex workers to divert the lascivious desires of "unsuspecting" men away from their respectable families, the city council validated this decision again and again throughout the Porfiriato, granting concessions to madams far more often than not and allowing them to continue working within the city's designated public spaces.

"Seductresses" and Corrupt Officials

City officials did, however, agree to increase the surveillance of the sex trade. Throughout the Porfiriato, officials passed legislation to increase the number of watchmen of prostitution. In particular, city officials viewed the growing number of nonregistered, clandestine sex workers as a menace to the city's inhabitants, "inflicting unwanted scandal on society."[90] Yet in an ironic turn of events, the watchmen themselves inflected their own scandals on the Porfirian city. The inconsistent and arbitrary work of watchmen and medical assistants shows that these minor officials were not simple extensions of the ruling class. Instead they served as "unintended intermediaries" between official regulations and the complicated reality of everyday life in the Emerald City.[91]

Following a report of a succession of fights in front of a city cafe in which officials blamed prostitutes (and not the men doing the fighting), the jefe político of the central district, acting as the police inspector general, requested the appointment of two additional watchmen in order to protect the "public morale."[92] In 1907 the municipal president proposed reforming Article 39 of the prostitution regulations in order to provide additional watchmen and nurses to assist the doctor of public health.[93] The doctor argued that he had too many patients to conduct examinations *and* write reports. He needed a nurse-scribe to enter the information for him.[94] Later that same year, the commission allowed medical students to assist the doctor in his work.[95]

The attempt to diminish the amount of vice in the city by increasing the surveillance of the sex trade eventually backfired. Student assistants and watchmen, seduced by their own "indecent" desires, compromised their positions as regulators of the sex trade and in so doing revealed the underlying contradictions in the government's official notion of a chaste modernity. While the government developed an elaborate regulatory apparatus to control "degenerate" sex workers, the regulators themselves often transgressed established norms of propriety. Beginning with the 1894 regulations, officials included a stipulation that watchmen in noncompliance with their duties faced fines of up to fifteen pesos and a two-week stay in the city jail.[96] In one example from 1907, the same year that medical students were added to the Commission on Public Health's payroll, the commission found that "a perverted student is conducting business and having regular sexual liaisons with the public women!" The commission fired the student and, as a result of the incident and others like it, amended the existing regulations to prohibit employees of the commission from privately engaging in business with sex workers. Furthermore, the commission required assistants to submit to an annual evaluation of their conduct or face dismissal.[97]

A lengthy city council debate four years earlier had exemplified the tensions within the commission itself and revealed the underlying gender and sexuality biases perpetuated by the government. Councilmen Andrés Castillo Bretón, Ingeniero Emilio Cruz, and Francisco Carrillo Folis, frustrated with the continued lawlessness of public women, had argued that the watchmen of the Commission on Public Health were unable to carry out their duties properly. The inability of the watchmen to work efficiently was not, they maintained, because the watchmen were dishonorable; rather, it was because they were unable to resist the seductive powers of the public women.

> The natural feminine graces; the studied seduction; the number of women in the brothels that the [watchmen] treat honorably; on the one hand, the love of liquor that attracts with its distinct colors and flavors, strong or weak; and on the other the lure of money. How easy it is to accept a peso or more or to demand them by force: these three causes — women, liquor, and money — sufficiently explain the enormous difficulty, the near impossibility of performing the duties of the watchman of prostitution.[98]

Thus, under the "spell" of the sex workers, watchmen ignored disorderly conduct and infractions by minors and clandestine prostitutes. They submitted false reports indicating that "nothing new" had occurred on their watch. Finally, the watchmen often drank on the job and stayed up all night to cavort with the sex workers.[99] The councilmen strongly suggested abolishing the position of watchman and replacing it with increased police surveillance and assistance to the doctor of public health. One councilman, Juan Varela, responded that abolishing the position of watchman would only lead to further disarray in the city. There were not, he argued, enough police in the city to properly maintain order among the prostitutes. Instead Varela suggested that although "some may find it a hilarious thought," the city should replace the young men working as watchmen with men who are "not vulnerable to the seductions of women," or homosexuals. The city council, not wanting to employ "pederasts," found Varela's suggestion "repugnant and unpleasant" and decided instead to include as watchmen "mature" women who would also not fall into the "dangers of seduction."[100] The example of the administration's response to the lascivious watchmen and students suggest a parallel with the incident of Antonio Z., the youth accused of estupro described earlier in this chapter. In both cases a dominant characteristic of masculinity hinged on the powerlessness of men vis-à-vis the perceived wiles of women. While the men are forgiven as helpless victims, the women are admonished as polluting seductresses.

The debate over the "dangerous" sexuality of women discloses the irony and hypocrisy of the city government's regulations. Although city councilors blamed women sex workers for a denigration of the city's moral purity, it was in fact the "innocent" men, acting with impunity, who compromised the system's integrity. The debate clearly shows that in the eyes of elite Porfirian society, only "mature" (read "elderly" or "widowed") women possessed a sexuality unthreatening enough to work in close proximity with the sex workers. After a certain age (forty-five, according to the prostitution regulations), women, in a sense, lost their sexuality and ceased to threaten the stability of the family. City councilors deemed homosexual and heterosexual men as too repulsive or too vulnerable (respectively) to work alongside the city's prostitutes. The council's decision reinforced the prevailing notions of gender and sexuality in the state capital. City officials, intractably wed to their gender- and sexuality-specific notion of modernity were unable to recognize the irony of their predicament.

These reforms came to a head in 1910 when a number of council members further amended the regulations to make the watchmen more accountable to their superiors. The councilmen argued that there was no way to determine whether or not the watchmen were carrying out their duties and thus imposed new regulations requiring them to submit regular reports of work progress to the city government.[101] The heightened surveillance of the brothels had spun out of control: city politicians now demanded that the watchmen themselves needed watching.

The city government's attempts to regulate the sex trade in response to the growing numbers of prostitutes culminated with the 1905 regulations of prostitution. The regulations, the last ones before the economic crisis of 1907 and the beginning of the decline in the numbers of prostitutes in the city, were the most stringent and comprehensive that the city had known.

Drawing on the "best regulations of sanitation [in the country],"[102] the new rules forced important changes in the lives of sex workers and madams in the city. The sheer detail of the 1905 regulations (the number of articles increased from forty in the 1894 regulations to sixty-eight) spoke to the heightened need to make the city's sex industry more "legible" to the governing elite. In order to satisfy the government's demands for legibility, officials required prostitutes to register in three different locations and submit their photographs (art. 4, para. 1). Hotels (chap. 5) and *casas de asignación* (chap. 4),[103] new legalized spaces for prostitution, received their own set of legislation.[104]

Yet, despite the new regulations and increased surveillance, control over the sex trade continued to weaken in the declining years of the Porfiriato. Corrupt watchmen persisted in submitting false reports and receiving bribes from sex workers and brothel madams. Prostitutes, although reduced in numbers, could be seen walking in central areas of the city and "committing scandals" in the city's suburbs.[105] During the Porfiriato, officials, unwilling to jeopardize the financial and perceived social benefits of the commercial sex trade, promoted it through regulations and practices.

The women workers had a different story to tell. During the Porfiriato prostitutes in the state capital experienced the city's attempt to regulate their bodies and businesses in increasingly detailed and more intrusive ways. Drawing on elite technologies and discourses and dominant notions of the respectable elite female, indigenous and nonindigenous sex workers altered their own identities to place themselves in positions of relative power. We will now examine the central role these women played in the construction of modernity in Oaxaca City.

CHAPTER FIVE

Portraits of a Lady
Visions of Modernity

Photographs are perhaps the most mysterious of all the objects that make up, and thicken, the environment we recognize as modern.
— Susan Sontag, *On Photography*, 1978

In November of 1896, Petrona O. entered a photography studio in the city of Oaxaca to pose for her photograph. Since she was a sex worker, the city council required her to submit photographs of herself to the registry of mujeres públicas (fig. 2). In the image, O. and the photographer attempted to represent her, an indigenous and illiterate woman from an outlying town, as a formally educated, respectable, and modern inhabitant of the state's capital. Her Victorian-era, bejeweled appearance, cropped hairstyle, the silk-draped table, and the garden scene backdrop all conspire to position her as a proper, high-society lady.

Elites and sex workers negotiated elements of the government's regulatory apparatus — photography and regulations of prostitution — to position themselves as part of the processes of modernity in the city. Elites, utilizing photographic registries, endeavored to contain and catalog the bodies and behavior of the city's "dangerous" women. By so doing, elites also established themselves as distinct from the "deviant" others of society. Workers like Petrona O. in the city's commercial sex trade appropriated photographs and other elements of the government's regulatory apparatus in an attempt to raise their class, gender, and racial status, and hence increase their level of social and political power. By mobilizing city regulations and the tools of a recently arrived photographic technology, both groups redefined the discourses and practices of tradition and modernity in reference to each other.

Women sex workers fought hard against barriers of discrimination to carve out a space for themselves in the Porfirian city. Oaxaca City sex workers were a diverse set of individuals well aware of their assigned space in society, a space they

Figure 2. Petrona O., 1896 (Etla, Oaxaca). AHMO, Registry of Prostitution, 1896

attempted, when possible, to claim for themselves. As we will see, they used the new techniques of rule to transform the ways in which they experienced their city. By challenging the regulatory measures in an increasingly institutionalized commercial sex trade, these members of the "world's oldest profession"[1] experienced the changes wrought by modernization and rearticulated dominant attitudes toward race, gender, and social status for their own benefit. In so doing, sex workers laid claim to elite respectability and certain elements of a "modern" lifestyle.

The Perilous Life of the Sex Worker

While city officials attempted to define the characteristics of a respectable and civilized society, sex workers tried to make a living for themselves despite the instability and frequent violence of their trade. Work in the commercial sex trade exacted a painful toll on women's bodies. In weekly reports to the city council throughout the Porfiriato, the doctor of public health never failed to mention the high number of sex workers suffering from hemorrhages, excoriated cervixes, uterine ulcers, and other painful and life-threatening ailments.[2]

Frequent assaults on the workers were part of the larger atmosphere of violence against women from all backgrounds, which was commonplace in the city during the Porfiriato. Criminal records and newspaper reports relate numerous stories of assaults by jealous lovers and husbands.[3] In this section I rely on the six extant registries of prostitution (*registros de prostitución*), which contain over six hundred individual entries, to construct narratives of the arduous lives of Oaxaca City sex workers.[4] The format of the registries reveals a wealth of information on the personal characteristics and daily life of a sex worker (fig. 3). The combination of visual and textual references to the prostitute helps to flesh out the often-obscured life of commoners in the city.

The professional career of Isabel F. exemplifies the desultory and hazardous path taken by many of Oaxaca's prostitutes within the tight confines of the sex trade. In the spring of 1892, F., a sixteen-year-old indigenous woman from the neighboring village of El Marquesado, went to work for Maximiana G., the proprietor of the city's largest brothel.[5] On May 9 of that same year, in compliance with regulations from the Commission on Public Health, F. posed for her photograph and registered as a public woman (fig. 3). We also learn from her entry in the registry that she was short and olive-skinned (*color trigueño*) with chestnut (*castaño*) colored hair, brownish-gray (*pardos*) eyes, a "regular" nose and mouth and a mole on her cheek. On June 21, 1893, she left the brothel of Maximiana G. for that of Ana María G. Subsequently she worked in the third-class brothels of Ursula G. (1894) and Francisca G. (1898). Finally, four days after Christmas in 1899 Isabel F. fell ill and went to the city hospital. She subsequently retired from the profession.

Most entries in the city's registries follow a trajectory similar to that of Isabel F. Other women, like Virginia Z. from the neighboring state of Puebla, not only moved from brothel to brothel, but also were constantly in flux "leaving" and "returning" to *el ramo* (the branch).[6] At different times, Z. left town, worked as a clandestine prostitute, and attempted to retire from the profession.

We also know, but not to what extent, that Oaxacan sex workers migrated not only to the capital city but also in and out of the surrounding towns and villages of the Central Valley.[7] This rural-urban migration underscores the fact that the city of Oaxaca was never a bounded geographic or political entity. Commerce of all forms flowed in and out of its borders. This fluidity of movement between the countryside and city raises the question, unanswered by the documents, of whether sex workers returned to their villages during harvest time or to village festivals to lend a hand, moving between lives as a peasant and as an urban worker.

It is also worth noting that a social fluidity may have existed. Luise White, in her work on colonial Nairobi, cautions us not to assume that prostitution caused the separation of families and the degradation of domestic structures. Instead prostitution could combine with other forms of women's work, especially agricultural, and foster an ongoing relationship between rural and urban areas.

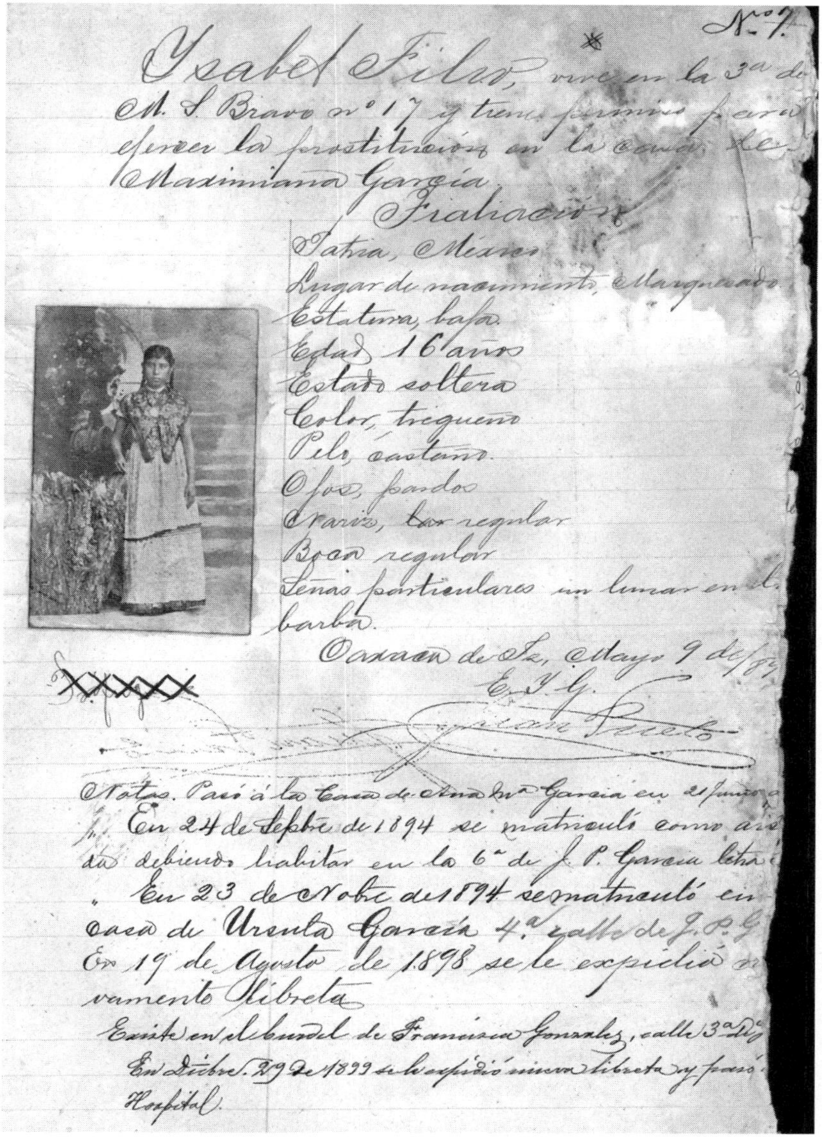

Ysabel Filio, vecina en la 3ª de
M. S. Bravo n.° 17 y tiene permiso para
ejercer la prostitución en la casa de
Maximiana García.

Filiación

Patria, Mexico
Lugar de nacimiento, Marquesado
Estatura, baja
Edad, 16 años
Estado soltera
Color, trigueño
Pelo, castaño
Ojos, pardos
Nariz, bra regular
Boca regular
Señas particulares un lunar en la
barba.

Oaxaca de Jz, Mayo 9 de 18__

E. J. G.

Notas. Pasó á la casa de Ana M.ª García en 21 junio
En 24 de Septbre de 1894 se matriculó como __
__ debiendo habitar en la 6ª de J. P. García letra __
En 23 de Nobre de 1894 se matriculó en
casa de Ursula García 4ª calle de J. P. G.
En 19 de Agosto de 1898, se le expidió n-
uamente Libreta

Existe en el burdel de Francisca Gonzalez, calle 3ª de __
En Dicbre. 29 de 1899 se le expidió nueva libreta y pasó
Hospital.

Figure 3. Page from *Registro de mujeres públicas*. AHMO,
Registry of Public Women, Isabel Filio, 1893

Mothers and daughters occasionally turned to prostitution to preserve the family structure. As such, prostitution represented not the destruction of family structures, but their restructuring and reconstitution.[8] While it is difficult to know the details of the domestic lives of the sex workers, there exists some evidence that transient workers were supporting their families. In their petitions to the city government, sex workers occasionally referred to their children and families.[9]

The brothels themselves were dangerous places for the women. Reports of drunken brawls in and outside of the establishments were not uncommon. Foreign males working in the mining industry usually arrived in the capital without their families. It was these men and their Mexican counterparts who created both the demand in the sex industry and the trouble that sometimes followed. In one case from July of 1893, the U.S. consular agent in Oaxaca, Charles H. Arthur, reported to the U.S. ambassador to Mexico, General Powell Clayton, that Robert Madden (a.k.a. John Conway), a U.S. citizen, had assaulted a sex worker. Madden had entered Merced V.'s brothel in an inebriated state, shooting off his gun and "striking one of the women with his revolver." Because he was a foreigner, the police did not arrest Madden.[10] V., on the other hand, spent fifteen days in prison and paid a fine to the city government for not paying her taxes during that period. Despite her protest that she had been punished for "what he did to me," the city government refused to exempt her from paying the taxes for the period she spent in jail.[11] Despite the city government's active support of the sex trade, the women workers received little protection. Frequent hospitalization of the women, resulting from a system of neglect and abuse, provided the government with yet another vehicle for the surveillance of women's bodies. Their bodies compromised by an unforgiving profession, sex workers fought to maintain a modicum of respectability despite the denigrating gaze of society.

Cultivating Honor

Porfirian notions of honor and respectability provided a fluid framework for the construction and maintenance of social class identities. Social class, never a static category, was contingent on a person's level of perceived honor. Honor, in turn, was based on the mutable, intersecting, and overlapping categories of class, race, gender, and sexuality. The form that these categories adopted depended on the place and historical era from which they emerged.[12] The increased presence of sex workers in Porfirian Oaxaca City forced elites and popular classes alike to continually reassert and redefend their notions of honor. Asserting one's sexual honor — in the face of overt displays of sexuality, lascivious behavior, and the like — became critical to establishing one's membership in modern society. Conversely, lack of sexual honor, especially among women, was deemed a threat to basic domestic stability that would in turn corrupt society and stymie progress.[13] As such honor, rooted in colonial society, represented a compromise between modernity and tradition.[14] Honor provided yet another way in which issues of gender and sexuality could enter into conceptualizations of tradition and modernity. Honor allowed people to root themselves in a seemingly natural and unbroken tradition while simultaneously proclaiming themselves as modern citizens and casting shame on those strategically excluded from living an honorable life.

Honor is, in a broader sense, part of what Antonio Gramsci terms the "ideological sectors" of society.[15] Elites, asserting control over symbolic and cultural expressions, delineated the limits of respectable behavior. "By creating and disseminating a universe of discourse and the concepts to go with it, by defining the standards of what is true, beautiful, moral, fair, and legitimate, [elites] build a symbolic climate that prevents subordinate classes from thinking their way free."[16] Sex workers actively modified their behavior in order to negotiate the moral prescriptions of respectable society. Constantly leaving and returning to work in the sex trade, they found themselves in the liminal space between social deviancy and decency as designated by the ruling classes. Social class hinged on specific notions of respectability.

Certain markers, aside from the obvious registration in the prostitute registries, indicated whether or not a woman belonged to the dangerous classes. Respectable women traveled the city streets with men of "decent character," never alone or with other women. Furthermore, women, if they were to be seen in public (as opposed to being public women), had to be chaste in their speech and actions. Compromising these standards of respectability could jeopardize a woman's social standing.[17] Dominant social codes of gender and sexuality tightly circumscribed acceptable behavior for women and men in Porfirian society. While the measuring of social honor and respectability was far from unique to the Porfiriato,[18] the steady rise of the city's sex industry caused a relative social crisis for elites, forcing them to "remap" the "moral boundaries" of the city more narrowly.[19]

The apprehension of Cecilia V. by watchmen from the Commission on Public Health inside a city theater exemplifies how rigid codes of honor determined the position of women in Porfirian society. In December 1904, Cecilia V. entered a theater in the city's central district, a refined public space, accompanied by two "honest" women. As V. subsequently dictated in a petition to the city council (she was illiterate), Luisa Mondragón, manager of the watchmen of prostitution,[20] forced her to leave the theater, then searched and arrested her. V. argued that Mondragón had not properly conducted her duty to "root out immoral social elements" but instead had "disdainfully" harassed her and accused her of being a *prostituta clandestina* (clandestine prostitute) – this despite her "reputation for being a *mujer honrada* [an honorable woman]." The Commission on Public Health then took charge of V. and conducted a routine vaginal examination on her at the city hospital. Discovering that she was suffering from the "second stage of syphilis," the commission immediately confined her to the hospital until she "recovered" from the disease and then ordered her to register as a prostitute with the city.[21] The commission's emphasis on V.'s physical condition underscored the government's concern for social hygiene and the maintenance of public order, as well as the medicalization of sex workers' bodies. Prostitution was deemed a disease in need of urgent treatment. But why had V. been apprehended in the first place? According to Mondragón, V.'s "improper behavior and immoral language revealed her to be a clandestine prostitute."[22] The fact that V. was accompanied by other women and exhibited dishonorable behavior in a public space was more than enough to mark her as part of the city's dangerous classes. This case, one among many, of a "mature" watchwoman's arrest of an "immoral" woman in a public space, reinforced dominant codes of Porfirian respectability and confined women to ever-smaller spaces in society.[23]

V.'s case also served to buttress elite male control over women and their bodies. If an "honorable" man had accompanied her, she would undoubtedly have been left to enjoy the theater performance. Similarly, the more stringent regulations of 1905 attempted to force prostitutes who tried to retire from the commercial sex trade and (re-) enter respectable society to continue their submission to male-dominated economic and sexual arrangements.[24] As we will see, city elites failed to keep sex workers under their surveillance more often than they succeeded.

Sex workers had many reasons to want to retire from their profession. In addition to wanting to spare their bodies further abuse, many women were concerned about their place in society. Sara H., through a scribe, eloquently explains her situation in a petition to the municipal president:

> I, Sara H., native of the capital of the Republic, with home in house number 3 on the first street of Hidalgo Avenue of this city, state before you with the utmost respect that for the past three or four years, more or less, I, a tragic victim of suffering and endangered health, have worked as a prostitute between this capital and the district seat of Ocotlán, not for reasons of carnal vice, but driven by [financial] necessity and other reasons that I will not bother mentioning here.
>
> I have a daughter who was born in the aforementioned district of Ocotlán, which, if necessary, I can legally prove. My daughter is now capable of judging my actions [i.e., old enough to judge them] and for this reason it is

necessary to educate her and provide her with a good example. If my mis-
fortune had inclined me to wickedness, I do not wish, in any way, to see her
in the same situation. I am resolved to face the necessities of life, *by way of
honest work* [H.'s emphasis] for our survival and her necessary education.[25]

There is, of course, an instrumental quality to H.'s missive. In the text she strategically engages with elite conceptions of motherhood and the deviant woman
by focusing on her daughter and her own hapless and, she alleges, unintentional
plight. There is a noticeable lack of religious rhetoric in these types of missives;
the women do not attempt to absolve themselves of their "sins" before God. Instead they tend to emphasize, most likely strategically, both their perceived domestic duties and their obligations of secular citizenship.

The 1905 prostitution regulations and subsequent amendments legislated that
prostitutes wanting to leave the profession required that an "honorable person"
post a bond with the city government (that would be returned upon the woman's
"rehabilitation" into respectable society), vouch for her character, and agree to
pay her expenses.[26] Yet it was often difficult for the women to obtain a guarantor
(*fiador*) in the city to vouch for their moral integrity, let alone provide financial
support. Many women, like Sara H., who migrated from outside the state capital, struggled to find someone to support them. She continues, "With respect to
the bond, it shames me to admit that, as a nonnative to this capital and given the
short time of my residence here, I have not been able to find someone to pay the
required fee."[27] After initially denying Sara H.'s request, the city agreed to release
her from "its care" (read, "surveillance") after she found a guarantor, Manuel C.,
a month later. In another case, despite having been "separated from the profession for six months," the city government was not ready to accept Francisca C. as
a "reformed" woman. The government denied her guarantor, Pedro G., the return
of his bond amount of twenty-five pesos.[28] The city government was reluctant to
release sex workers from its surveillance. When women were finally permitted to
leave the trade and enter respectable society it was almost always under the patronage of an established male, perpetuating the patriarchal power structure of
Porfirian society.[29] With the presence of an honorable male figure in their lives,
retired sex workers could, in the eyes of the government, restore their respectability and thus raise their social status.

Disrupting Modernity, Subverting Authority

Before leaving their profession, sex workers sometimes attempted to negotiate
their own space and experience in the modernizing city. While their access to
power was far more limited than that of city officials and their brothel madams,

sex workers did manage to challenge both superiors by using the tools of the city government's regulatory apparatus. As such, their efforts to challenge the government's policies played a fundamental role in constructing the framework in which the regulatory system developed and functioned.

Prostitutes responded in a variety of ways to the onslaught of government regulations and social denigration. While they did not collectively and coherently resist elite regulations, they did carry out isolated acts of subversion. The "fugitive political conduct" of subordinate groups like Oaxaca City sex workers amounted to what James Scott has called "everyday forms of . . . resistance." As Scott points out, the forms these "struggle[s] take stop well short of collective outright defiance, . . . require little or no coordinating or planning [and] . . . are unlikely to do more than marginally affect the various forms of exploitation that [the subordinates] confront." Yet, these forms of resistance are "far from trivial." Viewed collectively, the conduct of the city's prostitutes helped shape the government's regulatory processes.[30] The state's system of regulating prostitution in part buckled under its inherent weaknesses and its arbitrary definition of vice. Through acts of ridicule, absenteeism, tardiness, and defiance, sex workers further vexed the regulatory efforts of city elites and officials.

Sex workers paraded stridently in front of the offices of La voz de la verdad following the publication of a series of articles on the "scandal" of prostitution in the state capital.[31] Satirically flaunting their "perverse" sexuality in defiance of the Catholic Church's condemnation of their way of life, the women workers employed Rabelaisian techniques to upset the status quo, if only for the moment. They utilized the commonly perceived "grotesque" nature of their bodies to empower themselves.[32] Unsurprisingly, the spectacle did not amuse the paper's editors: "Last Tuesday, due to the undoubtedly noble quality of this organization, some 'cocottes' walked in front of 1 Guerrero Street, where our editing, administration, and printing offices are situated, conducting displays of impunity [alarde de impunidad] or of . . . who knows what! . . . It concerns us very little; such actions do not warrant our attention or our disdain. We take pity on those who commit them."[33] From the article and the regulations that subsequently attempted to stem the actions it reported, we learn that these forms of defiance occurred often, as sex workers tested the limits of social respectability.[34] Although in clear contradiction of the women's need, expressed elsewhere, to improve their social status, these moments of public ridicule provided sex workers with a medium to claim a space, albeit a precarious one, in the city. Far from being obedient and passive subjects of the state, sex workers taunted passersby with their indecorous and subordinated behavior, thereby integrating the public spectacle of prostitution into late Porfirian Oaxaca's modernizing process.

While some sex workers exposed their position in public space, most behaved as fugitives. Through tardiness and absenteeism, sex workers frustrated regulators' attempts to control their location and movement in the city. The process of monitoring and regulating prostitutes on a weekly basis proved more difficult than city bureaucrats had first envisioned. Although madams came to city officials with complaints and petitions, the brothel owners often broke the rules and sex workers frequently refused to register and submit themselves to weekly medical examinations. In July 1892, Jesús Ramón Campos, the doctor of public health, submitted his annual report to the city council.[35] In addition to providing a list of registered brothels and prostitutes, a tally of fines paid to the capital's treasury office, and reports on the health of sex workers, Campos explained how difficult it had been to maintain a consistent and reliable record of medical examinations; on average one-third of his "clients" failed to appear for their routine examination.[36] In his report to the council, the city treasurer reported similar difficulties in securing taxes and fines from sex workers. Instead of providing a simple list of delinquent payments, the treasurer, in order to convince the city council of the obstacles preventing him from submitting a balanced budget, filled his report with detailed narratives explaining why individual women were not able to pay on time. The reasons ranged from "physically incompetent" to "alcoholic" to "generally a disgrace." Almost all the women had served some time in the city prison. Many were *aisladas*, they had left their brothel to work independently. Campos complained that aisladas, because of their decentralized location in the city, were more difficult to track down for examinations. In one case, a sex worker, María J., and her mother, Rafaela D., were both imprisoned for fighting, leaving the treasurer without a close family member to turn to for compensation.[37]

Other prostitutes simply worked outside of the city's regulatory apparatus as *clandestinas*, clandestine prostitutes. While there are no clear data concerning the identities and numbers of clandestinas operating in the city, it is apparent, based on city council debates and provisions in the regulations of prostitution that they posed a considerable threat to the city's control of the commercial sex trade. Although there is also no record of prepubescent girls in the registries, their appearance in council debates indicates that they worked illegally as prostitutes in the city. The city council sentenced the apprehended girls to eight days in prison.[38] Officials also felt that the "conduct" of clandestinas "caused scandal in society and greatly damaged families."[39] In the 1895 annual city review, the municipal president indicated that of 199 registered prostitutes only 57 had complied with their inspection and tax payment requirements. The other 142 had "voluntarily separated from the profession on their own . . . or left the city without warning."[40] Working as a clandestina must have been doubly treacherous. Not only would the women have had to contend with the abuse and reviling glances of respectable society, they would have had no recourse to the limited assistance the city provided to safeguard their profession.

In the long run these incidents of moral transgression and fugitive conduct served only to reinforce dominant codes of behavior. As we have seen, throughout the Porfiriato city officials increasingly restricted the location and movement of sex workers. Nevertheless, these forms of insubordination also frustrated the government's attempts to regulate the commercial sex trade. On their own, these individual acts of everyday resistance did little to upset the operations of the Commission on Public Health. But cumulatively, in concert with the government's inability to reconcile its rigid notions of respectability with its need to promote the sex trade, they caused the regulatory system to flounder.

Portraits of a Lady: Visions of Modernity

Photographic registries of prostitution, another site within the boundaries of the government's regulatory apparatus, allow us to see how sex workers presented themselves as modern and respectable workers in the Emerald City. While government officials used photographic images as part of a larger effort to establish a visual order and rationalize the city's administration, both elite and popular groups employed photography to construct images of modernity in the Porfirian city. These constructions were multiple, and sometimes contradictory. Ironically, while city administrators worked to keep prostitutes outside of their visions of modernity, the photographic registries allowed these "dangerous" women to represent themselves as modern citizens of the capital.

City regulations obliged prostitutes to register with the Department of Sanitation and present three portraits. Considering the widespread resistance to and subversion of the regulatory system, the fact that sex workers submitted to medical examinations and posed for photographs in the registries at all is revealing.[41] While many must have feared punitive actions by the government, others may have co-opted the artifacts of the state's regulatory system, like the photographic images, to insert themselves into the wider discourse of Mexican modernity. The arrival of photography in Latin America gave both elites and common folk a new medium of imagining the world and being in it. Photographs as primary sources provide the historian with another tool to consider Gayatri Spivak's interrogative, "Can the subaltern speak?"[42] Since the experiences and expressions of subaltern or popular classes are usually mediated through elite-generated sources, it is necessary to read "against the grain" in order to cull out meanings from certain types of documents, photographs in particular.

Using Photographs as Primary Documents

> Photographs, after all, are complicated cultural artifacts. Though historical con-
> text is essential to their interpretation, they cannot be reduced to that context.
> Their use for documentary purposes is problematic. As historians, we are drawn
> to photographs because of their supposedly indexical character (or what Roland
> Barthes has called their denotative aspects) – because they seem to offer to tell us
> how people in the past "really looked," . . . but these denotative aspects cannot be
> separated from their connotative ones.
>
> — Nancy Leys Stepan, "Portraits of a Possible Nation," 1994

Following Stepan, the challenge, then, is to provide a multivalent analysis of the
image that considers not only its historical context, but also the meanings it both
indicates and implies. With this caveat in mind, photographic images must be
viewed as invaluable documents for narrating the social and cultural history of
Latin America.[43] In historical studies photographs are often used simply to illus-
trate, fill-in, or "spruce up" points made in the written text. The latter is privileged over the visual image, which is not treated as a text at all. Photographs tend
to be relegated to curio status and denied a truth-value on par with the written
document. It is crucial that we rethink this methodological approach to source
material. Photographic and other types of images can provide persuasive argu-
ments about the representation of (and by) historical subjects. When viewing an
historical image, we should ask what lies beyond it, how it was viewed, manufactured, distributed, and most important, why it was made.[44] Furthermore, this
"viewing" should not be limited to a gaze from above. As we will see, photographs
and other images in places like Porfirian Oaxaca, although produced by dominant groups, were often understood differently from below. This last point underscores a critical tension in the interpretation of historical photographs. On the
one hand, the perceived totalizing vision of government officials in places like
Oaxaca City produced and organized photographs in such a way to make individuals and groups static and "knowable."[45] On the other hand, following the
lead of theorists such as John Berger and Stuart Hall, we realize that the decontex-
tualized nature of photographs ultimately makes them "unknowable" or at least
subject to an infinite number of interpretations. Our recourse, then, is to supply
a historical context or "inventory" for these elusive artifacts and understand, as
best we can, the images' particular value.[46]

Popular groups, like Oaxacan sex workers, participated in what Deborah Poole
has called an "image world" – a visual discourse that includes interpretations of
images from multiple layers of society. Poole writes that there exists a "simulta-

neously material and social nature of both vision and representation. Seeing and representing are 'material,' insofar as they constitute means of intervening in the world. We do not simply 'see' what is there before us. Rather, the specific ways in which we see (and represent) the world determine how we act upon that world and, in so doing, create what that world is."[47]

Photographs played an intrinsic role in the expression and experience of modernity in Porfirian Mexico. Photographic images, visible in public announcements, newspapers, books, and city registries, were part of a variety of visual discourses of the late nineteenth century that included fashion, architecture, civic and religious festivals, and the arrangement of people and buildings in public spaces. Photographic images helped to represent and were shaped by the growth of industrial capitalism in the late nineteenth century. The serialized and interchangeable quality of photographs brought them new meaning and value in this rapidly changing historical environment.[48] Moreover, in a population of mixed literacy, the visual quality of images not based on text took on a broader significance. The camera was as much an apparatus as it was a symbol of Porfirian modernity. Finally, photographs were predominantly an urban phenomenon, contributing to the state capital's role as the major urbanized and modernized zone with which the state's population had contact. Photographic technology allowed inhabitants of the city of Oaxaca to imagine themselves as active participants in their changing world, to imagine themselves as modern citizens. Making a photograph in relation to its historical context is a political act imbued with the conscious and subconscious intent of the photographer and the photographed. Images exhibit a sense of the shifting power relations of the era, of the construction and interpretation of political and cultural dynamics.

Photography in Mexico: The Eyes of Modernity

The Mexican elite eagerly welcomed Louis-Jacques-Mandé Daguerre's 1839 Parisian announcement of the Daguerreotype photograph. By the end of that same year European-manufactured film had exposed its first images of Mexico. Louis Blanquart-Evrard's invention of the albumen print in 1850 yielded images that could be copied and mass produced. Photography spread quickly through the mainly urban areas of Mexico; in 1854 seven photography studios existed in Mexico City and by 1870 the number of studios increased to over seventy of varying quality and specialization.[49] The city of Oaxaca, never reaching more than forty thousand inhabitants during the Porfiriato, had four studios by 1908.[50] Albert Holm, the Portuguese consul for Oaxaca, who owned and managed the

Oaxaca Photo Supply House, often boasted in the city's English-language news-paper of his business's rich assortment of supplies: "Always on hand a full assort-ment of fresh films and plates, printing-out papers and everything else pertain-ing to Photography Eastman Kodaks. Plate-Cameras and whatever you may need. Price same as Mexico [City]. Films developed and prints made. Call or send your order to post office box 25 and they will be attended by return mail."[51]

Although the U.S. consul, Charles Arthur, lamented that there were only two photographers in the city, Felipe Torres and another "not so well known," the 1895 federal census records seven photographers practicing in the city.[52] In the city's prostitution registries Antonio Salazar is the only photographer whose name ap-pears.[53] More important, we know very few details of the photographer's role in taking the registry photographs. City regulations say nothing of the photogra-pher's function in the registration process; nor do they specify how photographs were to be contracted or remunerated. We can only infer from the inconsistent use of props and photographic formats used throughout the registries that a nonstandardized relationship existed between the photographer and the photo-graphed. Indeed, patterns emerged from the inconsistencies in the hundreds of photographs. As I will argue, in some cases, it is possible that sex workers, draw-ing on contemporary aesthetic conventions, determined the composition of their photographs.

Government elites in Oaxaca used photographic technology to rationalize the city's administration and organize its workers into discernable categories. Photo-graphs allowed officials to image the city's workers in neatly defined and control-lable units. The photograph was "the first technology to define – at the same time as it attempted to erase – the border between the private sphere and the public dimension."[54] The photographer, playing the role of the scientist, created photo-graphic images that were seen as paralleling reality. Photographs allowed offi-cials to produce a "frozen, disincarnated gaze on a scene completely external to itself."[55] That is, the images provided a seemingly objective and rationalized view of the people they displayed. The use of photography in Porfirian Oaxaca City was the epitome of the government's project of legibility.

During the latter half of the nineteenth century, government officials throughout Mexico and around the world had begun to employ photographs as part of larger systems of surveillance.[56] Images rendered of Mexicans assigned to specific categories or "types" existed from the colonial era.[57] Foreigners, curious to document the "exotic" Indian or mestizo, attempted to capture the country's in-habitants in static portraits.[58] The advent of the camera and the coinciding inter-vention of the French army in the 1860s allowed a natural continuation of the practice of making type images. In order better to understand Mexican culture, the imperial French government employed photographers like François Aubert to create a catalog of Mexican workers. His images, like the subsequent registry photographs in Oaxaca, portrayed men and women working in indispensable but fringe occupations (shoeshiners, street cleaners, basket sellers). Type photographs emerged with heightened industrialization and as part of a "global reorganization of society."[59] The fact that these transient workers existed on society's periphery further inspired elites to situate them in registries.

City photographic registries provided governing elites a medium with which to assert their notions of dominant (i.e., white, male, and elite) modernity while easing the anxieties produced by what they perceived as the threats to that modernity. Photographs helped to stabilize the territory of elites vis-à-vis the racialized and criminalized other by imposing a sense of order on the disorder caused by the country's Porfirian progress.[60]

The registries of sex workers were part of a larger collection of *registros de oficios* (trade registries) in which officials photographed the city's workers (e.g., water carriers, deliverymen, coachmen) and collected data on their physical characteristics and place of origin.[61] In the images (figs. 4–9), all the male workers appear in very similar, stiff, forward-looking poses against stiff backdrops, wearing traditional (white) uniforms, and frequently holding the tool of their trade. From image to image the appearance of the workers and their environment is basically unaltered. The striking similarity among the images reveals the underlying relevance of the registry photographs. City officials utilized photography to fix the otherwise fluid popular classes into distinct categories. These neatly defined groups could then be codified into statistically manageable units for purposes of surveillance, taxation, and discipline. In the photographic registries, city official turned the racial diversity of Oaxaca City workers into a catalog of a seemingly homogeneous population.[62] The registries subsumed men and women from diverse ethnic backgrounds into legible members of designated city occupations. The registries provided a medium with which the government could reinforce its rigid, class- and race-based notions of modernity. The photographs did not circulate outside of their immediate regulatory structure (i.e., in the form of commercial advertising). Although only city officials and perhaps the male workers and female prostitutes themselves viewed the registries, they nonetheless are an invaluable source for examining a subordinate group's engagement with elite discourses and practices.

Appropriating Photographs

> While the photograph was used to monitor and to control identity, it was also used
> to create new images and to posit new identities, proliferating the possibilities for
> representing and circulating the self.
> —Shawn Michelle Smith, *American Archives*, 1999

Unlike their male counterparts in the registros de oficios, one could argue that
after 1892 female sex workers began to utilize the images in the registries of public women to imagine as well as depict themselves as respectable members of
modern urban society. As in their acts of insubordination, prostitutes appropriated elite mechanisms of surveillance and administration to position themselves
as integral components of the turn-of-the-century city. The prostitutes' staged
adoption of characteristics of urbanized, respectable society had material consequences. By elevating their social status, indigenous sex workers from Oaxaca
sought to compete with the newly arrived, white prostitutes for the higher wages
in first- and second-class brothels.

The registries of prostitution also allow us uniquely to trace the shifting racial
contours of the city's commercial sex trade. As the state capital approached its
Porfirian zenith following the arrival of the Mexican Southern Railway and a concomitant boom in the mining industry, white, foreign prostitutes rapidly replaced indigenous prostitutes from the state's Central Valley. The images from
the registries provide ample evidence of the whitening of the city's sex trade and
reveal the relationship between ethnicity and the burgeoning economy. Photographic records of indigenous and nonindigenous sex workers reinforced the
dominant view of a respectable woman: she was to be white, demure, and affluent. To what extent were these women active agents in the design of their own
presentation? Did they merely succumb to the photographic conventions of the
times and dress and pose in compliance with contemporary fashions and the
moral prescriptions of an ambivalent government administration? Sex workers
never resolved these tensions. Instead, as the commercial sex industry grew in
the city, the manner in which sex workers portrayed themselves in the registries
varied.[63]

In the 1890 registry of public women, the city's first, all of the twenty-seven
women registered are indigenous and either from the state capital or the surrounding towns and villages. Their portraits in the registry follow the patterns
of the other workers in the registros de oficios: they are all almost identical in
pose and aesthetic content (figs. 10–13). Their dresses, shawls, braided hairstyles,
props, and gazes resemble each other. The women are immersed in the ostenta-

Figure 4. (*top left*) Amado J., 1905. AHMO, *Registro de aguadores* [water carriers], 1905

Figure 5. (*top right*) Victoriano R., 1903. AHMO, *Registro de aguadores* [water carriers], 1903

Figure 6. (*bottom*) Anastacio B., 1891. AHMO, *Registro de cargadores* [deliverymen], 1890

Figure 7. (*top right*) Alberto H., 1901. AHMO, *Registro de cargadores* [deliverymen], 1900

Figure 8. (*bottom left*) Cirilio L., 1903. AHMO, *Registro de cocheros* [coachmen], 1900

Figure 9. (*bottom right*) Orfino D., 1907. AHMO, *Registro de cocheros* [coachmen], 1905

Figure 10. Matilde C. AHMO, Registry of Prostitution, 1890

Figure 11. Isabel R. AHMO, Registry of Prostitution, 1890

Figure 12. Gregoria M. AHMO, Registry of Prostitution, 1890

Figure 13. Angela H. AHMO, Registry of Prostitution, 1890

tious trappings of Victorian-era Europe: a plush chair, velvet drapery, and a hand-kerchief daintily displayed in one hand while the other rests on a leather-bound tome supported by a padded bookstand. In these images the government is clearly attempting to define and catalog a specific sector of the city's population, thereby facilitating the surveillance of these members of the commercial sex trade.

After 1892 the images in the registries of prostitution radically changed. In a clear departure from the original, monotonous registries, the turn-of-the-century images depict women in a wide variety of poses, dress, and settings. The abrupt influx of capital into the city following the onset of the state's mining boom brought striking changes to the commercial sex industry. The face of the industry became increasingly white and foreign-born. Sex workers appropriated photographic technology in order to present themselves as respectable workers and members of a modern society.

The most remarkable aspect of the *registros de mujeres públicas* is the changing ethnicity of the women between 1890 and 1911. Starting in 1892, women from outside of the state began to replace Oaxaqueñas, and whites and mestizas took the place of indigenous women (figs. 14–17). Between 1901 and 1911 the majority of the registered prostitutes were from outside the predominantly indigenous state; they were older and white in appearance (table 3).[64]

The 1905 regulations responded to the increased presence of foreign sex workers by requiring them to register their nationality for the first time.[65] The increase in foreign and white prostitutes also coincided with the arrival of a "second wave" of foreign immigrants in the 1890s.[66] These predominantly male immigrants came from Spain, Germany, the United States, and a smattering of other countries.[67] Attracted by the new investment possibilities in the region, foreigners made their homes in Oaxaca and, in turn, most likely either brought or attracted foreign sex workers to the state capital.

Aesthetic conventions of foreign countries, especially France, set the standards of respectability for women in Porfirian Mexico. Fashion and the society pages in Oaxaca City magazines and newspapers depicted elite white women in Victorian-era finery. The images not only showcased the fashions à la mode and icons of a burgeoning middle-class consumer culture but also served as didactic reminders of a respectable aesthetic for women based on class, ethnicity, and sexuality.[68] By comparing figures 18 and 19, from the fashion pages of a Oaxaca City periodical, and the contemporaneous figures 20 and 21, from the registries of prostitution, we see the striking degree to which European fashions carried over into the seemingly unrelated realm of the commercial sex trade. Like the moral pronouncements of government and church officials, high-society images functioned as a touchstone of social propriety. In addition, the fashion pages were part of a new

Figure 14. Mercedes P., 1895 (Sevilla, Spain). AHMO, Registry of Prostitution, 1892

Figure 15. Francisca G., 1901 (Mexico City). AHMO, Registry of Prostitution, 1891–1903

Figure 16. Rosa B., 1905 (Barcelona, Spain). AHMO, Registry of Prostitution, 1901–3

Figure 17. Rosaura S., 1895 (Austria). AHMO, Registry of Prostitution, 1892

Table 3. Origin of Registered Sex Workers

Year(s) Registered	Total Number of Workers Whose Origin Is Known	Oaxaca City/Central Valley	Place of Origin Elsewhere in Mexico	Outside of Mexico
1890	27	27	0	0
1892	218	145	60	13
1901–3	93	17	71	5
1903	98	23	73	2
1905–9	169	29	133	7
1909–16	45	9	35	1

Source: AHMO, Orden 11, Grupo documental Registros fotográficos, Registros de prostitución, 1890, 1892, 1901–3, 1903, 1905–9, 1909–16.

aesthetic culture helping to create a society of consumers steeped in the "ostentatious consumption of goods and leisure that would demonstrate their personal, if not Mexico's, wealth and reputation."[69]

For the historical viewer these images may have also provided pleasure and functioned as "spaces of fantasy and desire."[70] In this respect they may have, as Poole suggests, disrupted not only the broader elite formulation of modernity but also the rationalized order of the registries. One can further imagine how the male officials cataloging this array of statistical type photographs may have utilized the images to fuel erotic fantasies.[71]

In the late 1890s and early 1900s, indigenous prostitutes from Oaxaca mobilized these elite aesthetic conventions in their photographic representation to work in first- and second-class brothels, which entailed higher pay and working in a more affluent section of the city, behind the church of Santo Domingo on Avenida Félix Díaz.[72] When compared with the images of sex workers from the 1890 registry (figs. 10–13), the images of Rafaela O., Luisa M., Rosa N., and Petrona O., (figs. 22–24 and fig. 2) are strikingly different. The women in the latter set of images, also indigenous women from Oaxaca City and the Central Valley, portray themselves not in formulaic poses but in ways that assert identities of respectable, modern women.[73] Following contemporary upper-class aesthetic trends, these women workers, wearing elegant dresses and hairstyles and standing confidently in unique poses against diverse backdrops, appear more like elite white women than their indigenous predecessors. In addition to age and experience, the city's regulations singled out appearance as a determining category for the class of brothel in which the prostitutes worked.[74] Rafaela O., Luisa M., Rosa N., and Petrona O. worked for Adelaida D., Manuel U., Virginia Z., and Bartola P., respectively, all owners of first- and second-class brothels. These sex work-

Figure 18. Fashion page from El *centenario:*
Revista mensual ilustrada, 1910

Figure 19. Fashion page from El *centenario:*
Revista mensual ilustrada, 1910

Figure 20. Josefina R. AHMO, Registry of
Prostitution, 1895

Figure 21. Herlinda M. AHMO, Registry of
Prostitution, 1901

Figure 22. (*top right*) Rafaela O., 1896
(Oaxaca City). AHMO, Registry of
Prostitution, 1892

Figure 23. (*bottom left*) Luisa M., 1901
(Oaxaca City). AHMO, Registry of
Prostitution, 1901–3

Figure 24. (*bottom right*) Rosa N., 1905
(Oaxaca City). AHMO, Registry of
Prostitution, 1905–9

ers successfully co-opted aspects of the state's regulatory apparatus to improve their relative social status in the commercial sex trade.[75] Appropriating dominant codes of Porfirian respectability, class, and ethnicity, registry photographs provided women workers with a means to reconcile their traditional images as indigenous and rural women with the progressive presentation as modern inhabitants of the city.[76]

While it is difficult to reconstruct the exact dynamic of the photographed and photographer in the studio, substantial evidence points to the active role of sex workers in the production of their own pictures.[77] As in the first registry of prostitutes in 1865 in Mexico City, mandated by the French occupation government, Oaxaca City officials did not regulate the portraiture of sex workers.[78] The women were instructed simply to turn in three copies of their photographs to the Commission on Public Health with no specific instruction concerning dress, pose, or aesthetic context. Unlike the prostitute images from 1890 and their counterparts in the trade registries, the wide variation in the photographs indicates that the women may have acted on their own behalf, and not solely at the behest of government officials and photographers. A large range of backdrops and props, dresses, poses, gestures, and glances in the images suggests cooperation between women and photographers (figs. 25-28). Again, unlike the earlier images (figs. 10-13), the women are relaxed and even playful in their appearance and expressions; they were most likely actively engaging the camera, appropriating its gaze of modernity for their own ends.

During the ethnic change that followed 1892, indigenous women attempted to portray themselves as decent white women by appropriating Victorian-style dress and background props in their photographs for the registros. The images resembled European *cartes de visite* (*tarjetas de visita*), a common photographic medium of the time used as a greeting card or collector's item.[79] The studio backdrops often replicated entrances to mansions, with sweeping staircases, bronze statues, columns, and paintings adorning the surrounding space. As Cuauhtémoc Medina points out, indigenous prostitutes were undoubtedly trying to Europeanize themselves and in so doing present themselves as honorable workers.[80]

It is also instructive to view the registries for what they are not. First, they do not include civil servants, lawyers, and doctors; they only record people from the lower economic strata of society. Second, in the registries sex workers do not appear destitute or bawdy. Prostitutes and photographers deployed props and backgrounds depicting elite finery (e.g., cloths, furniture, adornments) to accentuate *lo moderno*. While prostitutes asserted their position as respectable workers, they could only do so by reinforcing established codes of class and ethnicity. Not only did non-Oaxacan white and mestizo women form an increasingly large part of

Figure 25. Violeta G., 1895 (Havana, Cuba). AHMO, Registry of Prostitution, 1895

Figure 26. Juana A., 1892 (Ixtlán, Oaxaca). AHMO, Registry of Prostitution, 1892

Figure 27. Guadalupe F., 1892 (Oaxaca City). AHMO, Registry of Prostitution, 1892

Figure 28. Rosario M., 1902 (Mexico City). AHMO, Registry of Prostitution, 1901–3

the city's commercial sex trade in the later years of the Porfiriato, but the indigenous women who remained sought to portray themselves as white.

According to one historian, photographs provided a means for elites to "convince others and themselves that progress had been successfully imposed on formerly primitive and backward Latin American life."[81] In Oaxaca, as we have seen,
government officials used photographic technology as part of a larger effort to
rationalize the city's administration. At the same time, however, city sex workers
appropriated the same technology to inscribe themselves in municipal records in
a way that elevated their class and racial status and established their bona fides as
modern subjects.

Claiming Space: Brothel Madams

The commercial sex industry was by no means a monolithic experience or reality.
The different actors in the industry—owners of first-, second-, and third-class
brothels; sex workers in those brothels; clandestinas; owners of hotels and casas
de asignación; and, finally, government officials—all experienced the sex industry and the city in very different ways. Studies of prostitution that emphasize the
position of the sex workers in society as simply a foil to the forces of a regulatory
elite belie the multifaceted quality of the sex trade. Subaltern subjects experience
constantly changing relations of power vis-à-vis each other and dominant groups.
Subalternity is thus "a relational and a relative concept that refers to heterogeneous social actors that share a common condition of subordination."[82] In other
words, the positions of sex workers and madams relative to each other and relative to the state were constantly in flux, changing with the trajectory of Oaxaca's
dynamic Porfirian age. Brothel madams and sex workers had a unique relationship within the shifting dynamics of an emergent working-class population and
the sex trade.

Madams were mostly literate women from other states who were in Oaxaca
for the first time.[83] This is made evident by the fact that brothel owners, in petitions to the government, often (fallaciously) attempted to use the excuse of not
knowing the regulations to gain concessions from local officials.[84] While on the
one hand, brothel owners were entrepreneurial women struggling to establish
and maintain a legal business, on the other, they were outsiders, taking advantage
of a large pool of cheap labor.

Madams were very adept at utilizing the language of government regulations
to negotiate to their advantage, such as when they petitioned for new brothels
and deferred tax payments. In several cases, madams incorporated the liberal discourse of citizenship, individual rights and freedoms, citing selected articles from

the federal constitution.[85] Petitions from madams to the city council requesting the right to change the location of their brothels or a deferment on a tax or license payment were by far the most common during the Porfiriato.[86] In petitioning the municipal government for permission to retain her brothel in its present location, Concepción R. cited a variety of constitutional articles. Contesting the city's attempts, in the revised 1892 regulations, to relocate brothels, including her own, outside of the demarcated "red zone," R. argued that it was illegal to enact such regulations retroactively (Art. 14) and that they infringed on her individual freedoms and rights to private property (Arts. 16, 27, 101, 102; see appendix).[87] The city gave R. a two-month grace period but ultimately insisted that she relocate the brothel and pay fines. Although the government did not always grant concessions to brothel owners, its adherence to formal legal structures in reaching its decisions provided madams a means to challenge authority.

Like governing elites, madams also had a stake in controlling the space in which sex workers could ply their trade. Although brothel owners were not interested in designating a "moral geography of vice," they were very vigilant that their employees honor their debts and continue to work for them. Madams invested considerable time and money in feeding, clothing, and sheltering the women who worked for them; they also went to considerable and sometimes exploitative lengths to assure that prostitutes remained in their employ. Discussing the contemporaneous situation in Mexico City, Porfirian social hygienist Luis Lara y Pardo argued that madams were "evil exploiters of the degenerate *mujeres públicas*":

> The majority of the houses of prostitution in Mexico City are the property of practicing, old, or retired mujeres públicas who have had the character and sufficient good sense to move from the class of the exploited to the class of the exploiter in this . . . industry. These women know all of the vices, all of the weaknesses, all of the perversions that occur in these places, and they are very skilled at taking advantage of them.[88]

After being treated in the hospital, Oaxaca City sex workers sometimes fled, became clandestinas, and left their madams with the bill and one less source of income. Luz V., owner of the first-class brothel at 18 Allende Street, complained vehemently that, after receiving hospital treatment, the prostitutes under her charge had left the brothel without repaying her for the money she had spent on their medical care, clothes, and family support. V. requested that the city government either reduce the medical expenses she owed or require the watchmen or the police to track down the clandestinas and return them to her brothel. A debate ensued in the town council over whether or not to grant V.'s petition. While

some officials thought it fair to reduce her hospital debt, all agreed that ordering watchmen to return the errant sex workers to their former madams would
constitute an "attack [on] the individual rights of the prostitutes. The city council
tolerates prostitution as a necessary and inevitable evil; but [acknowledges that it]
runs contrary to the same institution that promotes, sanctions, and protects it."
Arguing that the relationship between brothel owners and prostitutes had to fall
under the law, the council ultimately denied V.'s request.[89]

Three years later V., working a familiar angle, submitted another petition to
the city government. Requesting a reduction in her liquor license, the madam
strategically acquiesced in her own criminalization and denigrated social status.[90]
In order to gain government assistance, V. referred to herself and her sex workers
as weak and morally compromised individuals in need of aid: "Honored Councilors, do not take into consideration the way in which my prostitutes and I provide resources for our subsistence. It was our fatal destiny. I beg you to remember that in the end we are women, and as such I believe we are worthy of some
consideration [in this matter]." This self-deprecatory appeal to patriarchal pater-
nalism often backfired. Reminded of the "moral depravity" of the sex industry,
city councilors were reticent to grant further concessions to the madams. Once
again the city council rejected V.'s petition. Councilor Amado Santibáñez argued
that combining alcohol and prostitution was too damaging to the clients.[91]

The increase in taxes and fines following the 1905 regulations concerned madams. Many were unable to pay their taxes and asked the city for assistance and
exemption from payment. In several cases, madams asked to change their brothel's rating from second to third class in order to fall into a lower tax bracket.[92]
Brothel madams paid taxes not only on their businesses but also on their property. Like the female owners in the city's retail alcohol business, madams benefited from the postindependence vestiges of the Spanish legal system that em-
powered women to administer property. Legal codes of 1870 and 1884 increased
women's access to property and power. The new codes freed widows and single
women from paternal control and provided them with the *patria potestad*, legal
powers over children or wards.[93]

While madams and sex workers receive ample attention in city records, a crucial protagonist in the commercial sex trade is notably absent: the male client.[94]
As mentioned in the previous chapter, the absence of men from the record underscores the extreme gender bias of the industry and its regulations. Officials
deemed women to be both threats to and sources of stability for the Porfirian
family. City watchmen never fined or arrested men for acting "inappropriately"
or for being infected with venereal disease, which they undoubtedly were pass-

ing on to their unsuspecting wives. Another mystery is the type of men who traded money for sex. The existence of three classes of brothels indicates a range of price for service, quality of establishment, and, according to regulations, the age, experience, and appearance of a business's prostitutes.[95] Because of their integrated professional and personal lives, it is probable that both foreign and local elites in the state capital sought out and thus promoted the business of the increasingly white and foreign-born prostitutes. It is unlikely that ordinary male workers could have afforded the prices of even third-class brothels, judging from the monthly taxes the city required madams to submit. Poorer male clients could only have afforded the unregulated *prostitutas prófugas* (fugitive prostitutes). In addition to a concern that these women were spreading disease and dishonor among the "proper" citizenry, authorities knew that they were evading the city's taxes and selling sex to men in unsanctioned, public spaces. As a result, city regulations (e.g., taxes and fines) grew tougher as officials feared the economic and moral impact these uncounted, "illegible" women had on the municipal coffers. Each *prostituta prófuga* meant a lost contribution of up to eleven pesos per month.

Twilight of the Regulated Sex Trade

The 1907 financial crisis led to the flight of much of the city's foreign capital and foreign population. The Oaxacan mining industry, vulnerable to international financial fluctuations and dependent on its export of silver and copper, was greatly weakened following a drop in the price of silver and the abandonment of the bimetallic (gold and silver) money standard for the gold standard.[96] Although the sex industry continued in one form or another, after 1907 the numbers of registered prostitutes rapidly declined. Between 1909 and 1911 only forty-five women registered as prostitutes in Oaxaca City. The golden era of the Oaxacan sex trade had come to an end. After 1907 and into the waning years of the Porfiriato, the primary petitions madams and sex workers addressed to the city were for permission to retire from the trade.[97] The decline of "luxury prostitution" continued in the years following the Mexican Revolution until 1969, year of the last extant prostitution registry in the city.[98]

Conclusions

Since they were not passive bearers of ideology, missionaries, colonists, slaves and royal authorities would create their own scripts out of the available discourses and

the material provided by their own past and present experiences. Yet they were all
trapped in a process that in great part escaped their control.
   — Emilia Viotti da Costa, *Crowns of Glory, Tears of Blood*, 1994

Da Costa's conclusions on the intersection of agency and contingency in the history of the slave revolt in Demerara closely echo the experience of prostitutes
working in the Emerald City's Porfirian commercial sex trade. Throughout the
Porfiriato, city officials and prostitutes working in the commercial sex trade negotiated access to power and public space. In chapter 4 we saw how the reciprocally
constructed relationship between the city government and sex workers helped to
define and regulate the commercial sex trade. City officials, eager to benefit from
the trade's profitability and stymied by their male-specific and sexually chaste
notions of modernity and the direct involvement of sex workers, were conflicted
in their attempts to monitor and regulate the business. In this chapter I have argued that the sex workers themselves, both prostitutes and their madams, appropriated elite regulatory apparatuses and discourses to negotiate the dominant
forms and processes of Porfirian modernity. Although out of analytical necessity
I have treated these domains separately, they were all interwoven.

   As a "necessary evil," Oaxaca City prostitutes were seen as an instrumental part
of the modern city. City officials felt that in order to extricate sin they had to feed,
ironically, what they saw as the city's vice. Despite the requests of some members of the city council, prostitution was not only allowed to exist in the city,
it was promoted through flexible regulations and concessions. The surveillance
of women's bodies in the city's public spaces and the accompanying regulations
served to reinforce dominant patterns of class, ethnicity, gender, and sexuality.
While Porfirian elites revered women as the "guardian angels" of the family and
hence of society, they also continued to limit women's access to power and public space. Sex workers in the state capital, working within those limited spaces,
actively adopted elite notions of class, ethnicity, gender, and sexuality in order to
gain access to spaces for themselves in the modernizing city and to promote their
position as respectable citizens.

The Consequences of Modernity

In the weeks surrounding the centennial celebration of the declaration of independence on September 16, 1910, colorful flags and spirited music filled the streets of the Emerald City. As we have seen, city officials promoted the festivities as the apotheosis of the Porfirian project. Event organizers scripted the city's inhabitants into a narrative of modernity that at once envisioned a prosperous future and extolled the virtues of the region's traditions, as best expressed in its indigenous past. The capital city was on display and meant to embody the class-, race-, and gender-specific forms of modern development prescribed by its ruling elites. Like many other provincial cities in Mexico and Latin America, Oaxaca City was the principal site of modernity for its region's inhabitants. Throughout the Porfiriato, the capital's citizens negotiated modernity in different ways to promote or consolidate their own positions in society. Ultimately, however, the multiplicity of these visions and the ruling class's discursive and material need to position itself apart from a denigrated "other" exposed the fragmented nature of modernity and undercut its claim to universality. While elites claimed that modernity brought stability and prosperity to the state capital (witness the Porfirian motto: "Order and Progress"), the constant need to revise knowledge and perceptions (what Anthony Giddens calls the "reflexivity") of fundamental social categories such as race and gender and a dependence on what is not "modern" paradoxically brought only disorder and anxiety.[1] When they envisioned modernity in the Emerald City, elites excluded the vast majority of the population. The consequences of modernity in Oaxaca City were grave and led to the undoing of the state capital's Porfirian-based government. The uneven advance and the contradictory, often paradoxical and contingent nature of "modernization" unsettled elite power and attempts to consolidate rule.

City officials took advantage of their connections with Díaz, state government officials, and foreign and Mexican capitalists to forge an elite vision of modernity and a sustained hegemony during the first half of the Porfiriato. Intermarriage, property ownership, rituals, tourism, print culture, and recreational activities all bolstered elite dominance and social status in the city. Urban elites sought to establish a visual order in the city's streets and neighborhoods by erasing and relocating its "traditional" indigenous elements. Officials enacted new regulations and surveillance to confine the popular classes to increasingly peripheral areas of the city. During the Porfiriato, city administrators initiated systems of legislation and surveillance. With these and other new projects, they attempted to recast the state capital and its inhabitants as "legible" subjects of a modern era. Ruling urban elites hoped that this rationalization of Oaxaca City's citizens would ease their own anxieties brought on by "progress" and facilitate their modernizing plans.

Archbishop Eulogio Gillow and other church leaders in the city and throughout Mexico attempted to reconcile their differences with secular elites in order to regain some of the power and influence they commanded before the anticlerical Reform years of the nineteenth century. Left with very little collective recourse, the city's workers turned to Gillow's Catholic Workers Circle for basic financial and health-care assistance. While ostensibly the Circle professed support for the capital's workers, in fact it served the controlling interests of the state, which sought to preempt worker unrest and forge a "modern" work ethic. The Catholic Workers Circle of Oaxaca exemplified the tensions between the conservative attitudes of the church and the developmentalist, secular projects of the Porfirian regime. The role of the Catholic Church in the transformation of the Porfirian city underscores the importance of the central religious institution in the formation of modern Mexico.

As government and church officials rallied to modernize spaces of the capital city and the citizenry itself, commoners negotiated and experienced modernity in their own, albeit circumscribed, ways. In the face of the government's attempt to forge a class-, race-, gender-, and sexuality-specific modernity, city prostitutes appropriated elements of the government's regulatory apparatus to position themselves as respectable women and to claim relative social power.

In the process, all of these groups—government officials, church leaders, the city's workers, and prostitutes—simultaneously constructed modernity in Porfirian Oaxaca City. Their varied experiences underscore the importance of examining modernity from multiple perspectives in secondary urban centers. Including Oaxaca City in the broader history of the Porfiriato also forces us to reconsider the notion of modernity as it formed in Mexico's South. Inhabitants of locations like Oaxaca City at the margins of less developed nations like Mexico played vital roles in Latin America's engagement with capitalism at the beginning of the twentieth century.

Much remains to be examined in this vein. Studies of roughly comparable Mexican provincial cities (e.g., San Cristóbal de las Casas in Chiapas and Chihuahua City) have yet to be completed.[2] Scholars would do well to draw on studies of modernity among so-called peripheral peoples living on the "margins" or "outside" of the developed world.[3] The role of visual order and legibility in the construction of modernity is particularly crucial to the process of modernization in late-nineteenth- and early-twentieth-century Latin American cities. The contemporaneous industrial expansion, the amplification of the state's administrative power, and visual technologies made visual regimes central to the process of state formation during this period. Furthermore, we need to know more about how these visual regimes interacted with society along intersecting lines of class, race, ethnicity, gender, and sexuality.

Modernity Disrupted: The Revolution in Oaxaca City

The process of modernization in Porfirian Oaxaca City showed signs of coming undone just as it began to develop. Díaz's selection and the subsequent election of Emilio Pimentel as governor of Oaxaca in 1902 marked the beginning of both a period of rapid modernization in the capital and its decline. As governor of Oaxaca, Pimentel used the expanding revenue from the state's mining and agricultural industries to consolidate Díaz's modernizing projects in his hometown. As we have seen, Pimentel initiated public works projects in the capital and oversaw the increased regulation of citizens and city businesses. Pimentel became the state's first Porfirian civilian governor. Part of the new *científico* elite, he made his way up the national political ranks.

Pimentel's election and subsequent nine-year tenure as governor exacerbated latent frustrations among the city's middle sectors. As governor, Pimentel's economic plan focused on foreign investment and the exploitation of an inexpensive labor force. The mining boom in the late Porfiriato created a short-lived but thriving economy and a new set of middle-sector occupations in the city. The capital's growing middle sectors were beginning to taste the possibility of economic and political advancement, but government elites like Pimentel kept any real power in either domain beyond their reach.

The increase in political instability in the final decade of the Porfiriato was not the only challenge to the dominance of Oaxaca City's ruling elites. A year after Pimentel's 1906 reelection, the state's mining industry, tied to global economic currents, reeled from a worldwide economic crisis. Foreign investment in Mexico, primarily from the United States, quickly diminished, metal prices declined, and national banks closed. Only a couple of the larger mines in Oaxaca

managed to continue operations in the years that followed.[4] Economic resilience
was also compromised by the absence of railway connections between Oaxaca
City and the Isthmus of Tehuantepec or between the capital and the ports on
the Pacific coast. These connections would have helped to stimulate internal markets, thus reducing dependency on international capitalism.[5] A 1908 article in the
Oaxaca Herald lamented the steady economic downturn: "There is no denying the
fact that business has not been as dull in Oaxaca as it is at the present time since
1897. It has been hoped with each passing month that conditions would improve,
but to date there has been a constant decline."[6]

Eventually, challenges from the middle sectors, in conjunction with revolutionary factions from the surrounding sierras, would undercut the hegemony of
Oaxaca City's ruling elites and cast them into the chaos of the Mexican Revolution (1910–20). Under Pimentel, the Porfirian project's almost exclusive focus on
economic development and its failure to include nonelite sectors made the middle
and lower classes desperate to right the imbalance of power.

By 1912, most of the state had already come under the control of the revolutionaries, leaving Oaxaca City as the last Porfirian bastion in the state. On May 27
of that year, five hundred members of the insurgent Sierra Juárez (Serrano) battalion approached the capital from the north. Famous for their chant of "death to
the *hacendados*," the Serrano rebels spent the next two years skirmishing with federal forces in and around the city. Eventually, after months of relentless fighting,
during much of which the capital's water and electricity were cut off, the rebels
entered the city on July 16, 1914.[7]

Visions of Modernity in Twenty-first-Century Oaxaca City

Following the Revolution in 1920 and for the remainder of the twentieth century,
Oaxaca City and its state struggled with a weak internal economy, a lack of federal
funds, and ongoing power struggles among federal and state politicians, problems that perpetuated the political and social inequalities of the Porfirian era.
Oaxaca remains one of Mexico's poorest states; its condition reflects the country's
poor south in general. As a result, starting in the 1940s large numbers of rural
Oaxacans began to migrate to Oaxaca City, Mexico City, and eventually to the
United States in search of employment. Today close to 40 percent of all *oaxaqueños* live elsewhere in Mexico or in the United States.[8] A deluge of rural migrants
to Oaxaca City has caused its population to swell. Rapid growth led to the expansion of the capital's physical borders as Oaxaca City spread out into the Central
Valley. Today the Emerald City is home to almost 350,000 people living in over two
hundred *colonias* or neighborhoods.

In the late 1980s Oaxaca City elites began to recast Porfirian-era visions of modernity and legibility. Like their historical predecessors, the capital's twenty-first-century officials continue to attempt to rationalize urban spaces while at once promoting an invented heroic indigenous past and rejecting aspects of contemporary indigenous life. Both the federal and state governments invested millions of pesos in the Oaxacan tourist industry, initiated during the Porfiriato. Since the late 1980s tourist visits have increased over 400 percent and become a primary source for revenue in the capital city.[9] Yet while some of this funding has found its way into communities that have launched their own projects of ecotourism and local history museums, most remains in the hands of larger, state-run, and state-subsidized businesses that showcase Oaxaca's "traditional" indigenous culture and crafts.[10]

Events like the annual Guelaguetza extravaganza in the Emerald City exemplify the state's latest race-exclusive vision of modernity. For two weeks each year indigenous "representatives" of Oaxaca's eight regions entertain tourists from around Mexico and the world with colorful performances of their "traditional" dances and rituals.[11] Like the famous Ballet Folklórico de México, the Guelaguetza's performances are "removed from their original contexts and packaged for touristic consumption, [permitting audiences to witness] a distanced and conflated staging of local cultural traditions marketed as national folklore." Contemporary elites have restaged Porfirian definitions of modernity that incorporated some aspects of rural/indigenous Mexico into urban centers while rejecting others. These elites have developed a new "cosmopolitan folklórico discourse," embodied in events like the Guelaguetza, to promote Mexican nationhood at home and abroad.[12]

Yet, other attempts by city elites to alleviate the anxiety of modernity in twenty-first-century Oaxaca have sought not to incorporate the indigenous and the popular but to expel and disperse them. In the days just prior to the Christmas and New Year's celebrations of 2004/2005, Oaxaca City officials built a purely touristic space in the capital's central zócalo. Starting in early December 2004, members of the state's largest panindigenous organization, the Popular Indigenous Council of Oaxaca "Ricardo Flores Magón" (CIPO-RFM), had staked out ground in front of the Palacio de Poder (statehouse) on the south edge of the square. Like their Zapatista counterparts in the neighboring state of Chiapas, CIPO adherents linked historical events and people (like Oaxaca's Porfirian-era antigovernment activist Ricardo Flores Magón) to contemporary protests against "the tyranny and corruption of the government of . . . the state of Oaxaca."[13] The group demanded, among other things, freedom for political prisoners, dismantlement of paramilitary groups in the Sierra Norte, and increased political autonomy and representation for Oaxaca's indigenous peoples. On December 22, the day before the famous Noche de Rábanos (Night of the Radishes, originated during the Porfiriato) festival in the zócalo, federal police forceably removed the CIPO protestors from in front of the statehouse.[14] According to the daily El imparcial, the government, attempting to legitimate its actions, had discovered that non-CIPO-related and, hence, unsanctioned protestors had integrated themselves among the ralliers.[15] Furthermore, the article reported, private business owners in the area had complained that the protestors hurt sales.

In the days surrounding this Christmas-time commotion, the government took the even bolder step of removing its offices from the statehouse (Palacio de Poder) and relocating them to separate locations around the city and state. In place of the offices, including that of the governor's, the government erected a banner proclaiming, "The City Is Building a Museum!" The intention was clear: officials hoped that by dispersing government offices away from the zócalo protestors would not only cease their activities in the central square, but that activists could no longer concentrate their efforts on a single locale. Ruling elites had, for the moment, succeeded in echoing the urban spatial designs of the Porfirian past. State officials, including the then-state governor José Murat, managed to temporarily transform the capital's central square into a legible touristic space free of disruption for the out-of-town guests.

The story, however, was far from over. Soon after the government expelled the indigenous protestors, six of Oaxaca's most prominent historians published a letter in Noticias, another of the capital's daily newspapers. The scholars vehemently disagreed with José Murat's authoritarian decision to alter the use of the statehouse.[16] In their letter, the professors argued in favor of retaining the historically established symbol of the statehouse as a political space, defending it as the "symbolic space of Oaxaca's State Government." They asserted that the governor's transformation of the government building into a "touristic and/or cultural space," a space beholden to tourists and store owners, flagrantly disregarded the historical struggles for freedom of expression in zócalos throughout Mexico.[17]

As if validating the inexorable importance of the Palacio de Poder and zócalo as symbolic political urban spaces, the CIPO protestors returned en masse, on January 9, 2005, only three weeks after the government had attempted to erase decades, if not centuries, of symbolic meaning. The protestors' return underscores the vital link between the historical construction of urban space, visual order, and the often competing claims of elites and popular groups. Elites attempted to ease their anxieties generated by modernity by rationalizing and making legible the city's spatial arrangements. Despite officials' efforts to counter the perceived problematic illegibility, the politically autonomous and ungovernable quality of unregulated spaces, the persistent demands of popular groups challenged and simultaneously formed new political visions of the Emerald City.

The citizens of Mexico in places like Oaxaca City continue to face the challenges of modernity amid the chaos, violence, and poverty of the early twenty-first century. As in their Porfirian history, Oaxacans demonstrate how life in the *provincia* is central to the development of modern Mexico. Since the Porfiriato, Oaxaca has become a center for tourism, U.S.-bound migration, and indigenous resistance and revolt—all critical elements in the formation of Mexico's continued encounter with modernity.[18]

Articles Cited from the 1857 Constitution

Title I. Section I. Of the Rights of Man.[1]

Art. 14: Laws can not be issued retroactively. No one may be judged nor sentenced, except according to the laws enacted prior to the fact and exactly applied to it by the tribunal previously established by law.

Art. 16: No one's person, family, house, papers, and possessions may be disturbed, except in accordance with a written order from the competent authorities that establishes the legal cause of the procedure. In the case of *delito infraganti* [flagrante delicto or red handed], anyone may be apprehended as the delinquent and his accomplices and placed without delay at the disposal of the immediate authorities.

Art. 27: The property of persons may not be occupied with out their consent, except in case of public utility and prior indemnity. The law determines the authority that must conduct the expropriation and the requirements with which this must be verified. No civil or ecclesiastic corporation, whatever its character, denomination or object, will have the legal capacity to acquire real estate in property or administration, with the only exception being that of buildings destined immediately and directly to the service or object of the institution.

Title III. Section III. Of Legal Powers

Art. 101: The tribunals of the federation will resolve all controversy that arises:
   I. From the laws or acts of any authority that protect the rights of the individual.
   II. From the laws or acts of the federal authority that violate or restrict the sovereignty of the states.
   III. From laws or acts of these authorities that invade the domain of the federal authority.

Art. 102: All of the judgments that the previous article speaks to will follow, on demand of the offended party, by means of procedures and forms of the juridical order that determine a law. The sentence will always be that which concerns only particular individuals, limiting itself to protecting and supporting them in the special case concerning that is found in the process, without making any general declaration with respect to the law or act that motivates it.

Notes

Preface

1. See Edward Said's article on the discursive fallout of the atrocities of September 11, 2001, where he excoriates Samuel Huntington's "clash of civilizations" thesis for its woefully uncritical characterization of modernity, late-twentieth-century geopolitics, and cultural difference. Said takes Huntington to task for naively pitting a monolithic "West" against an undifferentiated Islamic world; Said, "Clash of Ignorance"; Huntington, "Clash of Civilizations?"

Introduction

1. In his architectural study of Oaxaca City, Carlos Lira Vásquez points out that the capital owes much of its appearance to Porfirian-era construction and renovations. Visitors to Oaxaca City today usually marvel at its colonial-era churches and the surrounding precolonial indigenous pyramids. However, it was during the Porfiriato that city officials built and adorned many of the buildings and public spaces in the city that attract tourists from all over the world; Lira Vásquez, "Ciudad de Oaxaca," 415–37. All translations in this book are by the author unless indicated otherwise.

2. The moniker "the Emerald City" also resonates with L. Frank Baum's allegorical wizard of Oz. Like the deceptive wizard, Porfirio Díaz attempted to run his hometown from behind the scenes. While his modern technical and economic might may have seemed to a minority of ruling elites to be the magical solution to Mexico's century of instability, Díaz's gimmicks ultimately failed. He was unable to improve the lives of Mexico's middle class and destitute masses, both of which grew significantly under his regime. The 1910 revolution that resulted from this social unrest sealed the dictator's fate. Throughout this work I also refer to Oaxaca de Juárez interchangeably as "Oaxaca City" and "the city of Oaxaca."

3. Mitchell, "Stage of Modernity."

4. Piccato, City of Suspects, 47; Van Young, Conclusion, 346.

5. El centenario: Revista mensual ilustrada, October 15, 1910. According to the 1895 federal census, the average population in Mexico's thirty state and district capitals (excluding Mexico City) was 28,998. Oaxaca City had the country's eleventh-largest population; Resumen del primer censo.

6. Wells and Joseph, "Modernizing Visions," 180–81; Morse and Hardoy, Rethinking the Latin American City, 22; Scobie, "Growth of Latin American Cities."

Oaxaca City was part of a larger "urban network" in the state's central valleys, one that also included the towns Zaachila, Zimatlán, Tlacolula, Ejutla, and Miahuatlán; Chassen-López, "Liberal to Revolutionary Oaxaca," introduction, 2–3.

7. Wells and Joseph, "Modernizing Visions," 215.

8. Ruiz, *Great Rebellion*, 23.

9. Waterbury, "Non-revolutionary Peasants." Even more recently, George J. Sánchez, in his excellent work on the history of Mexican immigrants noted that "the southern states of Oaxaca and Chiapas . . . were relatively isolated from the profound changes taking place in Mexican society"; *Becoming Mexican American*, 24.

10. Taracena, *Apuntes históricos de Oaxaca*, 199. Other works by Oaxacan scholars writing in this vein include Iturribarría, *Oaxaca en la historia*; Brioso y Candiani, *Evolución del pueblo oaxaqueño*; and Tamayo, *Oaxaca en el siglo XX*.

11. In the Mexican adage, Cuauhtitlán represents the relatively unknown rural village in contrast to the nation's metropolis.

12. Chassen-López, "Liberal to Revolutionary Oaxaca"; Chassen-López, " 'Cheaper than Machines.' "

13. For examples of studies that critically champion Oaxaca's role in Mexico's modern history, see Dalton, *Oaxaca*; Sánchez Silva, *Indios, comerciantes y burocracia*; Martínez Vásquez et al., *Revolución en Oaxaca*; Martínez Vásquez, *Historia de la educación*; Arellanes Meixueiro, *Trabajos y guias*; Reina, *Historia de la cuestión agraria*; Ruiz Cervantes, *Revolución en Oaxaca*; Ruiz Cervantes, "Oaxaca"; Rubin, *Decentering the Regime*; Wright-Rios, "Piety and Progress"; Poole, "Image of 'Our Indian' "; and Sloan, "Runaway Daughters."

14. For a summary of the current historical scholarship on Oaxaca and Oaxaca City, see Overmyer-Velázquez and Yannakakis, "Renaissance."

15. Díaz served as state governor from 1881 to 1883.

16. Swingewood, *Cultural Theory*.

17. Stuart Hall furnishes an excellent overview of the term *modernity* and suggests some critical ways to think about the notion in his edited volume, *Modernity*, 3–18. In *Cosmopolis*, Stephen Toulmin provides an invaluable historical treatment of modernity. Toulmin notes that historians have been fickle in their attempts to locate modernity's origins. Its "start" has been variously dated from Gutenberg's adoption of moveable type (1436) to Freud's *The Interpretation of Dreams* (1895). Yet, for Toulmin, in order to understand the fundamental epistemological origin of modernity and all of its social, economic, political, and cultural permutations, we must look to Descartes's break with the philosophical tradition of humanism in the early seventeenth century. Descartes's philosophy of rationality and certainty privileged logic over rhetoric, generality over particularity, and permanence over transience. According to Toulmin, over time these "modern" characteristics infused themselves into the official and popular practices of our daily lives. See also Berman, *All That Is Solid*.

18. Hall, *Modernity*, 17. See also Giddens and Pierson, *Conversations with Anthony Giddens*; Harvey, *Condition of Postmodernity*.

19. As Dilip Parameshwar Gaonkar points out, the West is not a uniform and acultural place but a " 'culture' with a distinctive moral and scientific outlook consisting of a constellation of understandings of person, nature, society, reason, and the good that is different from both its predecessor cultures and non-Western cultures"; Gaonkar, "Alternative Modernities," 17.

20. Frank, *Capitalism and Underdevelopment*; Cardoso and Falleto, *Dependencia y desarrollo*.

21. Joseph, "Close Encounters," 12. Joseph explains in careful detail the history of development theories in Latin America.

22. Coronil, *Magical State*, 8.

23. Examples of some excellent recent historical studies on modern Mexico City include Rivera-Garza, "Masters of the Streets"; Lear, *Workers, Neighbors, and Citizens*; Bliss, *Compromised Positions*; and Piccato, *City of Suspects*.

24. Guerra, *México*, esp. 24 and 342. See also his *Modernidad e independencias*.

25. Gaonkar, "Alternative Modernities," 14.

26. Mitchell, Introduction, xii–xiii.

27. An excellent formulation of the simultaneous constructions of modernity and tradition can be found in Rubenstein, *Bad Language*.

28. Grandin, *Blood of Guatemala*, 165.

29. Mitchell, Introduction, xii–xiii.

30. Ibid., xiii. On the fragmented nature of Mexico's postrevolutionary "Golden Age" historical narrative, see Joseph et al., *Fragments of a Golden Age*.

31. Coronil, *Magical State*, 74.

32. In their discussion of global modernity, Jean and John Comaroff underscore the fact that, despite attempts to make it so, "the world has not been reduced to sameness." They argue for the multiplicity of modernities in the experience of colonized societies around the world, societies that have retained or at least steadfastly incorporated diverse notions of themselves in the face of global capitalism; Comaroff and Comaroff, *Modernity and Its Malcontents*, xi–xxxi.

33. During the Porfiriato, Oaxaca City's workers did not coalesce into a uniform working class. Instead, they labored as "proprietary producers" in small artisan shops throughout the capital. As such, I refer to "the city's workers" instead of "working-class groups" throughout.

34. In his article on modernity and popular religious customs, Edward Wright-Rios recasts Ignancio Altamirano as a proto-indigenista outside of the dominant intellectual currents of the Porfirian age; Wright-Rios, "Indian Saints."

35. In his discussion of Mexico's Aztec Palace exhibit at the 1889 World's Fair in Paris, Mauricio Tenorio-Trillo provides a clear example of Porfirian elites' ambivalence toward the role of indigenous society and culture in the construction of modern Mexico; Tenorio-Trillo, *Mexico at the World's Fairs*, esp. 64–80 and 92–95.

36. Bonfil Batalla, *México Profundo*, 103–7.

37. *Oaxaca Herald*, March 22, 1908. City newspapers devoted scores of pages to articles on the World's Fair. In addition to mining exhibits, state promoters displayed information on the Mexican Southern Railway and other symbols of modernity. See Tenorio-Trillo, *Mexico at the World's Fairs*.

38. French, *Peaceful and Working People*.

39. Buffington and French, "Culture of Modernity."

40. In 1872, Oaxaca City was officially named Oaxaca de Juárez in honor of Benito Juárez.

41. NAII, National Archives Microfilm Publications Microcopy no. 328 RG 59 M-328, Dispatches from U.S. Consuls in Oaxaca, 1869–1878. For another description of the region's disorder, see AGPEO, Memoria Administrativa, 1872, Mensaje leido por Miguel Castro (provisional governor).

42. Gay, *Historia de Oaxaca*, 437.

43. AGPEO, Memoria Administrativa, 1877, Mensaje leido por Governor Francisco Meijueiro [Meixueiro].

44. Oaxaca state was and continues to be divided into administrative districts (see map 2). Each district is administered by a *jefe politico*. Oaxaca City is located in the Central District.

45. AGPEO, Memoria Administrativa, 1872, Jefe Político Lic. Joaquín Mauleón.

46. *El diario del hogar*, November 8, 9, 13, 15, 17, 1892.

47. *El tiempo*, October 29, 1892.

48. Belmar, *Breve reseña*, 5.

49. Chassen-López, *Regiones y ferrocarriles*.

50. Chassen-López, "Liberal to Revolutionary Oaxaca," chap. 1. For a history of the railroad in Mexico during the Porfiriato, see Coatsworth, *Growth against Development*.

51. According to official statistics, two-thirds of the way into the Porfiriato the state's population had increased to 948,633. Although their number had declined since the 1870s, indigenous inhabitants still remained in the majority, accounting for 66 percent of the population; *Memoria administrativa*.

52. Arellanes Meixueiro, *Trabajos y guias*, 44.

53. Southworth, *Estado de Oaxaca*, 54.

54. Da Costa, *Crowns of Glory*, xviii.

55. Throughout this study, I steer clear of imposing my own authoritative "narrative logic" onto the disparate series of events in Oaxaca City's Porfirian history. While it is impossible to avoid completely certain rigid and "official" discursive, spatial, and temporal conventions, I have found it important to remember along with Stuart Hall that "the history of modern societies had no absolute beginning or predetermined goal"; Hall, *Modernity*, 13–14.

56. In *The Country and the City*, Raymond Williams, attempting to demystify stereotypes of the subject, examines the "astonishingly varied" histories of cities and the countryside.

57. Chassen-López assiduously interrogates the prevailing scholarly notion of Oaxaca's "passive" peasantry and shows that indigenous villagers staked their own claims to land, education, and the liberal ideologies of the late nineteenth century; Chassen-López, "View from the South."

1. Oaxaca's Ruling Class

1. I use the terms *elite class* and *ruling class* to denote those individuals in control of the state capital's government and industry. These elites included members of both the upper and upper-middle socioeconomic class.

2. Giddens and Stanworth, *Elites and Power*; Falcón, "Force and the Search for Consent."

3. Gordon, "Governmental Rationality," 3.

4. Díaz unsuccessfully had tried to unseat Juárez and his predecessor, President Sebastián Lerdo de Tejada (1872–76), through the ballot box and by force. When Lerdo announced that he was seeking reelection in 1876, Díaz quickly responded with the *Plan de Tuxtepec*, asserting that Lerdo had violated, among other things, the no-reelection principles of the 1857 constitution. In his following three decades as president, however, Díaz would flout his own proclamation to free himself and his supporters from term limits in state and federal governments.

5. For more on the "dual legacy," see Chassen-López, "Liberal to Revolutionary Oaxaca," conclusion, 9; for an analysis of the "unifying liberal myth," see Hale, *Transformation of Liberalism*.

6. In addition to Pimentel in Oaxaca, Pablo Escandón in the state of Morelos, Enrique Creel in Chihuahua, and Olegario Molina in Yucatán served as científico governors in support of Díaz.

7. Wells and Joseph, *Summer of Discontent*.

8. Falcón, "Force and the Search for Consent," 134.

9. Wells and Joseph, "Modernizing Visions," 167–215.

10. Chassen-López, "Liberal to Revolutionary Oaxaca," chap. 8, 9n27; chap. 7, 12–14.

11. Bulnes, *Verdadero Díaz*, 181–82.

12. Topik, "Economic Domination."

13. *Manual de gobernadores*. For a detailed outline of the city's administrative structures, see AHMO, Orden 03, Grupo documental Secretaría municipal, Ordenanzas municipales de la Ciudad de Oaxaca de Juárez, 1890.

14. With the exception of four civilian interims, all the governors of Oaxaca from 1876 to 1902 were generals loyal to Díaz. They were Fidencio Hernández, Francisco Meixueiro, Mariano Jiménez, Luis Mier y Terán, Albino Zertuche, Gregorio Chávez, and Martín González.

15. CPD, L7 C1 D000050 and CPD L7 C1 D000046–48.

16. CPD, L 0014, C 0002, D 000906, D 000907, and D 000908, January 1889.

17. See, e.g., CPD, L 005, C 001, 000194; L 005, C 004, D 001716-A; L 005, C 005, D 002045; L 0014, C 00016, D 007543. See also Kuecker, "Desert in a Tropical Wilderness," 106.

18. AHMO, Orden 22, Grupo documental Biblioteca, Mensaje leido por el C. Lic Emilio Pimentel, 1904. For a complete run of the governors' annual administrative reports during the Porfiriato, see AGPEO, *Memorias administrativas*, 1876–1911.

19. Díaz's political reach also extended to the highest levels of Oaxaca's Catholic Church. Díaz and the state's archbishop, Eulogio Gillow, maintained a strong relationship throughout the period. This dynamic is discussed in chapter 3.

20. Buffington and French, "Culture of Modernity," 385.

21. Falcón, "Force and the Search for Consent," 107–34.

22. Examples of this pervasive involvement can be found in AHMO, Orden 03, Grupo documental Secretaría municipal, dossier [legajo] 1879.3, file [expediente] 10, and under "jefe político" throughout the Docemp. database in the AHMO.

23. AHMO, Orden 03, Grupo documental Secretaría municipal, dossier 1894, vol. 5.

24. *La unión*, June 30, 1907.

25. AHMO, Orden 03, Grupo documental Secretaría municipal, dossier 1905.3, file 78. Gómez would have his turn as municipal president two years later.

26. AHMO, Orden 05, Grupo documental Padrones, artículos de la ley electoral federal, 1901.

27. On the history of late-colonial and independence-era elites, see Sánchez Silva, *Indios, comerciantes y burocracia.*

28. Arellanes Meixueiro, *Trabajos y guias*, 12. The term was first used in de la Cruz, "Razones de Juchitán."

29. According to the 1895 federal census, 174 foreign nationals lived in the city. Most foreigners came from Germany, Spain, France, Italy, England, and the United States; *Resumen del primer censo*. Ross Parmenter notes that "in the halcyon days of Porfirio Diaz" the number of North American and British families alone grew to "as many as 300"; Parmenter, *Lawrence in Oaxaca*, 1. For a discussion of the precursors to Oaxaca City's Porfirian elite, see Chassen-López, "Liberal to Revolutionary Oaxaca," chap. 5; Berry, *Reform in Oaxaca*; and Sánchez-Silva, *Indios, comerciantes y burocracia.*

30. Foreigners were prominent industrialists throughout Mexico during this period. They were particularly numerous in Mexico City, Veracruz, and Puebla. See Collado Herrera, *Burguesía mexicana*; García Díaz, *Pueblo fabril*, 11–19; and Torres Bautista, *Familia Maurer*, 9–22.

31. After 1892, Oaxaca's *Periódico oficial* is replete with weekly announcements of the purchase of new *pertenencias* by foreigners and Oaxacans alike.

32. AHMO, Orden 22, Grupo documental Biblioteca, Mensaje leido por el C. General Porfirio Díaz, 1882.

33. AGPEO, Grupo documental Fomento, dossier 9, file 3, 1901.

34. Wasserman, *Capitalists, Caciques, and Revolution*, 84–86.

35. *La unión*, July 29, 1907.

36. Guillermo Bonfil Batalla argues that this was the attitude of most elite Mexican *pensadores*, who felt that "there was nothing left to do with the spoken languages of the Indians except bury them, along with everything else Indian"; Bonfil Batalla, *México Profundo*, 105.

37. AHMO, Orden 22, Grupo documental Biblioteca, Mensaje leido por el Gobernador Emilio Pimentel, 1904. Several foreign countries maintained consular agencies in Oaxaca City throughout the Porfiriato. Representatives for the United States, France, Great Britain, Germany, Spain, Portugal, and, for a time, Greece worked in the capital on behalf of their countries. The consular agents were mostly businessmen who enjoyed the prestige and strategic economic privilege that the posts afforded them. In the case of the United States, consular officers like Charles Arthur and Ezra Lawton owned mines and businesses in the state. Regular inspectors' reports indicated that the post, especially during the mining boom, provided important services to North Americans in the region. The consuls also kept busy responding to letters from U.S. companies hoping to expand their businesses to Oaxaca and its capital. During his tenure (1908–13), Lawton attempted to raise the status of the agency to a consulate, which meant it would receive more than the nominal financial support it had been receiving. The request came too late. By 1910 economic

and political unrest had destabilized the region. The U.S. embassy in Mexico City turned its energies away from Oaxaca; Mark Leyes, U.S. consular agent, Oaxaca de Juárez, interview with author, January 10, 2000; NAII, Record Group 59, Consular Post Records, Oaxaca, 1869–1915.

38. Kuecker, "Desert in a Tropical Wilderness," 58.

39. Similar family networks operated in Yucatán, Chihuahua, and Monterrey. See Joseph, *Revolution from Without*; Wasserman, *Persistent Oligarchs*; and Saragoza, *Monterrey Elite*.

40. Medina Gómez, "Introducción de la luz," 51–52; Sánchez Silva, "Don José Zorrilla Trápaga."

41. AGPEO, Informe de gobierno, 1878.

42. *Periódico oficial del Estado de Oaxaca*, May 14, 1885.

43. *El Estado de Oaxaca: Diario independiente*, June 27, 1895.

44. Ibid., May 17, 1895.

45. Zorrilla also worked as an agent for the Banco Nacional de México; AGPEO, Grupo documental Fomento, various files, 1897.

46. *Periódico oficial*, May 25, 1897.

47. Sánchez Silva, "Don José Zorrilla Trápaga."

48. AGNE, Ledger entry by notary Antonio Iturribarría, file 28, January 29, 1903.

49. *El correo del sur*, September 5, 1909.

50. Medina Gómez, "Introducción de la luz," 99. See also concluding chapter.

51. AGNE, Ledger entry by Juan Varela, file 91, February 28, 1903. The city government's *Boletín municipal* regularly carried articles revealing the elites' overlapping roles as politicians and businessmen. See, e.g., *Boletín municipal*, February 24, 1903, and January 1, 1905.

52. Kuecker finds a similar convergence of politics and business in elite families in Tampico, Veracruz; Kuecker, "Desert in a Tropical Wilderness," 67–68.

53. *El centenario: Revista mensual ilustrada*, August 15, 1910, 35. See also Chassen-López, "Liberal to Revolutionary Oaxaca," chap. 5, 21–25. Chassen-López discusses in detail the political economy of the middle and upper classes of Oaxaca and how the two sectors interacted and overlapped. For other analyses of class mobility and interaction during the Porfiriato, see Wells and Joseph, *Summer of Discontent*; Saragoza, *Monterrey Elite*; and Wasserman, *Persistent Oligarchs*.

54. Chassen-López, "Liberal to Revolutionary Oaxaca," chap. 5. The fall of the ruling class is discussed in the concluding chapter of this book.

55. AHMO, Orden 03, Grupo documental Secretaría municipal, dossier 86, file 2, December 14, 1894.

56. Portillo, *Oaxaca en el centenario*. Examples of women selling property abound in the notary records of the Archivo General de Notarías del Estado; AGNE, Escribano Jesús Apolonio Vásquez, notario público no. 14, entry nos. 45, 47, 57.

57. Chassen-López points out that "while women legally maintained the ownership of their inheritance, dowry or *arras* (property given to the bride by the groom on marriage), their husbands generally exercised virtual control over their property short of selling it. Poor administration could be challenged by wives in court, but this was rarely the case. Property acquired during marriage was jointly owned, and only *bienes parafernales*

(clothes, jewels, or property received during the marriage through inheritance or dona-tion) were under the wife's control. Elite women had always been sizable property owners in Mexico. Thus, despite considerable restrictions, women did gain some advances in legal rights. . . . With respect to agriculture, in late nineteenth and early twentieth century Oaxaca, women were not only elite hacendadas but also owners of medium and small-sized tracts of lands. In the wave of land speculation that hit the state during the presi-dency of Porfirio Díaz, women bought up newly privatized lands"; Chassen-López, "Lib-eral to Revolutionary Oaxaca," chap. 5, 6–7; see also Arrom, *Women of Mexico City.*

58. Lira Vásquez discusses the development of the city's Porfirian architecture at length in his master's thesis, "Ciudad de Oaxaca," esp. 415–502.

59. *Oaxaca Herald,* July 26, 1908. See also numerous articles in *La unión* and *El Estado de Oaxaca.*

60. A true tourist *industry* did not begin in Oaxaca until the 1930s, and not until the 1980s did it become a substantial economic force in the state and its capital.

61. *El Estado de Oaxaca,* February 9, 1895.

62. *Mexican Herald,* March 10, 1903.

63. Southworth, *Estado de Oaxaca,* 8.

64. *Oaxaca Herald,* September 15, 1907.

65. Oaxacan travel accounts from the nineteenth century include Mühlenpfordt, *En-sayo de una descripción;* Fossey, *Viage a Méjico;* Seler-Sachs, *Auf alten Wegen in Mexiko und Guatemala.*

66. Mostkoff-Linares, "Foreign Visions." Despite the Mexican government's failure to attract large numbers of foreign immigrants during the Porfiriato, a substantial and dis-proportionately influential North American population settled in Oaxaca and other urban centers in Mexico. For the Mexico City case, see Schell, *Integral Outsiders.*

67. *Oaxaca Herald,* January 13, 1907.

68. The Guelaguetza, an annual spectacle in the city's Fortín amphitheater, brings together dancers and musicians from discrete, government-designated indigenous groups inhabiting the state. Spectators are confronted with what are represented as displays of Oaxaca's "traditional" native cultures. For a cultural analysis of the festival, see Poole, "Tipos 'raciales.' "

69. For a discussion of the elite Porfirian leisure culture, see Beezley, "Porfirian Smart Set."

70. For a study of the Cuban-imported game in Yucatán, see Joseph, "Forging the Re-gional Pastime," 29–61.

71. Arbena, "Sport," 1–14.

72. *Oaxaca progresista,* June 1909.

73. Ferguson, *Anti-politics Machine,* esp. chap. 9.

74. *Oaxaca Herald,* January 13, 1907. Governor Pimentel celebrated his birthday with a baseball game in 1907 and the American colony initiated Fourth of July festivities with a game; *La unión,* June 2, 1907.

75. *Oaxaca Herald,* February 24, 1907. El *score* was published from the offices of the *Oaxaca Herald.* Other city newspapers carried regular sports sections reporting highlights from games in the city, elsewhere in Mexico, and in the United States.

76. *El correo del sur*, November 5, 1909.

77. Ibid., April 24, November 24, 1910.

78. Beezley, *Judas at the Jockey Club*, 45.

79. Beezley goes as far as to argue that the new culture of *ciclismo* in Mexico provided women with a means to rebuke "tradition" (and challenge established gender norms) by modernizing their wardrobe with the inclusion of pants and bloomers. Although he argues that the "señoritas looked on the sport as an opportunity for a broader, freer life," he does little to support this claim except to say that critics argued that the rebellious women should be held responsible for the accidents they caused by distracting motorists; Beezley, "Bicycles," 15-28, esp. 23.

80. The highlight of the theater's inauguration included a performance by the Italian opera company Sigaldi; *El correo del sur*, September 5, 1909.

81. Muñoz Cabrejo, "New Order," 160.

82. Connell, *Masculinities*, 35-39.

83. The turn of the century witnessed a rapid increase in journalistic publications in the United States and Europe as well. Between 1880 and 1914 in France, for example, the circulation of Parisian dailies increased 250 percent; Schwartz, *Spectacular Realities*, 27-28.

84. The majority of these periodicals can be found in three archives. The Hemeroteca de la Universidad "Benito Juárez" de Oaxaca and the Fondo Manuel Brioso y Candiani, Law Library, Universidad "Benito Juárez" de Oaxaca contain the most complete collections of newspapers and magazines from Porfirian Oaxaca City. Unfortunately, the Brioso y Candiani collection has been closed to researchers for several years. The Hemeroteca General de la Nación holds thirty-six titles, most of which are short run papers (one to four editions). The Hemeroteca de la Ciudad de Oaxaca de Juárez, the Colección Porfirio Díaz, Universidad Iberoamericana, and the Archivo General de la Nación also have small collections of periodicals published in Oaxaca City. For a general description of the collections in Oaxaca City, see Sánchez Silva, "Prensa en Oaxaca."

85. Benedict Anderson, *Imagined Communities*, chap. 2.

86. Iturribarría, *Oaxaca en la historia*.

87. Taracena, "Imprenta en Oaxaca."

88. Henkin, *City Reading*, x.

89. Ibid., 21.

90. Sánchez Silva, "Prensa en Oaxaca," 8.

91. Complete census records exist for only three of the eight municipal districts. I have, therefore, necessarily extrapolated from the extant data. A comparison of two square blocks provides a reliable example of the general pattern of literacy rates in the city. Of the one hundred people living in block 31 (located one block to the east of the zócalo and bordered by Guerrero and Armenta y López streets), forty-six registered as literate, eighteen as semiliterate, and thirty-six as illiterate. The literate subset are almost all listed as "blanco" (white), own businesses in the city, and hail from either foreign countries, other states of Mexico, or Oaxaca City itself. Members of the illiterate subset in block 31 are all from towns in the Central Valley, registered as "mixta" (mixed) under the category of "race," and work as servants. By contrast, the inhabitants of block 25 (located on the city's southern edge and bordered by Melchor Ocampo and La Noria streets) are all

workers, "mixta," and except for some of the household heads, are all illiterate. The other difference between these two blocks is gendered: older men are much more likely to be literate or semiliterate than are women. "Mixta" here most likely refers to indigenous inhabitants. See chapter 4 for a discussion of racial categorization in this and other official demographic indexes. The enumeration of city blocks is taken from an 1887 map of the city, *Plano topográfico*. The 1887 census also draws on this spatial organization; AHMO, Orden 05, Grupo documental Padrones, census from 1887.

92. *Resumen del primer censo.* According to the census, 6,873 men and 4,596 women could both read and write, whereas 988 men and 2,325 women could only read. Of the 12,940 illiterates, 4,738 were men and 8, 202 were women.

93. *La unión*, July 28, 1907. In the first edition of *La unión* the editors proclaimed that, "obeying the general tendency of the era toward progress," the newspaper's objective was to educate the masses and to improve their moral and intellectual status.

94. *Oaxaca Herald*, April 22, 1906.

95. As I discuss in chapters 4 and 5, papers like the *Oaxaca Herald* devoted much ink to the promotion of "proper" female conduct and the condemnation of "scandalous" public behavior by prostitutes and other "dangerous" elements in modern society.

96. Buffington and French, "Culture of Modernity," 425.

97. Schwartz, *Spectacular Realities*, 27.

98. Taracena, "Imprenta en Oaxaca," 35. Similarly, Governor Gregorio Chávez (1890–94) imprisoned Juan de Esesarte and Esteban Castellanos for reporting in El *ferrocarril* that the construction of the "Porfirio Díaz" city market had been conducted using "fraudulent and hidden schemes." Governor Emilio Pimentel followed suit by arresting numerous journalists in the state capital for their political positions; Brioso y Candiani, *Evolución del pueblo oaxaqueño*, 71, 76–77.

99. Díaz, "Satiric Penny Press," 499. See the discussion of workers and the Catholic Church in chapter 3.

100. After its initial runs, *La voz de la justicia* changed its subtitle from "Liberal and Independent Newspaper" to the more biting "Liberal, Independent, Antigovernment, and Destined to Defend the Interests of the People."

101. *La voz de la justicia*, August 1, 1907.

102. Sánchez Silva, "Prensa en Oaxaca," 10–11.

103. *El voto público*, July 17, 1909.

104. González, *San José de Gracia*, 101.

2. Legible City

1. The earthquake of May 11, 1870, was felt throughout the state. In the city it affected mainly the homes of laborers south of the zócalo. Many churches and government buildings also suffered considerable damage. City residents who had lost their homes spent several nights camped out at the Llano de Guadalupe, a large park in the northern half of the city. For a detailed description of the earthquake, see Gay, *Historia de Oaxaca*, 442; and Vásquez, *Para la historia del terruño*, 6–7.

2. Scott, *Seeing Like a State*, 3. Although Scott's emphasis is on high-modernist state

schemes in places such as the Stalinist Soviet Union and Brasilia, and on urban planners like Le Corbusier (Charles-Edouard Jeanneret), it still provides an excellent lens through which to view the processes of Porfirian-era scientific politics.

3. Ibid., 54.

4. In *The Lettered City*, Angel Rama discusses the colonial origins of what he calls the "ordered city," the New World city rationalized by Creole elites to fit a vision of progress and modernity; see esp. 1–15. See also Carrera, *Imagining Identity*, 107–35.

5. See Marx, *Machine in the Garden*; and Bender, *Toward an Urban Vision*. Both works are cited in Tenorio-Trillo, "1910 Mexico City," 88.

6. Tenorio-Trillo, "1910 Mexico City," 79.

7. The examination of space has long been treated as subordinate to that of time in critical studies. For a comprehensive discussion of the literature surrounding the debate about time and space, see Craib, *Cartographic Mexico*, 2–7.

8. Harvey, *Condition of Postmodernity*, 203.

9. Soja, *Postmodern Geographies*, 6.

10. I have found only three exceptions to this in the city records. The first is a petition by government officials to regulate the schedules of public officials; AHMO, Orden 03, Grupo documental Secretaría municipal, dossier 1897, file 50. The second is a request by two prison guards that the city increase their break time during their shift; AHMO, Orden 03, Grupo documental Secretaría municipal, dossier 1904.3, file 67. And the third is the case discussed below of prisoner schedules in the new city penitentiary. Gloria Medina Gómez also mentions that, with the arrival of electric lighting, the city's small textile, beer, and cigarette factories began to change the shift times of workers and extend the workday until nine from five in the evening; Medina Gómez, "Introducción de la luz," 101.

11. Thompson, "Time," 70–71.

12. AHMO, Orden 19, Grupo documental Carteles, May 26, 1890.

13. See the detailed narrative of mid-nineteenth-century life in the city of Oaxaca in Vasconcelos, *Apuntes históricos*. In the novel, two Porfirian-era women reflect on life in the state capital at midcentury.

14. On Mérida, Yucatán, see Wells and Joseph, "Modernizing Visions," 167–215. For studies of Morelia and other cities and towns in Michoacán, see Sánchez Díaz, "Ciudades michoacanas." The collection in which this essay is included, Muro, *Ciudades provincianas*, also contains brief treatments of Guanajuato and Aguascalientes during the Porfiriato.

15. In addition to Mexico City, Gómez visited Guanajuato, Guadalajara, Aguascalientes, Querétaro, and Morelia; *La unión*, July 23, 1907.

16. Tenorio-Trillo, "1910 Mexico City," 88.

17. Craib, *Cartographic Mexico*, 164–68.

18. A relative of General Díaz Ordaz, Luis Díaz Ordaz, donated twenty thousand pesos to the city government to build an orphanage, El Hospicio de la Vega (the location of the present day Municipal Archive), along the borders of the colonia.

19. Scott, *Seeing Like a State*, 58.

20. Developers determined lot class depending on the lots' proximity to main avenues (*principales vías de comunicación*). Those closest to Calle Progreso received first-class status. Since the Díaz-Ordaz expansion was outside and separate from the city center, where lot

value depended on the relation to the central plaza (decreasing in concentric circles of distance from the center), city authorities were forced, much to their chagrin, to design this new system of evaluation.

21. For a sampling of elite bidders, see AHMO, Orden 03, Grupo documental Secretaría municipal, dossier 1898.3, file 54; and dossier 1904.2, files 36, 48, and 83.

22. AHMO, Orden: 03, Grupo documental Secretaría municipal, dossier 1903.4, file 271. The velodrome was eventually constructed in 1909.

23. *El correo del sur*, May 19, 1909.

24. Pulque, sold in pulquerías, is a frothy-white alcoholic drink made from fermented agave leaves.

25. AHMO, Ralfredo, February 1899.

26. *La unión*, July 21, 1907.

27. According to state records, the three gold mines had very small yields. The mines and their owners were La Soledad, Francisco Casano; El Brasil, Luis García Najera; and El Capricho, Waldo Figueroa; AGPEO, dossier 14, files 3–6, 1900.

28. AHMO, Orden 03, Grupo documental Secretaría municipal, dossier 1894.5.

29. AHMO, Orden 22, Grupo documental Biblioteca, Mensaje leido por el C. Lic. Emilio Pimentel, March 1906.

30. AHMO, Orden 03, Grupo documental Secretaría municipal, Docemp. 1876.4.

31. Ibid., 1889.1.

32. AGPEO, Padrón General, Marquesado, Julio 28, 1890; AHMO, Orden: 5: Grupo documental: Padrones: Padrón de elecciones de la Villa del Marquezado, 1894; AHMO Orden: 5; Grupo documental: Padrones: Padrón de la Villa del Marquezado, 1900; AHMO, Orden: 5, Grupo documental: Padrones: Padrón de elecciones de la Villa del Marquezado, February and June 1907; AHMO, Orden: 13; Grupo documental: Registro civil; Actas de nacimiento, Villa de Santa María Oaxaca el Marquesado, 1869–1908; AHMO, Orden: 13; Grupo documental: Registro civil; Testimonio de defunciones; Santa María del Marquesado, 1875–1908.

33. The available sources provided contradictory information on El Marquesado's growth. The complete census record from 1890 indicates that a total of 1,931 (999 men and 932 women) lived in El Marquesado. A less detailed summary record shows that a decade later the population had increased to 2,885 (1,307 men, 1,578 women). A third and fourth source contradict the first two, demonstrating that the population had a negative growth rate throughout the Porfiriato. The number of annual deaths far outnumbered the number of births. Since all of the sources agree that there was almost no in-migration (circa 90 percent of all inhabitants were born in El Marquesado), I am inclined to believe that the village either declined or grew marginally in population during this period. AGPEO, Padrón General, Marquesado, July 28, 1890; AHMO, Orden 5, Grupo documental Padrones, Padrón de la Villa del Marquezado, 1900; AHMO, Orden 13, Grupo documental Registro civil, Actas de nacimiento, Villa de Santa María Oaxaca el Marquesado, 1869–1908; AHMO, Orden 13, Grupo documental Registro civil, Testimonio de defunciones, Santa María del Marquesado, 1875–1908.

34. Compare the census and electoral records from San Matías Jalatlaco, San Felipe del Agua, Hacienda de San Luis Beltrán, and the Hacienda de Pansuela; AGPEO, Padrones generales.

35. This, as we shall see in chapter 4, is a problematic racial category that most likely included Zapotec and Mixtec individuals.

36. AHMO, Orden 22, Grupo documental Biblioteca, Memoria del Estado de Oaxaca, 1900.

37. Decreto no. 11, Secretaría del Gobierno del Estado Libre y Soberano de Oaxaca, in Portillo, *Oaxaca en el centenario*, 10.

38. *El correo del sur*, May 15, 1909.

39. *Oaxaca Herald*, May 23, 1909.

40. *El correo del sur*, May 15, 1909.

41. Ibid., May 19, 1909.

42. For examples of scholarship that treats urban areas from without, see Williams, *Country and City*; and Cronon, *Nature's Metropolis*. Also, the historical literature of the Mexican-American experience in the United States is replete with examples of transnational urban-rural migration. See, e.g., Romo, *History of a Barrio*; Hondagneu-Sotelo, *Gendered Transitions*; Gutiérrez, *Walls and Mirrors*; and Vargas, *Proletarians*.

43. AHMO, Orden 03, Grupo documental Secretaría municipal, dossier 79, file 1.

44. *Oaxaca Herald*, November 3, 1907.

45. NAII – Oaxaca, Oax – Consular Posts RG 84/stack 35/row 07/compartment 02 – Miscellaneous Record Book, – vol. 6.

46. Lira Vásquez, "Jardines de la Oaxaca porfiriana," 15–22.

47. Lira Vásquez, "Ciudad de Oaxaca," 321–23.

48. Manuel Martinez Gracida in Portillo, *Oaxaca en el centenario*, 157.

49. Cf. Grandin, *Blood of Guatemala*, 162.

50. An exception that confirms the rule is Archbishop Eulogio Gillow's establishment of a recreation center for the city's workers in the former convent of Carmen Alto.

51. AHMO, Orden 03, Grupo documental Secretaría municipal, dossier 1897.4, file 178, Reglamento para paseos y jardines públicos.

52. AHMO, Primer Concurso de Floricultura y Horticultura – Celebrado en la Ciudad de Oaxaca el 10 de mayo de 1898.

53. Scott, *Seeing Like a State*, 92.

54. *Periódico oficial*, Oaxaca de Juárez, October 22, 1885, 1.

55. AHMO, Orden 03, Grupo documental Secretaría municipal, letter from C. Conzatti to the president and aldermen of the city council. Oaxaca de Juárez, January 30, 1903. In 1999 the city government went ahead with a version of Conzatti's garden. On the grounds of the well-known former convent of Santo Domingo, the city and state constructed a garden consisting of plants and flowers from the state's many regions.

56. *Periódico oficial*, Oaxaca de Juárez, April 10, 1890, 2.

57. Olsen, *City as Work of Art*, ix; cited in Tenenbaum, "Streetwise History," 127.

58. In an interview in *La unión*, municipal president Adolfo Silva discusses the contract he made with a gardener from Mexico City who had worked on the Paseo de la Reforma; *La unión*, January 12, 1908.

59. *Periódico oficial*, Oaxaca de Juárez, August 1, 1889, 2. Scheleske was also commissioned by Archbishop Gillow to restore parts of the interior of the capital city's cathedral in the late 1890s; Esparza, *Gillow y el poder*, 96.

60. AHMO, Orden 03, Grupo documental, Secretaría municipal, dossier 1895.1, file 1, 1895 Memoria.

61. Tenenbaum, *Streetwise History*, 135.

62. *Periódico oficial*, Oaxaca de Juárez, September 22, 1885, 1. The statue of Juárez was moved in 1914 to San Pablo Guelatao, Juárez's birthplace.

63. *Periódico oficial*, Oaxaca de Juárez, March 13, 1890, 1.

64. Uribe, "Entre el rosa y el gris," 418–41.

65. Tenenbaum, *Streetwise History*, 143.

66. AHMO, Orden 03, Grupo documental Secretaría municipal, letter from C. Conzatti to the president and aldermen of the city council, Oaxaca de Juárez, January 30, 1903.

67. Gilberto Torres, *Periódico oficial*, Oaxaca de Juárez, May 15, 1889, 1.

68. *Periódico oficial*, Oaxaca de Juárez, May 18, 1883.

69. AHMO, Orden 03, Grupo documental Secretaría municipal, dossier 1895, file 1, 1895 Memoria.

70. *La alerta*, April 11, 1912.

71. *Periódico oficial*, Oaxaca de Juárez, July 13, 1883.

72. Archivo General de la Nación, Gobernación, Nacionalización y Desamortización de Bienes Nacionales, 1856–1910.

73. Gilberto Torres, *Periódico oficial*, Oaxaca de Juárez, September 16, 1889, 1.

74. Lira Vásquez, "Ciudad de Oaxaca." Lira mentions that many of the buildings erected during the Porfiriato drew on the architectural trend of eclecticism. According to Lira, eclecticism was a late-nineteenth-century architectural idiom based on an often random mix of elements from the classical, medieval, baroque, mannerist, Renaissance, and neoclassical periods along with influences from Islam, Byzantium, Egypt, and Mesopotamia. In Oaxaca during the Porfiriato, elites tentatively began to employ the style of eclecticism and incorporated some of the art nouveau style then at the vanguard of European design. Lira discusses in detail the novel architecture of Porfirian Oaxaca in "Oaxaca porfiriana," 12–17.

75. Gilberto Torres, *Periódico oficial*, Oaxaca de Juárez, September 16, 1889, 1.

76. Beezley, Martin, and French, Introduction, xiii.

77. Corrigan and Sayer, *Great Arch*.

78. Beezley, "Porfirian Smart Set," 175.

79. In an effort to support Pimentel in his bid for a third term as governor, Angel San Germán, a prominent businessman and owner of the capital's largest printing company, published a "list of some of the material works completed during the two administrative periods [1902–10] of Sr. Lic. Don Emilio Pimentel." The list includes detailed descriptions of completed construction projects in the capital and in all of the state's districts as proof of Pimentel's success as governor; *Lista de algunas obras materiales*.

80. *Periódico oficial*, Oaxaca de Juárez, January 10, 1889, 1.

81. Portillo, *Oaxaca en el centenario*, 104ff.

82. Ibid., 106.

83. National Archives–Oaxaca City, Oaxaca–Consular Posts, RG 84/stack 35/row 07/compartment 02–Miscellaneous Record Book–vol. 1. Glen Kuecker points out that the

Juárez myth became a kind of civic religion "in which the official interpretation of Juárez's life and legacy was presented for popular consumption. The official interpretation of Juárez constructed Díaz as the modernizing patriarch whose confident hand was needed to construct the national foundations of economic growth and political stability upon which the liberal promise of Juárez could be safely built"; Kuecker, "Desert in a Tropical Wilderness," 108. See also Weeks, *Juárez Myth*.

84. *La unión*, June 2, 1907.

85. Ibid., September 22, 1907.

86. Tenorio-Trillo, "1910 Mexico City," 75.

87. National Archives – Oaxaca City, Oaxaca – Consular Posts, RG 84/stack 35/row 07/compartment 02 – Miscellaneous Record Book, vol. 1.

88. Ibid.

89. Deborah Poole's discussion of Manuel Martínez Gracida's treatise on the Indians of Oaxaca explores his elaborate construction of race in Oaxaca (centering on the primacy of the Zapotec race) and a form of Oaxacan regional exclusivity; Poole, "Image of 'Our Indian.'"

90. Urías Horcaditas, "Etnología y filantropía."

91. *El centenario: Revista mensual ilustrada*, December 31, 1910. The opening speech was delivered by Francisco Canseco, a much despised state judge who led the fight against the opposition to Governor Emilio Pimentel; Chassen-López, "Liberal to Revolutionary Oaxaca," chap. 9.

92. *El centenario: Revista mensual ilustrada*, December 31, 1910.

93. Van Young, Conclusion, 349.

94. Falcón, "Force and the Search for Consent," 116.

95. See, e.g., Sánchez Díaz, "Ciudades michoacanas," 31–44; Tenorio-Trillo, "1910 Mexico City," 76; and, although a treatment of postrevolutionary Mexico, Newcomer, *Reconciling Modernity*.

96. Esparza, *Ordenanza*, 1–2.

97. For a more detailed discussion of the cartographic history of Oaxaca City, see Ruiz Cervantes and Sánchez Silva, *Ciudad de Oaxaca*.

98. The map is located in the Mapoteca Orozco y Berra, 2826, no. 64.

99. In the previous decade, city elites could obtain maps at four pesos apiece. See the advertisement by Albino López Garzón in the *Periódico oficial*, Oaxaca de Juárez, January 21, 1892, 4.

100. Ruiz Cervantes, "Ciudad de Oaxaca," 7–15.

101. This is made evident by the content of and use of English in business advertisements, e.g., "Sucs. de José Zorrilla Co. Bankers and Merchants. Transacts and General Banking Business. Buy Drafts on all parts of the United States, England, Germany, France and Spain."

102. As Chassen-López has pointed out, "the elite and middle classes often lied about the extension of their holdings in order to cheat on taxes and miners were able to negotiate the sum of mining taxes with the government. At the same time, all the working population had to pay the hated *capitación*, the monthly head tax of about 20 centavos, a

campesino or a laborer paying the same as a merchant or miner"; Chassen-López, "Liberal to Revolutionary Oaxaca," chap. 7, 20.

103. AHMO, Actas de cabildo, February 20, 1883.

104. Unlike for Mexico City, there appears to be no record among Oaxaca City's urban poor of resistance to or discontent with the renaming of their city streets. The initial renaming project of Oaxaca's capital, predating Mexico City's by five years, seems to have gone unchallenged by city residents; Piccato, *City of Suspects*, 45–47.

105. AHMO, Orden 03, Grupo documental Secretaría municipal, dossier 1903.4, file 300.

106. For an excellent analysis of Porfirian vice and state formation in northern Mexico, see French, *Peaceful and Working People*, esp. 63–85.

107. AGPEO, Memoria constitucional presentada por el Ejecutivo del Estado de Oaxaca al H. Congreso, September 17, 1882.

108. Carlos Sánchez Silva suggests that a study has yet to be done comparing the political careers of Díaz and Lázaro Cárdenas. As governor of the state of Michoacán, Cárdenas, like Díaz, used his home state as a testing ground for new projects and policies that he would later carry out as president; Sánchez Silva, personal correspondence with author.

109. Belmar, *Breve reseña*, 99.

110. AGPEO, Libro de leyes y decretos del Gobierno del Estado de Oaxaca, vol. 9, 159, June 15, 1882.

111. AHMO, Orden 02, Grupo documental Juzgado, dossier 1882.15, unnumbered file.

112. AHMO, Ralfredo, no. 22, January 22, 1907.

113. For a study of the development of military and police forces during the Porfiriato, see Hernández Chávez, "Origen y ocaso," 257–96.

114. AHMO, Orden 03, Grupo documental Secretaría municipal, dossiers 1876.19, 1876.12, 1876.13, 1878.16, 1879.10; AHMO, Actas de Cabildo, June 19, 1882.

115. An analysis of Oaxaca's state budgets from 1869 to 1910 shows a steady decline in military spending following the wars of the Reform and into the Porfiriato; AGPEO, *Memorias administrativas*, 1869–1910.

116. AGPEO, *Memoria administrativa*, 1899.

117. *Periódico oficial*, Oaxaca de Juárez, September 17, 1904; AHMO, Orden 22, Grupo documental Biblioteca, Mensaje leido por el C. Lic Emilio Pimentel, December 29, 1903. See also *Boletín municipal de Oaxaca de Juárez*, March 11, 1903, for a complete list of officers and auxiliaries in the city.

118. For an in-depth discussion of the role of jefes políticos in the Porfirian political apparatus, see Falcón, "Force and the Search for Consent," 107–34.

119. The emergence of a formalized gendarmerie in Oaxaca City followed a similar restructuring of law enforcement in Mexico City that had begun in 1879, only three years earlier; Piccato, *City of Suspects*, esp. 41–45. Quote on 45.

120. Portillo, *Oaxaca en el centenario*, 155.

121. El *Estado de Oaxaca*, March 15, 1895. On the degenerate condition of the state's prison system before the Porfiriato, see AGPEO, *Memoria administrativa*, 1872.

122. AHMO, Orden 19, Grupo documental Carteles, Reglamento para el régimen interior de las cárceles de esta ciudad, 1910.

123. Buffington, "Revolutionary Reform," 169–93.

124. Ibid., 173.

125. Today, water scarcity continues to be a problem in the capital. While residents of the city's periphery struggle to obtain water on a daily basis, the major hotels and elite families in the city center are the only groups to receive water 365 days a year. For an in-depth analysis of the capital's hydrological history, see Riley, "Liquid Inequity."

126. National Archives – Oaxaca City, Oaxaca – Consular Posts RG 84/stack 35/row 07/ compartment 02 – Miscellaneous Record Book – vol. 7.

127. AHMO, Orden 13, Grupo documental Registro civil, *Cuadro estadístico que manifiesta la mortalidad, clasificada por enfermedades en el estado*, 1896; AHMO, Orden 12, Grupo documental Panteones, 1878–1909; AHMO, Orden 13, Grupo documental Registro civil, testimo-nio de defunciones Santa María del Marquesado y Jalatlaco.

128. Starting in November 1875 the city government established a water commission and a set of regulations to stem the continuous pilfering of water from the city's main lines. Throughout the Porfiriato, city government worked to repair outdated lines (e.g., uncovered wood and clay water channels). Requests to the municipal government for private access to water mains came almost entirely from businesses and residences in the city's affluent central areas; AHMO, Documentos empastados, Agua, 1876.1–1905.3. See also Riley, "Liquid Inequity." It was not until 1910 that the government began to work on improving the sewage system in the city. Officials contracted the Mexico City engi-neer Enrique Schöndube to construct an underground system in Oaxaca City. Before then sewage flowed uncovered through street-side gutters, occasionally washed out by over-flow water; AHMO, Ralfredo, no. 10, 1910.

129. Voekel, "Peeing on the Palace," 202.

130. For a discussion of how Mexico City elites merged their projects of public hygiene and spatial symbolization, see Agostoni, *Monuments of Progress*.

131. Both Catholic and Protestant church leaders also had a very significant stake in the city's morality campaigns. I discuss this and other aspects of the capital's religious life and leadership in chapter 3.

132. Rohlfes, "Police and Penal Reform"; Bretas, "You Can't!"; Kalmanowiecki, "Mili-tary Power"; Vanderwood, *Disorder and Progress*; Holloway, *Policing Rio de Janeiro*; Johnson, *Problem of Order*.

133. Flores, *Tratado especial*; *Prontuario de las obligaciones*.

134. *La victoria*, August 24, 1877.

135. Piccato, "Urbanistas, Ambulantes, and Mendigos," 113–48.

136. *La unión*, September 12, 1908.

137. *El correo del sur*, March 12, 1910.

138. Flores, *Tratado especial*, 18.

139. Falcón, "Force and the Search for Consent," 117.

140. Ibid., 118.

141. AHMO, Orden 19, Grupo documental Carteles, 1877–1912.

142. AHMO, Orden: 03, Grupo documental Secretaría municipal, dossier 1892.2, file 100.

143. A *vara* and a *jarra* are roughly equivalent to one yard and one U.S. gallon, respec-

tively. Their exact measurements were determined locally and thus varied from region to region.

144. AHMO, Orden: 03, Grupo documental Secretaría municipal, dossier 1905.1, un-numbered file.

145. AHMO, Orden: 03, Grupo documental Secretaría municipal, dossier 1903.2, file 24.

3. Church, State, and Workers

1. On the study of religion in the social scientific and historical literature, see Pessar, *Fanatics to Folk*, 6–7.

2. In his work, Talal Asad criticizes scholarly conventions that assume the transition to secularism in modern societies; see Asad, *Formations of the Secular*.

3. *Resumen del primer censo.*

4. There is little in the literature that connects the state with religious institutions, let alone religious practices. Most often, the church tends to disappear after the Reform period (1855–75) and then reemerge during the Cristero War of 1926–29. In a few studies, most notably Paul Vanderwood's recent narrative history of Porfirian-era Tomochic, the church, as both a cultural and political actor, plays a predominant role in the analysis; Vanderwood, *Power of God*. See also Wright-Rios, "Piety and Progress"; Voekel, *Alone before God*; Goddard, *Pensamiento político y social*; Bastian, *Disidentes*; Bastian, *Breve historia*; Bastian, "Metodismo y clase obrera"; Ceballos Ramírez, *Historia de Rerum novarum*; Ceballos Ramírez, *Catolicismo social*; and O'Dogherty Madrazo, *Urnas y sotanas*.

5. O'Dogherty Madrazo, *Urnas y sotanas*, 21.

6. Berry, "Ficción y realidad," 328.

7. Juárez did gradually permit some church leaders to return to their posts with lessened powers; Goddard, *Pensamiento político y social*, 8–17, 95–96.

8. Esparza, *Gillow durante el porfiriato*, 24.

9. Esparza, *Padrón de capitación*.

10. In his detailed study of Oaxaca's Catholic Church during this period, Wright-Rios maintains that the prelate Gillow and his closest adherents successfully implemented a local version of modern European Catholicism in Oaxaca City. He goes on to explain that this was not the case outside the state capital, where indigenous villagers grafted long-standing local religious traditions onto the new structures and practices promoted by Gillow; see Wright-Rios, "Piety and Progress," esp. chap. 3.

11. Gill, *Rendering unto Caesar*, 32–36. Late-nineteenth-century reforms in the Mexican Catholic Church closely paralleled reforms during the same period in Europe; see Lannon, *Privilege, Persecution, and Prophecy*; and Ralph Gibson, *Social History*.

12. Voekel, *Alone before God*, esp. 1–16.

13. Although no government functionary officially attended the lavish celebrations, the mere fact that they took place in the nation's capital bridged the gap between church and state. For historical treatment of the Virgin of Guadalupe, see Brading, *Mexican Phoenix*; and Lafaye, *Quetzalcoatl and Guadalupe*.

14. *La voz de México*, October 7, 1899; *La voz de la verdad*, November 19, 1899. Until the 1890s the Catholic press continued to challenge Díaz's attempts at reconciliation. The suc-

cess of new policies as well as a burgeoning economy convinced editors to support the government, albeit with caution; Ceballos Ramirez, *Catolicismo social*, 50.

15. Letter to Porfirio Díaz from Bishop Eulogio Gillow, February 17, 1888, CPD, L 0013, C 0004, D 001951.

16. Iturribarría, "Política de conciliación," 100. Manuel Esparza attributes some of Gillow's success at recuperating church property to his close relationship with President Díaz; Esparza, *Gillow y el poder*, 69–77.

17. The national ratio of people to churches was much higher at 1,211 to 1; Chassen-López, "Liberal to Revolutionary Oaxaca," chap. 5, 31.

18. CPD, 1896; L 40, C 7, D 388.

19. On the day before the coronation, Canon Agustín Echeverría's "official" history of the Virgin of Solitude appeared in the *Oaxaca Herald*. The story tells of a mule driver transporting goods from Veracruz to Guatemala "thirty years after the landing of Cortés on Mexican soil." As he approaches Oaxaca City (then Antequera), he notices a lone mule from another train alongside his own. After searching for the mule's owner at length and without success, the driver, "being a conscientious man," decides to turn it and its burden over to the authorities. But before the driver can make it to the city, the mule collapses. When the mayor arrives at the site, he opens a package strapped to the mule and inside is an image of the virgin inscribed with the words "Our lady of the solitude at the foot of the cross": "The mule rose again, relieved of its burden, but then trembled and died." Oaxaca's bishop quickly comes and delivers the miraculous virgin to the capital.

Over the centuries, people flocked to the virgin to benefit from her reputed healing powers. In 1683 the city began construction of a church dedicated to the virgin. In the next century, Augustinian nuns came from the state of Puebla to act as the statue's caretakers; *Oaxaca Herald*, January 17, 1909. The virgin, on display at the Templo de la Soledad in Oaxaca City, continues to attract pilgrims and followers to this day. For a comprehensive discussion of the coronation, see Wright-Rios, "Piety and Progress," chap. 4.

20. Ibid. The *Herald* reported that "never before in the history of Oaxaca have as many people been congregated in the city at one time. Last night there was not a public bench in any of the parks of the city that did not have from one to four occupants. Many were forced to sleep in the angles of the walls of churches and other buildings. Never before in the history of Oaxaca have there been as many famous churchmen in the city" (*Oaxaca Herald*, January 17, 1909).

21. *Albúm de la coronación*. The *Albúm* is replete with photographs commemorating the event.

22. *Boletín oficial y revista eclesiástica*, April 4, 1909.

23. *La voz de la verdad*, January 18, 1910.

24. There are strong parallels between the role of the church in Oaxaca City and other urban centers in Mexico. See, e.g., Salmerón Castro, "Aguascalientes."

25. This is not to say that religious faith in general declined among the capital's residents. Private expressions of faith more than likely endured throughout these tumultuous years for the church.

26. *Boletín oficial y revista eclesiástica*, March 15, 1901, November 22, 1908. These "official" reports also staked a claim to the church's growing influence among the city's faithful.

27. *La voz de la verdad*, June 1, 1896.

28. Archivo de la Arquidiócesis, Oaxaca City (AA), Diócesis, Gobierno, Correspondencia, 1876–1912, letters from June 14, 1876, and July 13, 1876.

29. Ibid., letters from July 8, 1876, and December 22, 1882.

30. Ibid., letters from April 23, 1882, and March 22, 1882.

31. In his research, Charles Berry discovered one case from 1861 of an individual who conducted a "simulated operation" of purchasing disentailed church property only to make it available to the church once the "turbulence [of the initial anticlerical laws] had passed." This "fraudulent sale" allowed the church to continue using its original property and portrayed the purchaser as a devotee of the Reform laws. I found no similar cases for the Porfiriato. As Berry points out, it would be difficult to find such "operations," since they would necessarily involve admission of breaking the law and as such would not appear in the notary archives; Berry, "Ficción y realidad," 339–41.

32. Gillow's father, Thomas Gillow, originally from Liverpool, England, was a wealthy jeweler, entrepreneur, and landowner. He introduced new agricultural equipment from England to Mexico and established Mexico's first agricultural society in 1860. Gillow's mother, doña María J. Zavalza y Gutiérrez, was the ex-marquise of Mexico's Selva Nevada.

33. Esparza, *Gillow durante el porfiriato*, 4, 169.

34. Gillow also worked closely with Thomas Braniff, the British manager of the Ferrocarril de México.

35. The information for this biographical sketch comes from four sources, *Boletín oficial y revista eclesiástica*, October 1, 1908; Iturribarría, "Política de conciliación"; Esparza, *Gillow durante el porfiriato*; and Esparza, "Mediación," 79–83.

36. Esparza argues that not only did Gillow forge a new relationship with civil authorities, he actively subordinated the church to Díaz's government; Esparza, "Arzobispo Eulogio G. Gillow," 197–217.

37. Gillow spent thousands of pesos of his own money sprucing up the diocese. For the city's cathedral alone he spent nine thousand pesos for an ornate curtain from Rome, five thousand pesos for candles from Paris, and an undisclosed sum for twelve bronze busts representing saints and church fathers; *Boletín oficial y revista eclesiástica*, October 1, 1908. Further details concerning Gillow's efforts to renovate and beautify the city's ecclesiastical infrastructure can be found in Esparza, *Gillow y el poder*, 91–117. For a description of his journeys in the Oaxacan countryside, see Gillow, *Reminiscencias*. It is important to cast a critical eye on Gillow's proclamations. Although he was responsible for much change in Oaxaca's church, he often portrays his successes in a careerist manner that calls into question the veracity of his claims (Gillow, *Apuntes históricos*).

38. *Boletín oficial y revista eclesiástica*, March 15, 1901.

39. See chapter 5 for a discussion of the Catholic Church's attitudes on "proper" gender roles.

40. *Boletín oficial y revista eclesiástica*, March 15, 1901.

41. Eulogio Gillow to Porfirio Díaz, December 1894; cited in Esparza, *Gillow y el poder*, 15.

42. Ramón Ramírez to Eulogio Gillow, November 21, 1907; cited ibid., 11.

43. AHMO, Orden 03, Grupo documental Secretaría municipal, dossier 1903.3, file 3, 1903.

44. A detailed study of Valle de Oaxaca markets in the Porfiriato needs to be conducted. Although anthropologists have studied contemporary markets (see, e.g., Cook and Diskin, *Markets in Oaxaca*), historians have only briefly discussed the role of the market system in the valley. See the references in Berry, *Reform in Oaxaca*, 18; and Taylor, *Landlord and Peasant*, 47, 81, 91, and 247.

45. I avoid the term *working class* because there did not exist a cohesive workers' consciousness or movement in the state capital. *Artisan* and John Womack's term *proprietary producer* better describe the type of workers in Porfirian Oaxaca City. I am grateful to Womack for his comments on an earlier version of this chapter.

46. Ruiz Cervantes and Arellanes Meixueiro, "Orígenes del movimiento obrero," 388.

47. AGPEO, Special data for the 1903 Universal Exposition at Saint Louis, Mo., 1903, Fomento, dossier 7, file 13, 1902; Arellanes Meixueiro, *Trabajos y guías*, 46–53.

48. Esparza, *Padrón de capitación; Resumen del primer censo*; AHMO, *Padrón para elecciones*, Orden 03, Grupo documental Secretaría municipal, dossier 1901.11, December 1901; AGPEO, Office of General Statistics, Industrial Statistics, Fomento, dossier 37, file 3, 1902.

49. NAII, Oaxaca City, Oaxaca, Consular Posts, RG 84/stack 35/row 07/compartment 02 – Miscellaneous Record Book – Vol. 3, see letters from December 12 and 29, 1904.

50. AHMO, Orden 03, Grupo documental Secretaría municipal, dossier 1882.1, file 1.

51. AGPEO, Office of General Statistics, Industrial Statistics, Fomento, dossier 37, file 3, 1902; AGPEO, Name, quantity, and value of products or articles of industry in the city of Oaxaca de Juárez, Fomento, dossier 37, file 3.

52. Chassen-López, " 'Cheaper than Machines,' " 27–50.

53. For more on the deskilling of labor within the evolution of an industrial work force, see Braverman, *Labor and Monopoly Capital*, esp. 169–83.

54. A weak and disorganized labor movement (hence vulnerable to employer domination) persisted throughout most of Mexico during the Porfiriato, especially in nonindustrial centers like Oaxaca; see Knight, *Mexican Revolution*, Vol. 1, 431–32.

55. Francisco Vasconcelos became municipal president in 1880 and served again from 1897 to 1898. AHMO, Orden 03, Grupo documental Secretaría municipal, dossier 1890.7, file 7, 1890. In 1904 Tomás Sánchez, who had served as municipal president in 1885, became the society's president.

56. *El correo del sur*, January 14, 1910.

57. Chassen-López, "Liberal to Revolutionary Oaxaca," chap. 5, 31.

58. Ibid. The society continues to this day.

59. AHMO, Orden 03, Grupo documental Secretaría municipal, Ralfredo, no. 31, July 23, 1897.

60. The city required workers to display clearly a circular brass shield of at least five centimeters in diameter at all times.

61. AHMO, Orden 5, Grupo documental Padrones, Registro de cargadores, 1889–1914; Orden 5, Grupo documental Padrones, Registro de aguadores, 1903–9; Orden 22, Grupo documental Biblioteca, Reglamento a que se sujetaran los que se dediquen al ejercicio de aguadores en la ciudad de Oaxaca, 1903.

62. AHMO, Orden 03, Grupo documental Secretaría municipal, dossier 1879.8, file 8, 1879.

63. Ibid., 1895.3, file 123.

64. For examples of these petitions, see ibid., Orden 03, Grupo documental Secretaría municipal, dossier 1877.3, file 1; dossier 1881.4, file 5; dossier 1891.3, unnumbered file; dossier 1894.3, file 122; dossier 1897.1, file 15.

65. NAII, Oaxaca City, Oaxaca, Consular Posts, RG 84/stack 35/row 07/compartment 02 – Miscellaneous Record Book – vol. 4, July 5, 1906.

66. *La voz de la verdad*, September 4, 1910.

67. As we can see from the epigraph, the pope relies on tropes of nature and the body to argue for the existence of "natural" harmony among social classes. Throughout the text, he describes a "natural" social order of class and gender, one that, according to him, requires divine intervention from the Christian God if it is to survive. This powerful motif adroitly fuses the Christian doctrine of stewardship with the immediate needs of social action and service.

68. Molony, *Worker Question*, 2–3.

69. Ceballos Ramírez, *Historia de Rerum novarum*, 123.

70. Sowell, "Political Impulses," 15–29; Baer, "Buenos Aires," 129–52.

71. In the case of Mexico City, Tony Morgan argues that religion and religious celebrations played only very minor roles in connecting workers to emergent industrial capital. He adds, however, that this was not the case in other, less secular, parts of the country; Morgan, "Proletarians, Politicos, and Patriarchs," 159.

72. Wright-Rios argues that "Gillow should be understood first and foremost as an important conduit and facilitator of militant modern Catholicism in Mexico"; Wright-Rios, "Piety and Progress," 238.

73. For guidance, society founders also turned to the predecessor of the *Rerum Novarum*, Pope Leo XIII's 1884 encyclical, *Humanum Genus*. In the earlier encyclical, the pope argued that the best way to defend the Catholic Church against its secularizing enemies was to foster the growth of Christianity among the working class.

74. Arellanes Meixueiro, *Trabajos y guías*, 36–40.

75. In May 1905 Gillow and other members of the auxiliary committee of the Second Catholic Congress of Mexico (Morelia, October 1904) met and formulated the CCOO.

76. *Boletín oficial y revista eclesiástica*, January 2, 1906.

77. The *gremios* represented builders, potters, quarriers, carpenters, tanners, shopkeepers, copper workers, cart drivers, deliverymen, sculptors, blacksmiths, tinsmiths, printers, plasterers, gardeners, soapmakers, general laborers, musicians, painters, bakers, silversmiths, watchmakers, tailors, hatmakers, saddlers, weavers, shoemakers, and a group of assorted workers.

78. Undoubtedly inappropriate reading material included the newspaper and propaganda issued by the city's Protestant community.

79. *Reglamento del Círculo católico.*

80. In 1909, as part of a resurgence of national political involvement, which included the construction of new schools and churches, the holding of national conferences, and the publishing of periodicals, the Mexican Catholic Church formed the Círculo Católico Nacional (National Catholic Circle, CCN). The CCN imitated contemporary European political parties and involved itself in the growing Mexican electoral crisis. In 1911

the CCN became the Partido Católico Nacional (National Catholic Party), the predecessor of the Partido de Acción Nacional (National Action Party, PAN)—the party of President Vicente Fox Quesada.

81. Chief among the directors was José Othón Núñez y Zárate. Under Gillow's tutelage, Núñez played a key role in the modernization of Oaxaca's church. He was a central figure in the diocese's publications and in the Círculo Católico, as well as in other aspects of the Catholic labor movement. In 1909 Gillow aided his promotion to bishop of Zamora, Michoacán; Wright-Rios, "Piety and Progress," chap. 3.

82. Perhaps most important for Gillow and Oaxaca's church leaders, the CCOO also functioned as one of many new religious associations and sodalities established during the Porfiriato and meant to rally the state's Catholics around the revitalized church; see ibid., chap. 5.

83. French, *Peaceful and Working People*, 36, 67–68.

84. *Reglamento del Círculo católico*.

85. *La unión*, October 20, 1907; *La voz de la verdad*, August 29, 1908.

86. *Boletín oficial y revista eclesiástica*, January 1, 1907.

87. *La voz de la verdad*, June 24, 1907.

88. Ibid.

89. *Rerum Novarum*, 26–27.

90. *La voz de la verdad*, August 18, 1907.

91. These deposits and benefits were significant considering that workers earned an average of three pesos per week.

92. *Boletín oficial y revista eclesiástica*, January 1, 1910.

93. Ibid., November 11, 1907.

94. *Oaxaca Herald*, March 10, 1907.

95. The city government issued more stringent regulations in 1904; AHMO, Reglamento de las casas de empeño, Orden 03, Grupo documental Secretaría municipal, dossier 1881.4, file 4, 1881, and dossier 1905.1, file 1, 1905.

96. AHMO, Orden 22, Grupo documental Biblioteca, Mensaje leido por el Gobernador Emilio Pimentel, 1904.

97. Sowell, "Caja de Ahorros," 617, 623, 635.

98. The historian Marie François notes that very little work has been done on the history of pawnshops in Latin America as a whole; François, "When Pawnshops Talk," and "Vivir de prestado."

99. Archbishop Gillow played a key role by transporting the bank's initial funds to the state capital. While en route to Oaxaca, Gillow hid the eight hundred thousand pesos in his coach; Chassen-López, "Liberal to Revolutionary Oaxaca," chap. 4, 40.

100. AHMO, Orden 22, Grupo documental Biblioteca, Mensaje leido por el Gobernador Emilio Pimentel, 1904.

101. See, e.g., "El taller y la taverna" (The workshop and the tavern), ibid., May 13, 1906.

102. Sánchez Santos, *Obrero católico*.

103. *La voz de la verdad*, August 30, 1908.

104. See ibid., August 18, 1907.

105. Esparza, *Gillow durante el porfiriato*, 85–87; quotation on 86.

106. *La unión*, July 14, 1907.

107. For details on the years of Porfirian labor unrest, see Rodney Anderson, "Díaz y la crisis laboral," 513–35.

108. Chassen-López, "Liberal to Revolutionary Oaxaca," chap. 5, 36.

109. Ruiz Cervantes and Arellanes Meixueiro, "Orígenes del movimiento obrero," 385–86.

110. The principal cities included Guadalajara, Mexico City, Morelia, León, Aguascalientes, and Zamora.

111. *Oaxaca Herald*, January 31, 1909.

112. Only a few lay people attended the first three congresses. By contrast, the Oaxaca conference included seventy-eight lay people out of ninety total participants.

113. The conclusions of the conference are published in the *Boletín oficial y revista eclesiástica*, May, June, and July 1909.

114. Ceballos Ramírez, *Catolicismo social*, 227.

115. Bastian, *Disidentes*, 11–12.

116. *La unión*, November 24, 1907.

117. AGPEO, Gobernación, dossier 120, file 4, 1907.

118. *La hoja del pueblo*, January 8, 1884.

119. *La voz de la verdad*, November 12, 1901. Another reason for anti-U.S. sentiment could have been the false promises of North American labor scouts. The Mexican federal government sent a circular to Oaxaca's governor in 1904 urging him to warn the state's workers of labor contractors from California, Texas, and Arizona. According to the circular, once the workers reached the job sites in the United States (usually railroad lines), they were abused and soon found themselves unemployed; AGPEO, Gobernación, dossier 117, file 3, 1904.

120. *La hoja del pueblo*, December 1, 1883.

121. Bastian, *Disidentes*, 259.

122. See letter to C. E. Guyant, American vice and deputy consul general in charge, Mexico, Federal District in NAII, Oaxaca, Oaxaca, Consular Posts, RG 84/stack 35/row 07/compartment 02, Miscellaneous Record Book, vol. 8. Since the 1970s the number of Protestants in Oaxaca has increased rapidly. The state of Oaxaca now has the sixth-largest concentration of Protestants in Mexico; see Marroquín, ed. *¿Persecución religiosa?*; and Hartch, "Service of the State."

123. Ruiz Cervantes, "Carlos Gracida," 34.

124. Arellanes Meixueiro, *Trabajos y guías*, 91–152.

4. Public Space and Public Women

1. Despite the fact that the term *sex work* can encompass more than just prostitution, I employ it here to avoid contributing to the pervasive historical stigmatization of these women. Official documents refer to the sex workers with a plethora of names including *mujeres públicas*, *prostitutas*, *púpilas*, *meretrices*, and *matronas*. Terms like these belie the fact that these women were workers and business people struggling like other workers and entrepreneurs with increased regulation by the state but, unlike others, addition-

ally confronted with constant stigmatization and the dangers of disease and physical and psychological abuse. The label *mujer pública*, among others, is part of a terminology of deviance that the state promulgated to make different sectors of society "legible" or definable for regulatory and administrative purposes. The term *sex worker* allows for a more balanced, service-provider, client/customer relationship that illustrates the involvement, in this case, of both women and men. Nevertheless, as we shall see, in municipal petitions the women appropriate the state's designations and refer to themselves as "prostitutas." Furthermore, they attempt to improve their access to government concessions by acquiescing in their own stigmatization. In letters to the municipal council they refer to themselves as "dishonest" workers and "weak" women who require special attention. See examples of these letters in AHMO, Orden 03, Grupo documental Secretaría municipal, unnumbered file, December 11, 1909; dossier 1910, unnumbered file, April 29, 1910; dossier 1911, unnumbered file, July 29, 1911.

2. AHMO, Orden 03, Grupo documental Secretaría municipal, dossier 1893, file 31, July 8, 1893; dossier 1893, file 166, July 21, 1893; dossier 1894, file 88, January 17, 1894; dossier 1894, file 42, March 31, 1894; dossier 1894, file 130, September 8, 1894.

3. See, e.g., Guy, *Sex and Danger*; Garon, "World's Oldest Debate?"; and Bernstein, *Sonia's Daughters*.

4. Rivera-Garza, "Masters of the Streets," esp. chap. 2.

5. French, "Imagining," 264. On the fragility of the state's hegemony, see Roseberry, "Hegemony."

6. I have only found records concerning female, heterosexual prostitutes in the city's archives. While it is possible that male heterosexual and male and female homo- and transsexual prostitutes existed, it is unlikely if not impossible that the Oaxacan state government would have sanctioned their practice. Katherine Bliss discusses lesbian relationships among female prostitutes in Porfirian Mexico City in *Compromised Positions*, 44–45. Two recent works of sociology treat the presence of male (transvestite) sex workers in contemporary Mexico; see Prieur, *Mema's House*; and Higgins and Cohen, *Streets, Bedrooms, Patios*, esp. chap. 3.

7. AHMO, Orden 03, Grupo documental Secretaría municipal, dossier 1893, file 107, May 31, 1893.

8. Voekel, "Peeing on the Palace," 183–208.

9. Stallybrass and White, *Politics and Poetics*, esp. 192.

10. On the intersection of race and gender, see Stephenson, *Gender and Modernity*, 2–8.

11. A notable exception is Eileen Suárez Findlay's excellent study of the intersection of gender, race, sexuality, and colonialism in Puerto Rico, *Imposing Decency*.

12. Examples of this recent literature include Bell, *Reading, Writing, Rewriting*; Caulfield, *Defense of Honor*; French, *Peaceful and Working People*; Rivera-Garza, "Masters of the Streets"; Rago, *Prazeres da noite*; Corbin, *Women for Hire*; Mary Gibson, *Prostitution and the State*; Guy, *Sex and Danger*; White, *Comforts of Home*; Bliss, *Compromised Positions*; Bliss, "'Guided'"; Bliss, "Science of Redemption"; McCreery, "'Life of Misery and Shame'"; and Overmyer-Velázquez, "Espacios públicos."

13. Gilfoyle, "Prostitutes in History." The current literature on prostitution intersects with recent works on gender and state formation in modern Latin America. Elizabeth

Dore provides a useful summary and analysis in her essay "One Step Forward, Two Steps Back." See also Quay Hutchinson, "Add Gender and Stir?"; and Caulfield, "History of Gender."

14. AHMO, Orden 03, Grupo documental Secretaría municipal, dossier 1880–1881–1882, 143. I am grateful to Manuel Esparza for bringing my attention to these earlier references of the city's sex trade.

15. Massé Zenejas, "Photographs of Mexican Prostitutes"; Bliss, " 'Guided,' " 169. For an excellent study of the history of sexual commerce in nineteenth- and early-twentieth-century France, see Corbin, Women for Hire.

16. Bell, Reading, Writing, Rewriting, 41.

17. Morris and Patton, Michel Foucault.

18. Except for church periodicals, Oaxaca City newspapers rarely printed stories concerning prostitution. The state capital's population, however, most likely would have had access to the stories circulated in the Mexico City press from the groups of people (elites and commoners) traveling between the two locations; Gamboa, Santa. See also Sagredo Baeza, María Villa (a) La Chiquita, no. 4002; and the article by Buffington and Piccato, "Tales of Two Women," that examines that narrative construction of Porfirian life in serials, novels, and criminological texts. In Os prazeres da noite, Margareth Rago analyzes in detail the real and symbolic lives of prostitutes in São Paulo from 1890 to 1930. Rago emphasizes the mythic and allegorical dimensions of prostitution and its role in the construction of femininity and modernity in an industrializing urban area.

19. Lara y Pardo, Prostitución en Mexico, 130–31.

20. Piccato argues that criminological explanations of society forwarded by theorists like Lara y Pardo "emerged from an unstable combination of fear, eclecticism, and fascination that did not conform to the complexity of everyday life." City of Suspects, 50–72.

21. See, e.g., Roumagnac, Crímenes sexuales y pasionales; and Guerrero, Génesis del crimen.

22. Mary Gibson, Prostitution and the State, 4. Lombroso, Crime.

23. Joseph, Forward, xi.

24. Bliss, "Science of Redemption," 15.

25. El diario oficial del Estado de Oaxaca, February 8, 1892.

26. Calderón, Crimen según las leyes naturales.

27. Mexican scholars have challenged the notion of the archetypal Mexican woman (virgin vs. whore). In this light, several studies reexamine the history of women in Mexico during the Porfiriato. See, e.g., Ramos Escandón, "Señoritas porfirianas"; Tuñón Pablos, Mujeres en México, esp. chap. 4. More recent studies building on the influential feminist theories of Joan Wallach Scott include González and Tuñón, Familias y mujeres; Cano and Valenzuela, Cuatro estudios de género; Cano, "Género y construcción cultural"; and Cano, "Porfiriato."

28. French, Peaceful and Working People, 87. In her work on late-nineteenth- and early-twentieth-century Italy, Mary Gibson refers to sex workers as part of the "dangerous class." Dangerous because they posed a threat to "decent women" and their families: "The increasing visibility of these 'independent' women on city streets reinforced general anxieties about female emancipation. It is not surprising that an era that uneasily witnessed

changes in the status of women should be preoccupied with female deviance"; Mary Gibson, *Prostitution and the State*, 4.

29. McCreery, " 'Life of Misery and Shame,' " 335.

30. *La voz de la verdad*, March 22, 1896, June 1, 1896.

31. *La libertad*, April 7, 1896.

32. See figures 18 and 19.

33. *El eco mercantil*, September 20, 1891.

34. Lauderdale Graham, *House and Street*, 15. See also Stephenson, *Gender and Modernity*, 5.

35. AHMO, Orden 02, Grupo documental Juzgados, Varios delitos, 1882.

36. For further examples of *delitos en contra de la moralidad pública*, see AHMO, Orden 02, Grupo documental Juzgados, Delitos varios, 1876–1900.

37. Chazkel, "Laws of Chance." Chazkel argues that Brazilian misdemeanor laws existed as part of an arsenal that was used somewhat arbitrarily to harass (and, with the advent of legal medicine, increasingly to keep track of and study) the poor. This is confirmed for her by the fact that many of these types of cases resulted in acquittals for lack of suitable evidence.

38. While it is likely that female homosexuals participated in the development of Oaxaca City's Porfirian-era modernities, I have found no documents that either directly or indirectly discuss them. City officials did not use the terms *homosexual* and *heterosexual*. *Homosexual*, despite its initial usage in a publication by the German physician Karl Friedrich Otto von Westphal in 1869, was not used as a conceptual category in Mexico until the 1930s. Officials referred to homosexuals in Porfirian Oaxaca not as members of a definable social group, but through their actions. Documents mention men committing "scandalous acts" with other men or men who are not vulnerable to the "dangers of female seduction." I have also found no material indicating how men having sex with men referred to each other. The terms *puto* and *homosexual* were and continue to be mutable and contingent on a wide range of local factors. Jeffrey Rubin describes a "third category" of gender, the *muxe*, in Oaxaca's Isthmus of Tehuantepec. A transvestite sexual identity, the *muxe*, according to Rubin, are localized to the isthmus region, especially in Juchitán. See Rubin, *Decentering the Regime*; and also Miano Borruso, *Hombre, mujer y muxe'*. On the fluid and historical nature of homosexual terminology, see the excellent work by Chauncey, *Gay New York*, 12–23. See also Nesvig, "Complicated Terrain" and "Lure of the Perverse." On the criminological study and construction of homosexuality in pre- and postrevolutionary Mexico, see Buffington, *Criminal and Citizen*, 130–40.

39. The rise of Protestantism during the Porfiriato led to virulent anti-Protestant attacks by the Catholic press. *Regeneración*, a pro-Félix Díaz newspaper, ran an article titled "Los pederastas protestantes" (The Protestant Pederasts) comparing the sexuality of Protestants in the city to that of stray dogs; *Regeneración*, June 2, 1911. Similarly, *La voz de la verdad* compared Protestantism to prostitution. The paper claimed that if left unchecked both institutions would bring the ruin of Catholic society; *La voz de la verdad*, March 22, 1896.

40. See, e.g., AHMO, Orden 02, Grupo documental Juzgados, Varios delitos, 1888.

41. AHMO, Orden 02, Grupo documental Juzgados, Varios delitos, 1889. Cf. Chazkel, *Laws of Chance*.

42. For a review of recent works on gender and sexuality in Mexico, see Bliss, "Sexual Revolution."

43. The judge charged Antonio Z. but released him to the custody of his parents. AHMO, Orden 02, Grupo documental Juzgados, Delitos sexuales, April 20, 1876. One hundred and eight similar cases are documented through 1884. Sloan discusses the sexual politics of Porfirian Oaxaca City in "Runaway Daughters."

44. Connell, *Masculinities*, 35, 71.

45. McCreery, " 'Life of Misery and Shame,' " 333. Similar conditions in the small and medium-size cities in the state of Michoacán also helped to promote a growing sex trade. See Sánchez Díaz, "Ciudades michoacanas," 40.

46. Liberal reformers, determined to fashion a propitious environment for the expansion of a capitalist economy, believed that the privatization and hence commodification of public lands were necessary. For a revisionist analysis of land tenure in nineteenth-century Oaxaca, see Chassen-López, "Liberal to Revolutionary Oaxaca," chap. 2. Chassen-López shows that liberal laws mandated the disentailment of communal lands prior to the Lerdo Law during the early part of the century and especially during Benito Juárez's tenure as state governor in the 1850s.

47. AHMO, Orden 11, Grupo documental Registros fotográficos, Registros de oficios, 1881–1913; AHMO, Orden 11, Grupo documental Registros fotográficos, Registros de prostitución, 1890, 1892, 1901–3, 1903, 1905–9, 1909–16.

48. *Resumen del primer censo.*

49. AHMO, Orden 05, Grupo documental Padrones, Padrones, 1887, 1890. Barabas and Bartolomé, *Etnicidad y pluralismo cultural.*

50. Leading intellectual figures of the Porfiriato include José Limantour, Francisco Bulnes, and Justo Sierra; Raat, "Intelectuales."

51. This goal was in many ways reversed by their postrevolutionary *indigenista* successors. In the 1920s and 1930s, proponents of *indigenismo* such as Manuel Gamio and Moisés Sáenz were bent on *including* Indians in Mexico's twentieth-century state-building project. Unlike their Porfirian predecessors, they proclaimed the Indian as "a model for, and subject of, democritisation," with the "intellect and capacity for modernity"; Dawson, "Models," 291.

52. Van Young, Conclusion, 356. For an excellent study of the "Indian question" in mid-nineteenth-century Oaxaca, see Traffano, "Cuestión indígena," 123–32.

53. Deborah Poole finds that Manuel Atanasio Fuentes's work also excluded Indians from mid-nineteenth-century Lima; Poole, *Vision, Race, Modernity*, 142–67, esp. 166.

54. AHMO, Orden 03, Grupo documental Secretaría municipal, dossier 1885.3, file 1.

55. AHMO, Orden 05, Grupo documental Padrones, Padrones municipales Jalatlaco and El Marquesado, 1890.

56. Despite his biased approach and a lack of corroborating evidence, Lara y Pardo suggests a plausible reason for women's turn to prostitution in the context of Mexico City. He argues that madams, hoping to fill their brothels with attractive, marketable women, searched "the hospitals, jails, and other places where destitute women are, looking for

new employees for their brothels. And every time they encountered a pleasant face and a body that could give the appearance of youth and beauty, they would begin their work of conquest that almost always bore fruit"; Lara y Pardo, *Prostitución en México*, 92.

57. See, e.g., AHMO, Orden 03, Grupo documental Secretaría municipal, dossier 1909, unnumbered file, December 11, 1909; dossier 1910, unnumbered file, April 29, 1910; dossier 1911, unnumbered file, July 29, 1911. Lara y Pardo argues that women in domestic service, more than in other occupations, turned to prostitution: "Almost all the middle- and upper-class families [in Mexico City] employ more than one woman in this service [i.e., as servants]." According to Lara y Pardo, the poorly paid servants are drawn to the seemingly lucrative profession of prostitution. He goes even further to suggest, through a study of the occupations of the sex workers' fathers, that sex workers are most likely to come from working-class parentage; Lara y Pardo, *Prostitución en México*, 26–27, 44–46.

58. Esparza, *Padrón de capitación*; AHMO, Orden 05, Grupo documental Padrones, Padrones 1887, 1890.

59. Bliss, "Prostitution," 71. In another example, the young title protagonist in Federico Gamboa's Porfirian-era novel *Santa* (1903), enters the nation's capital from the *provincia*, is corrupted by the city, and turns to prostitution.

60. While hundreds of women came to the state capital and worked as prostitutes, some also left the city and state and entered the sex trade elsewhere. John Turner, in his muckraking account of slavery in Oaxaca's Valle Nacional, relates a story of "eleven girls who had come [to the Valle Nacional] in a single shipment from Oaxaca." Apparently, the jefe político needed money, so he had them sent to work as prostitutes; Turner, *Barbarous Mexico*, 87. In his somewhat dubious statistics, Lara y Pardo also shows the presence of sex workers of Oaxacan origin working in Mexico City. He notes that in 1905 a total of eleven prostitutes hailed from the state of Oaxaca; Lara y Pardo, *Prostitución en México*, 49–50.

61. McCreery, " 'Life of Misery and Shame,' " 337, 339. AHMO, Registros de mugeres [sic] públicas, 1890, 1892, 1901–3, 1903, 1905–9, 1909–16. Although the numbers do not include clandestine or fugitive prostitutes, that is, nonregistered women, the sheer increase in numbers is hard to dispute.

62. The village's regulations included lower taxation rates for sex workers and madams and fewer responsibilities for the inspector (not a doctor) of public health; Archivo General del Poder Ejecutivo del Estado de Oaxaca (AGPEO), Reglamento de prostitución de Sta. María Oaxaca (a) El Marquesado, 1907.

63. Haber, *Industry and Underdevelopment*.

64. *La voz de la verdad*, June 7, 1908.

65. Ibid.

66. The *ambivalence* of city elites toward the regulation of the sex trade strongly echoes Homi Bhabha's use of the term. In his analysis of systems of power in colonial settings, Bhabha notes that the colonizers' failed attempts to make the colonized "mimic" the dominant culture lead to an ambivalent and unstable relationship between the two groups. Far from a dichotomous interaction, this shifting and fluid relationship necessarily becomes "hybrid" as both colonizer and colonized mutually construct each other's historical identity and experience in many ways, as did Oaxaca City's officials and sex workers. See Bhabha, *Location of Culture*, 85–92.

67. Rivera-Garza, "Masters of the Streets," 145–46.

68. For a discussion of the development of the interconnecting discourses and practices of hygiene and prostitution regulation in revolutionary and postrevolutionary Mexico City, see Bliss, "Science of Redemption."

69. AHMO, Orden 03, Grupo documental Secretaría municipal, Ordenanzas municipales de la ciudad de Oaxaca de Juárez, 1907; Orden 5, Grupo documental Padrones, Padrón de niños de los pueblos de la jurisdicción del Centro, 1903.

70. AHMO, Orden 03, Grupo documental Secretaría municipal, dossier 1884.4, file 1, 1894.1; dossier 1905.1, file 21.

71. AHMO, Orden 03, Grupo documental Secretaría municipal, dossier 1880–1881–1882, 143.

72. According to McCreery, turn-of-the-century sex workers in Guatemala City were "held by debts, a structure which faithfully reproduced the broader patterns of extraeconomic exploitation in the general economy"; McCreery, " 'Life of Misery and Shame,' " 342. For a discussion of extraeconomic labor exploitation in Oaxaca during the Porfiriato, see Sigüenza Orozco, Minería.

73. AHMO, Reglamento de prostitución, 1894, art. 1, paras. 1 and 2.

74. AHMO, Proyecto de ordenanzas municipales de la ciudad de Oaxaca, January 1, 1890, chap. 5, sec. 6.

75. See AHMO, Orden 03, Grupo documental Secretaría municipal, Reglamentos de prostitución, March 1892, August 1894.

76. According to Donna Guy, tax revenue from legal prostitution also generated substantial income for the municipal government in turn-of-the-century Buenos Aires; Guy, Sex and Danger, 53.

77. AHMO, Reglamento de prostitución, 1892, sec. 2, art. 11, sec. 5, art. 14, sec. 6.

78. AHMO, Reglamento de prostitución, 1894, secs. 6, 7.

79. The history of the sale and regulation of alcohol in Porfirian Oaxaca City follows a very similar trajectory to that of the sex trade. The year 1893 marked the first time that revenue from both sex work and alcohol sales appeared in the city's budget. Dominated by older, often widowed, women, alcohol vendors in the city jockeyed for position in the increasingly regulated industry. As with prostitution, city officials were torn between what they perceived as the "immoral" and "degenerative" effects of alcohol on society and its financial benefits. As a result, as regulations grew in scope and detail, so did the taxation and hence revenue from alcohol sales. Viewing alcohol as an "enemy of modern society," the government required "antialcohol" classes in state schools. A local educator published a booklet detailing the curriculum for the schools that linked alcoholism to crime and physical deformities; Menéndez, Enseñanza antialcohólica. Alcohol also proved to be a lucrative commodity for the state and federal governments. Oaxaca ranked eighth among Mexican states in production of alcohol. It paid thirty-two thousand pesos in annual taxes to the federal government, sixteen hundred of which came from the Central District; Oaxaca Herald, May 30, 1909. For a study of alcohol regulation in the Porfiriato, see Piccato, "Paso de Venus." In her study of colonial Mexico City, Gabriel Haslip-Viera draws conclusions similar to the Porfirian Oaxaca case, noting that among elites "the con-

sumption of alcoholic beverages was not only tolerated, but encouraged because it bene-fited private entrepreneurs and the government"; Haslip-Viera, *Crime and Punishment*, 65–66.

80. AHMO, Orden 03, Grupo documental Secretaría municipal, dossier 1894.3, file 83; dossier 1894, unnumbered file; Orden 03, Grupo documental Secretaría municipal, dossier 1894.3, file 146; *Periódico oficial*, December 1, 1904. The "vice-ridden" industries added nearly six thousand pesos per year (or five percent) to the city coffers.

81. AHMO, Orden 03, Grupo documental Secretaría municipal, Ralfredo, February 26, 1906.

82. In his work on urban European prostitution, Philip Howell calls for a "geo-graphical understanding of the phenomenon of prostitution." See Howell, "Prostitutional Space."

83. AHMO, Orden 03, Grupo documental Secretaría municipal, Reglamento de pros-titución, March 1892, art. 5, para. 5. Police regulations stipulated that the "scandalous women" could be apprehended and detained with little provocation. See *Prontuario de las obligaciones*; and the later compilation of regulations in Flores, *Tratado especial*.

84. AHMO, Orden 03, Grupo documental Secretaría municipal, dossier 1893, file 97, May 13, 1893.

85. AHMO, Orden 11, Grupo documental Registros fotográficos, Registro de prostitu-ción, 1890, 1892, 1901–3, 1903, 1905–9, 1909–16.

86. French, *Peaceful and Working People*; Soja, *Journeys to Los Angeles*, 110.

87. AHMO, Orden 03, Grupo documental Secretaría municipal, dossier 1893, file 107, May 31, 1893, 1.

88. AHMO, Orden 03, Grupo documental Secretaría municipal, Reglamento de prosti-tución, 1905, art. 48.

89. AHMO, Orden 03, Grupo documental Secretaría municipal, dossier 1893, file 107, May 31, 1893, 3.

90. AHMO, Orden 03, Grupo documental Secretaría municipal, dossier 1893, file 127, July 29, 1893.

91. Piccato, *City of Suspects*, 45.

92. AHMO, Orden 03, Grupo documental Secretaría municipal, dossier 1894, file 81, May 8, 1894.

93. AHMO, Orden 03, Grupo documental Secretaría municipal, Reglamento de prosti-tución, 1905, chap. 8, art. 39.

94. AHMO, Orden 03, Grupo documental Secretaría municipal, dossier 1907, unnum-bered file, March 19, 1907.

95. AHMO, Orden 03, Grupo documental Secretaría municipal, Ralfredo, no. 89, 1907.

96. AHMO, Reglamento de prostitución, 1894, sec. 7, art. 38.

97. AHMO, Orden 03, Grupo documental Secretaría municipal, Ralfredo, no. 1, 1907.

98. AHMO, Orden 03, Grupo documental Secretaría municipal, dossier 4, file 262.

99. AHMO, Orden 03, Grupo documental Secretaría municipal, dossier 1910, unnum-bered file, June 8, 1910.

100. Ibid.

101. Ibid.

102. AHMO, Orden 03, Grupo documental Secretaría municipal, dossier 1905.1, unnumbered file.

103. The casas de asignación are described by Lara y Pardo as "those in which prostitutes work but do not live. These houses are in reality grubby, foul hotels where rooms are rented for either a short stay or for the whole night, at a relatively high price"; Lara y Pardo, *Prostitución en México*, 18, 93.

104. AHMO, Orden 03, Grupo documental Secretaría municipal, Reglamento de prostitución, 1905.

105. AHMO, Orden 03, Grupo documental Secretaría municipal, Ralfredo 1913, no. 27.

5. Portraits of a Lady

1. I use this expression in order to debunk it. I concur with Mary Gibson that the term "world's oldest profession" conveys an inaccurate notion of fixity belying the historically and geographically contingent meanings and experiences of sex workers; Mary Gibson, *Prostitution and the State*, 6.

2. For examples of this type of report, see AHMO, exp. 192, January–June 1892. I am grateful to Jorge Luis Cortés for his help in deciphering medical terms in the documents.

3. See, e.g., AHMO, Orden 02, Grupo documental Juzgados, criminal, lesiones, sections 876–99; *La unión*, July 28, 1907; *La alerta*, June 18, 1912.

4. AHMO, Orden 11, Grupo documental Registros fotográficos, Registros de prostitución, 1890, 1892, 1901, 1903, 1905–9, 1909–16.

5. The fact F. is an *indigenous* woman is not clearly indicated by the documents. Based on her appearance and place of origin, I determine that she was most likely a Zapotec Indian. While I acknowledge the problematic nature of the construction of ethnic identities, especially in the predominantly indigenous state of Oaxaca, what is important here is not the specific way F. identifies herself or the way the state identifies her, but her experience and how she is perceived as a nonwhite woman in the city's sex trade. For a discussion of ethnic categorization in the state of Oaxaca, see Chassen-López, "Liberal to Revolutionary Oaxaca," chap. 6.

6. AHMO, Orden 11, Grupo documental Registros fotográficos, Registros de prostitución, 1892.

7. An article in *La voz de la verdad* mentions the practice of prostitution in nearby towns (*pueblecillos cercanos*); *La voz de la verdad*, June 7, 1908. Also see AHMO, unnumbered dossier, July 29, 1911, and AGPEO, Reglamento de prostitución de Sta. María Oaxaca (a) El Marquesado, 1907.

8. White, *Comforts of Home*.

9. See, e.g., the forthcoming case of Sara Hernández; AHMO, Orden 03, Grupo documental Secretaría municipal, dossier 1911, unnumbered file, July 29, 1911.

10. Madden was in Oaxaca to find work in the mining industry. Through a connection provided by the consular agent, Madden found employment at the mine of another U.S. citizen, Adolphus D. King, as an "Indian Overseer." Madden drank his wages, left his job, and, a month after the brothel incident, killed King to "vindicate [his] family's honor."

After spending a year in the Oaxaca City jail, Madden was executed. Madden wrote a letter to U.S. Ambassador Clayton asking him to intervene with the Oaxacan officials; NAII –Oaxaca, Oax.–Consular Posts, RG 84/stack 35/row 07/compartment 02–Miscellaneous Record Book–vol. 3.

11. AHMO, Orden 03, Grupo documental Secretaría municipal, dossier 1904, unnumbered file, January 28, 1904.

12. Ana María Alonso traces the shifting conception of honor along Mexico's northern border during the late colonial period; Alonso, *Thread of Blood*.

13. In her book *In Defense of Honor*, Sueann Caulfield explores the relationship between popular and elite conceptions of sexual honor and state intervention in the construction of gender, race, and class difference in modern Brazil.

14. Piccato, *City of Suspects*, 80.

15. Gramsci, *Selections*, 123–209.

16. Scott, *Weapons of the Weak*, 39.

17. AHMO, Orden 03, Grupo documental Secretaría municipal, Reglamento de prostitución, chap. 2, art. 4.

18. For examples of works on honor and shame in colonial Latin America, see Seed, *To Love*; Stern, *Secret History*; Johnson and Lipsett-Rivera, *Faces of Honor*; and Twinam, *Public Lives*. Sarah Chambers argues that notions of honor shifted as Peruvians "transformed themselves from colonial subjects into republican citizens"; Chambers, *Subjects to Citizens*.

19. Stoler, *Race and Education of Desire*.

20. By 1904 surveillance of the city's sex trade had increased and "mature" women worked alongside their "vulnerable" male counterparts. See chapter 4.

21. It is unclear how successfully these women were treated for venereal diseases, especially in the diseases' secondary and tertiary stages. Doctors most likely prescribed the inconsistently effective chemical potassium iodide. The women themselves may have used the highly acidic solution of potassium permanganate as a prophylactic. It was not until 1905, the year after V.'s arrest, that scientists isolated the bacterium that causes syphilis. Penicillin, far more successful than all previous treatments, was not discovered until 1928; Brandt, *No Magic Bullet*. See also Bliss, "Science of Redemption," 8.

22. AHMO, Orden 03, Grupo documental Secretaría municipal, dossier 1905.1, unnumbered file, December 28, 1904.

23. AHMO, Orden 03, Grupo documental Secretaría municipal, dossier 1910, unnumbered file, June 8, 1910, and throughout Orden 03, Grupo documental Secretaría municipal, dossiers 1876–1911.

24. Suárez Findlay, *Imposing Decency*, 97.

25. AHMO, Orden 03, Grupo documental Secretaría municipal, dossier 1911, unnumbered file, July 29, 1911.

26. AHMO, Orden 03, Grupo documental Secretaría municipal, Reglamento de prostitución, 1905, Art. 64.

27. AHMO, Orden 03, Grupo documental Secretaría municipal, dossier 1911, unnumbered file, July 29, 1911.

28. AHMO, Orden 03, Grupo documental Secretaría municipal, dossier 1909, 29 file, December 11, 1909. See also dossier 1910, unnumbered file, September 23, 1910.

29. On rare occasions the person "responsible" for the retired sex worker was a female family member (a mother, sister, or aunt); AHMO, Orden 11, Grupo documental Registros fotográficos, Registro de prostitución, 1892, nos. 18, 14, 32, 45, 53, 57, 81.

30. Scott, *Domination*, 183-201, esp. 183-84, and 28-47, esp. 30, 32.

31. The fact that these women workers acted in response to the newspaper's articles is a clear indication that, although predominantly illiterate, they participated in the city's news media culture.

32. Bakhtin, *Rabelais*; Scott, *Domination*, 172-82.

33. *La voz de la verdad*, June 14, 1908. The article was written by "Filodemos," a psuedonym used by the Oaxacan lawyer and journalist Lorenzo Mayoral.

34. Ibid.; AHMO, Orden 03, Grupo documental Secretaría municipal, Reglamento de prostitución, 1905, chap. 2, arts. 5-12.

35. The duties of the doctor of public health are outlined in section 5 of the 1894 Reglamento de prostitución and chapters 7 and 8 of the 1905 Reglamento de prostitución; AHMO, Orden 03, Grupo documental Secretaría municipal, Reglamentos de prostitución, 1894, 1905.

36. AHMO, Orden 03, Grupo documental Secretaría municipal, dossier 1892, file 192, July 1892.

37. AHMO, Orden 03, Grupo documental Secretaría municipal, dossier 1908, unnumbered file, February 10, 1908.

38. "Clandestine prostitutes discovered working in brothels, casas de asignación, or hotels will be registered with the Commission on Sanitation and must comply with the regulations of prostitution"; AHMO, Orden 03, Grupo documental Secretaría municipal, Reglamento de prostitución, 1905, chap. 6, arts. 31-33.

39. AHMO, Orden 03, Grupo documental Secretaría municipal, dossier 1893, file 127, July 29, 1893.

40. Memoria de los trabajos del H. Ayuntamiento de 1894, leido por el Presidente municipal, January 1, 1895, Orden 03, Grupo documental Secretaría municipal, dossier 1895.1, file 1.

41. While it is conceivable that some sex workers saw benefits from medical examinations, the enforced routine visits and the crude methods employed by the city's doctors must have deterred attendance.

42. Spivak, "Can the Subaltern Speak?" Challenging elite and West-centered (Occidentalist) histories, Spivak and the other members of the Subaltern Studies project have studied the subaltern class as legitimate historical subjects/actors. These scholars' emphasis on decentering and deconstructing social relations and the corresponding historical texts in order to "make the subaltern classes the subjects of their own history" is relevant to the study of society in Porfirian Oaxaca. For examples of the use of the methods of Subaltern Studies in the Latin American history, see Joseph, "Trail of Latin American Bandits"; and Mallon, "Promise and Dilemma."

43. See the papers and commentary by Gregory Grandin, Daniel James, Mark Overmyer-Velázquez, and Deborah Poole from the panel on this subject, "Every Picture Tells a Story (Don't It?): The Use of Family and Public Photographs in the Writing of Latin

American Social History," presented at the American Historical Association meetings, Boston, January 7, 2001.

44. Here and elsewhere, I am grateful to John Mraz for his thoughtful comments on earlier versions of this chapter.

45. Haraway argues for a "partial vision" leading to a "feminist objectivity" as an antidote to the totalizing vision. See her article "Persistence of Vision."

46. James and Lobato, "Family Photos."

47. Poole, *Vision, Race, Modernity,* 7.

48. On this score, see Walter Benjamin's discussion of photography's role in the political transformation of art in "Work of Art."

49. Debroise, *Fuga mexicana,* 24.

50. The four studios were: Oaxaca Photo Developing Co., Salas Arguelles, the Oaxaca Photo Supply House, and Photo Developing by Francisco Vásquez.

51. *Oaxaca Herald,* April 4, 1909.

52. National Archives – Oaxaca City, Oaxaca – Consular Posts, RG 84/stack 35/row 07/ compartment 02 – Miscellaneous Record Book – vol. 6; *Resumen del primer censo.* The 1875 census lists one photographer, Manuel Reyes, operating in the city; Manuel Esparza, *Padrón de capitación.*

53. The photographs in the registries are firmly glued to their paper backing. Salazar's name is only legible thanks to a detached photo.

54. Debroise, *Fuga mexicana,* 25.

55. Jay, *Downcast Eyes,* 127. See also Tagg, *Burden of Representation.*

56. Susan Sontag points out that "starting with their use by the Paris police in the murderous roundup of Communards in June 1871, photographs became a useful tool of modern states in the surveillance and control of their increasingly mobile populations"; Sontag, *On Photography,* 23. In Mexico, the Porfirian criminologist Carlos Roumagnac used photographs as evidence of mental and physical degeneracy; Roumagnac, *Criminales en México.* The techniques of the French criminal anthropologist Alphonse Bertillon, developed in the 1880s, were published widely. Like Roumagnac, Bertillon identified criminals by their physiognomies recorded in photographic records. By the turn of the century his work was available in Latin America. See Barros Ovalle, *Manual de antropometría.* See also Jay, *Downcast Eyes,* 143; and Buffington, *Criminal and Citizen,* 72.

57. Magali M. Carrera discusses the visual regulatory practices embedded in the casta paintings of late-colonial New Spain in *Imagining Identity.*

58. In 1828, the Italian Claudio Linati published lithographs of "traditional" costumes in his book, *Trajes civiles, militares y religiosos.* Representation of Mexican "types" was not limited to the image. Travel literature abounds with terse descriptions of the inhabitants of Mexico. In her 1901 memoir, *Mexico as I Saw It,* Ethel Brilliana Tweedie describes her travels through Oaxaca and her attempts to reconcile what she sees as the "paradox of Mexico." She writes, "In some aspects, Mexico, in this year of grace 1901, is highly civilized, but in others, it remains completely barbaric. It really is a country of paradoxes"; cited in Ramey, "Visión victoriana," 54. Other examples of travel accounts include those of Señora Calderón de la Barca, Carson, and Mathieu de Fossey; Ochoa, *Fotografía,* 116.

59. Debroise, *Fuga mexicana*, 106.

60. Sekula, "Body and Archive"; Smith, *American Archives*, 3–10.

61. AHMO, Orden 11, Grupo documental Registros fotográficos, Registros de oficios, 1881–1913.

62. Poole, "Cultural Diversity," 10, 13; see also Poole, "Image of 'Our Indian.'"

63. Gregory Grandin examines similar tension in his study of K'iche' families; Grandin, *Blood of Guatemala*, 182–91.

64. According to official (albeit imprecise) statistics, in 1878, 77 percent of the state was indigenous; in 1890, the figure was 78 percent; González Navarro, *Estadísticas sociales*, 150.

65. AHMO, Orden 03, Grupo documental Secretaría municipal, Reglamento de prostitución, 1905, art. 4, para. 2.

66. Chassen-López, "Liberal to Revolutionary Oaxaca," chap. 5, 12.

67. Ibid., 12–13. Chassen-López notes that the number of foreigners in the state grew rapidly, from 260 in 1878 to 814 in 1900 and 2,026 in 1910. In 1910 the number of foreign men, 1,622, was four times greater than that of foreign women, 404. As a result, many foreign men married young Oaxacan women.

68. In her study of Mexico City (which admittedly had a different relationship to capitalist development than Oaxaca), Rivera-Garza submits another reading of the prostitute's appearance in light of a growing consumer culture in Mexico. She finds that the commodification of the body and its adornment in fashionable dress linked the prostitute to a sexist view that women were obsessed with consumer goods. Summarizing an anonymous author of the era, Rivera-Garza writes, "Consumerism promoted prostitution through an intricate process involving vanity, irrational wants, credit and debts. Vain women left their homes with no money in their purses but lots of charm in their bodies. By seducing inexperienced or conning male clerks, they managed to come back to their houses with packages of the fancied goods on credit. The debt thus led to prostitution since it was more often than not eventually paid with sexual favors"; Rivera-Garza, "Masters of the Streets," 175.

69. Beezley, "Porfirian Smart Set," 178.

70. Poole, *Vision, Race, Modernity*, 18–20.

71. Poole, "Image of Our 'Indian,'" 47–48.

72. Although the elevated brothel status did afford these women certain comforts, they were still financially tied to their madams in a form of debt peonage. For the Mexico City case, see Bliss, *Compromised Positions*, 55.

73. Due to the relative absence of indigenous prostitutes in the registries after 1901, one can only speculate as to their whereabouts. Although some managed to alter their status by appropriating outward elite, white traits and enter second- and first-class brothels, others, unable to pay increasing taxes, most likely worked as unregistered and hence illegal *prostitutas clandestinas*.

74. AHMO, Orden 03, Grupo documental Secretaría municipal, Reglamento de prostitución, 1905, chap. 1, art. 3.

75. Unlike the poor, black, Pentecostal Brazilian women whom John Burdick describes appropriating modest dress and a white aesthetic as an empowering alternative to the stereotype of the sexually available black woman, there is no evidence that Oaxaca's in-

digenous prostitutes appropriated the whiteness of modernity to lessen their sexual appeal. On the contrary, their adaptation of an elite, white aesthetic enhanced their value as sellers of sex; Burdick, *Women, Race, Popular Christianity*, esp. 6, 29–31.

76. In her study of courtesans in Shanghai, Gail Hershatter examines how Chinese sex workers adopted Western fashions and presented themselves in photographs as a way to "display not only refinement, but also knowledge of the modern"; Hershatter, *Dangerous Pleasures*, 83–84.

77. See Poole, *Vision, Race, Modernity*, 201.

78. Massé Zenejas, "Photographs of Mexican Prostitutes."

79. For studies of bourgeoise portraiture in tarjetas de visita, see Massé Zenejas, *Cruces y Campa* and *Simulacro y elegancia*. See also Levine, *Images of History*.

80. Medina, "Vigilar y retratar," 7.

81. Levine, *Images of History*, 312.

82. Coronil, *Magical State*, 16.

83. For a different view of the origins and professional trajectory of madams, see Katherine Bliss's work on Mexico City; Bliss, " 'Guided,' " 176–77.

84. See, e.g., AHMO, Orden 03, Grupo documental Secretaría municipal, dossier 1905, file 31, July 9, 1893; dossier 1894, file 71, June 1, 1894.

85. In two parallel examples, Jennie Purnell and Patrick McNamara discuss how peasants and indigenous landowners in Oaxaca state utilized the terms of a liberal discourse during the Porfiriato to negotiate claims to property and their own history; Purnell, "Negotiating the Nation"; McNamara, "Time of Unspeakable Hardship." See also Alan Knight's original discussion of folk liberalism in *The Mexican Revolution*; as well as Lear, "Mexico City," 39–41.

86. For examples of these types of petitions, see AHMO, Orden 03, Grupo documental Secretaría municipal, 1905, file 43, March 9, 1894; dossier 1894, file 162, April 6, 1894; dossier, 1907, unnumbered file, January 3, 1907; dossier 1908, unnumbered file, June 27, 1908; dossier 1911, unnumbered file, December 20, 1911.

87. AHMO, Orden 03, Grupo documental Secretaría municipal, dossier 1893, file 159, May 29, 1893.

88. Lara y Pardo, *Prostitución en México*, 81. See discussion of Lara y Pardo in chapter 4.

89. AHMO, Orden 03, Grupo documental Secretaría municipal, dossier 1907, unnumbered file, July 7, 1907; dossier 1907, unnumbered file, July 12, 1907.

90. Bliss, " 'Guided,' " 167. Kathryn Sloan has found similar examples in Oaxaca's archives concerning women's manipulation of the legal system in cases of rape and bridal abduction; Sloan, "Runaway Daughters."

91. AHMO, Orden 03, Grupo documental Secretaría municipal, dossier 1910, unnumbered file, April 29, 1910.

92. See, e.g., AHMO, Orden 03, Grupo documental Secretaría municipal, dossier 1907, unnumbered files, April 10 and August 7, 1907; dossier 1911, unnumbered files, April 4, July 4, and August 4, 1911.

93. Here I am not supporting the overly teleological myth that women advanced generally as a result of independence and the subsequent era of liberal reforms and modernization. As Elizabeth Dore explains, republican movements throughout Latin America

often served to bolster patriarchal arrangements rather than dismantle them. See "One Step Forward" in *Hidden Histories of Gender and the State in Latin America*.

94. This is not an uncommon phenomenon. Men are typically absent in the prostitution records throughout Latin America. See Suárez Findlay, *Imposing Decency*, 94; and Green, *Beyond Carnival*.

95. AHMO, Orden 03, Grupo documental Secretaría municipal, Reglamento de prostitución, 1905, chap. 1, art. 3.

96. Sigüenza Orozco, *Minería*, 36; Chassen-López, "Oaxaca," 188–91.

97. See AHMO, Orden 03, Grupo documental Secretaría municipal, Ralfredo, nos. 99 and 100, 1912, and Ralfredo, 1910–12, passim.

98. Medina, *Vigilar y retratar*, 9.

Conclusions

1. Giddens, *Consequences of Modernity* is cited in Buffington and Piccato, "Tale of Two Women," 403.

2. An exception is the excellent study of Morelia, Michoacán, by Christina Jimenez, "Making the City Their Own."

3. Two outstanding collections that rigorously examine the notion of modernity from the vantage points of "less developed" regions are Gaonkar, *Alternative Modernities*; and Mitchell, *Questions of Modernity*.

4. Orozco, *Minería y comunidad indígena*.

5. Chassen-López, "Liberal to Revolutionary Oaxaca," chap. 1, 57.

6. *Oaxaca Herald*, October 11, 1908.

7. *La situación*, May–October 1912; *El trueno*, July 17, 1914.

8. The history of the Mixtec community of Oaxaca exemplifies this migratory trend. See Nagengast, Stavenhagen, and Kearney, *Human Rights and Indigenous Workers*; and Cohen, *Culture of Migration*.

9. Whipperman, *Oaxaca*. Tourism ranks third after petroleum exports and migrant remittances in level of economic importance in Mexico; Clancy, *Exporting Paradise*. In recent years, an average of 250,000 foreign tourists and over 1.5 million Mexican tourists has visited Oaxaca City annually; SECTUR (Mexican Sectretary of Tourism), Data Tur Certeza Estratégica, at http://datatur.sectur.gob.mex/jsp/index.jsp.

10. Two anthropologists working for the National Institute for Anthropology and History (INAH) conceived of and initiated Oaxaca's community museums or *museos comunitarios*. See Camarena Ocampo and Morales Lersch, *Fortaleciendo lo propio*.

11. "Mini" Guelaguetzas continue throughout the year in hotel courtyards in Oaxaca City. The Guelaguetza celebration in its present form developed as early as the 1930s. It was, however, only after Oaxaca's more recent touristic renaissance that the event became such a prominent and lucrative promotional element of contemporary Oaxaca.

12. Zolov, "Discovering a Land," 242.

13. Excerpt from CIPO flyer titled (in the English-language copy provided for non-Mexican tourists) "To National and International Media, Citizens of Oaxaca, Tourists, People of the World, Organizations of Good Will, Brothers and Sisters."

14. Although claiming origins from at least colonial times, el Noche de Rábanos became institutionalized during the Porfiriato and the age of scientific agriculture (see chap. 2). The event consists of a competition among artists to create the best scene constructed solely of red radishes.

15. El imparcial, "Podrían desalojar al CIPO," December 22, 2004.

16. On January 1, 2005, Oaxaca's new governor, Ulises Ruiz, was sworn into office. The election of Ruiz, a member of the Institutional Revolutionary Party (PRI), was widely deemed as fraudulent, especially by the largely anti-PRI inhabitants of Oaxaca City.

17. Letter signed by Anselmo Arellanes Meixueiro, Manuel Esparza Camargo, Victor Raúl Martínez Vásquez, María de los Angeles Romero Frizzi, Francisco José Ruiz Cervantes, and Carlos Sánchez Silva in Noticias, December 27, 2004.

18. Overmyer-Velázquez, "Traspasando las fronteras."

Appendix

1. Constituciones de México.

Bibliography

ARCHIVES

Oaxaca City

Archivo de la Arquidiócesis de Oaxaca (AA)
Archivo General de Notarías del Estado de Oaxaca (AGNE)
Archivo General del Poder Ejecutivo del Estado de Oaxaca (AGPEO)
Archivo Histórico Municipal "Manuel R. Palacios" de Oaxaca (AHMO)
Archivo Poder Judicial (APJ)
Fundación Dr. Juan I. Bustamante Vasconcelos (FBV)
    Colección Privada
Hemeroteca de la Ciudad de Oaxaca de Juárez (HCO)
Hemeroteca de la Universidad "Benito Juárez" de Oaxaca (HUO)

Mexico City

Archivo General de la Nación (AGN)
    Ramo de Fomento
    Ramo de Gobernación
    Ramo de Obras Públicas
Biblioteca Miguel Lerdo de Tejada (BMLT)
    Fondo Reservado
    Hemeroteca
Centro de Estudios de la Historia de México (CONDUMEX)
Colección Porfirio Díaz, Universidad Iberoamericana (CPD)
Hemeroteca General de la Nación (HGN)
Hemeroteca del Instituto Nacional de Antropología e Historia (HINAH)
Mapoteca Manuel Orozco y Berra (MOB)

United States

National Archives II, College Park, Maryland (NAII)
    Record Group 59, Consular Post Records, Oaxaca, 1869–1915.
Yale University, New Haven, Connecticut
    Manuscripts and Archives Collection, Sterling Memorial Library (SML)
    Seeley G. Mudd Library (Mudd)

NEWSPAPERS

Oaxaca City

El adelanto
La alerta
El avance
La bandera del evangelio
El bien público
Boletín municipal de Oaxaca de Juárez
El centenario
El club Benito Juárez
El correo del comercio
El correo del sur
El defensor del pueblo
El eco mercantil
El Estado de Oaxaca
El estandarte
La hoja del pueblo
El huarache
El imparcial

La libertad
La linterna de Diógenes
Noticias
Oaxaca Herald
Oaxaca Moderno
Oaxaca progresista
La patria
Periódico oficial del Estado de Oaxaca
Regeneración
Revista de Oaxaca
La semecracia
La situación
El trueno
La unión
La victoria
La voz de la verdad

Mexico City

El diario del hogar
El imparcial
Mexican Herald
El país

El siglo diez y nueve
El tiempo
El universal
La voz de México

PUBLISHED PRIMARY SOURCES

Albúm de la coronación de la santísima Virgen de la Soledad que se verá en Oaxaca. Oaxaca City: Talleres de Imprenta, La Voz de la Verdad, 1911.

Barros Ovalle, Pedro N. Manual de antropometría criminal y general, escrito según el sistema de A. Bertillon para la identificación personal y destinado al uso de los establecimientos penitenciarios, autoridades judiciales, compañías de seguros, cuerpos, armados, etc. Santiago de Chile: E. Blanchard-Chessi, 1900.

Belmar, Francisco. Breve reseña histórica y geográfica del Estado de Oaxaca. Oaxaca City: Imprenta del Comerico, 1901.

Boletín oficial y revista eclesiástica de la provincia de Antequera. 6 vols. Oaxaca City: La Voz de la Verdad, 1901–10.

Bulnes, Francisco. El verdadero Díaz y la revolución. Mexico City: E. Gómez de la Puente, 1920.

Calderón, Miguel. El crimen según las leyes naturales. Instituto de Ciencias y Artes del Estado. Oaxaca City: Imprenta de Francisco Márquez, 1908.

Carson, W. E. Mexico: The Wonderland of the South. Detroit: MacMillan, 1909.

Las constituciones de México, 1814–1989. Mexico City: H. Congreso de la Unión, Comité de Asuntos Editoriales, 1989.

Estadísticas sociales del porfiriato. Mexico City: Secretaría de Economía, 1956.

Flores, Adalberto. Tratado especial de policía de la capital del Estado de Oaxaca. Oaxaca City: Imprenta del Estado, 1908.

Fossey, Mathieu de. Viage a Méjico. Translation from the French. Mexico City: I. Cumplido, 1884.

Gamboa, Federico. Santa. Mexico City: Eusebio Gómez de la Puente, 1922 [1903].

Gay, José Antonio. Historia de Oaxaca. Mexico City: Porrúa, 1990 [1881].

Gillow, Eulogio. Apuntes históricos. Mexico City: Imprenta del Sagrado Corazón de Jesus, 1889.

———. Reminiscencias. Mexico City: Imprenta del Sagrado Corazón de Jesus, 1919.

González Navarro, Moisés. Estadísticas sociales del porfiriato. Mexico City: Secretaría de Economía, 1956.

Guerrero, Julio. La génesis del crimen en México. Paris and Mexico City: Librería de la viuda de Ch. Bouret, 1901.

Lara y Pardo, Luis. La prostitución en México. Mexico City: Estudios de Higiene Social, 1908.

Lista de algunas obras materiales, llevadas a cabo en el Estado, durante los dos períodos de la administración del Sr. Lic. Don Emilio Pimentel. Oaxaca City: Nuevos Talleres de Imprenta y Rayados de San Germán, 1910.

Lombroso, Cesare. Crime: Its Causes and Remedies. Boston: Little, Brown, 1911.

Manual de gobernadores y de jefes políticos. Mexico City: Ildefonso Estrada y Zenea, 1878.

Memoria administrativa presentada por el gobernador interino, Lic. Miguel Bolaños Cacho al H. Congreso del Estado. Oaxaca: Imprenta del Comercio, 1902.

Menéndez, Rodolfo. Enseñanza antialcohólica. Oaxaca City: Librería y Papelería de Julián S. Soto, 1904.

Mühlenpfordt, Eduard. Ensayo de una descripción fiel de la República de Méjico, con especial referencia a su geografía, etnografía y estadística. Translated by María del Carmen Salinas and Elizabeth Siefer. Mexico City: Codex, 1993.

Plano topográfico de la ciudad de Oaxaca de Juárez. Oaxaca: J. P. Guzmán, 1887.

Prontuario de las obligaciones del policía. Oaxaca: Imprenta del Estado, 1891.

Portillo, Andrés. Oaxaca en el centenario de la independencia nacional: Noticias históricas y estadísticas de la ciudad de Oaxaca y algunas leyendas tradicionales. Oaxaca City: Imprenta del Estado, 1910.

Reglamento del Círculo católico de obreros de Oaxaca. Oaxaca: La Voz de la Verdad, 1907.

Rerum Novarum (On the Condition of the Working Classes): Encyclical of His Holiness Pope Leo XIII. New York: America, 1936 [1891].

Resumen del primer censo general de habitantes. Secretaría de Fomento, Colonización e Industria, Dirección General de Estadística de la República Mexicana, 1896.

Roumagnac, Carlos. Los criminales en México: Ensayo de psicología criminal. Mexico City: Tipografía, 1904.

———. Crímenes sexuales y pasionales: estudio de psicología morbosa. Mexico City: Charles Bouret, 1906.

Sánchez Santos, Trinidad. El obrero católico ante el socialismo revolucionario: Discurso ante el

Gran círculo católico de obreros, celebrado el día 20 de enero de 1909 en la Ciudad de Oajaca. Oaxaca City: Voz de la Verdad, 1909.

Seler-Sachs, Caecilie. *Auf alten Wegen in Mexiko und Guatemala: Reiseerinnerungen und Eindrücke aus den Jahren 1895–1897.* Berlin: D. Reimer, 1900.

Southworth, J. R. *El Estado de Oaxaca: Ilustrada México — Su historia, comercio, minería, agricultura e industrias — Sus elementos naturales.* Liverpool: Blake and MacKenzie, 1901.

Turner, John K. *Barbarous Mexico.* Austin: University of Texas Press, 1990 [1910].

Vasconcelos, Francisco. *Apuntes históricos de la vida en Oaxaca en el siglo XIX.* N.d. Ediciones Bibliográficas del Ayuntamiento de Oaxaca de Juárez. AC. Fco Vasconcelos No. 2.

SECONDARY SOURCES

Agostoni, Claudia. *Monuments of Progress: Modernization and Public Health in Mexico City, 1876–1910.* Calgary: University of Calgary Press, 2003.

Alonso, Ana María. *Thread of Blood: Colonialism, Revolution, and Gender on Mexico's Northern Frontier.* Tucson: University of Arizona Press, 1995.

Anderson, Benedict. *Imagined Communities: Reflections on the Origin and Spread of Nationalism.* London: Verso, 1993.

Anderson, Rodney D. "Díaz y la crisis laboral de 1906." *Historia mexicana* 19 (1970): 513–35.

Arbena, Joseph L. "Sport and the Study of Latin American Society: An Overview." In Arbena, ed., *Sport and Society in Latin America: Diffusion, Dependency, and the Rise of Mass Culture.* New York: Greenwood, 1988.

Arellanes Meixueiro, Anselmo. *Los trabajos y los guías: Mutualismo y sindicalismo en Oaxaca, 1870–1930.* Oaxaca City: Instituto Tecnológico de Oaxaca, 1990.

Arrom, Silvia. *The Women of Mexico City, 1790–1857.* Stanford, Calif.: Stanford University Press, 1985.

Asad, Talal. *Formations of the Secular: Christianity, Islam, Modernity.* Stanford, Calif.: Stanford University Press, 2003.

Baer, James A. "Buenos Aires: Housing Reform and the Decline of the Liberal State in Argentina." In Baer and Ronn Pineo, eds., *Cities of Hope: People, Protests, and Progress in Urbanizing Latin America, 1870–1930.* Boulder, Colo.: Westview, 1998.

Bakhtin, Mikhail. *Rabelais and His World.* Translated by Hélène Iswolksy. Bloomington: Indiana University Press, 1984.

Barabas, Alicia, and Miguel Bartolomé, eds. *Etnicidad y pluralismo cultural: La dinámica étnica en Oaxaca.* Mexico City: Instituto Nacional de Antropología e Historia, 1990.

Bastian, Jean-Pierre. "Metodismo y clase obrera durante el porfiriato." *Historia mexicana* 33 (1983): 39–71.

———. *Breve historia del protestantismo en América Latina.* Mexico City: Casa Unida de Publicaciones, 1986.

———. *Los disidentes: Sociedades protestantes y revolución en México, 1872–1911.* Mexico City: Colegio de México, 1989.

Beezley, William H. *Judas at the Jockey Club and Other Episodes of Porfirian Mexico.* Lincoln: University of Nebraska Press, 1987.

———. "Bicycles, Modernization, and Mexico." In Joseph L. Arbena, ed., *Sport and Society in*

Latin America: Diffusion, Dependency, and the Rise of Mass Culture. New York: Greenwood, 1988.

———. "The Porfirian Smart Set Anticipates Thorstein Veblen in Guadalajara." In Beezley, Cheryl English Martin, and William E. French, eds., Rituals of Rule, Rituals of Resistance: Public Celebrations and Popular Culture in Mexico. Wilmington, Del.: Scholarly Resources, 1994.

Beezley, William H., Cheryl English Martin, and William E. French. Introduction to Beezley, Martin, and French, eds., Rituals of Rule, Rituals of Resistance: Public Celebrations and Popular Culture in Mexico. Wilmington, Del.: Scholarly Resources, 1994.

Bell, Shannon. Reading, Writing, and Rewriting the Prostitute Body. Bloomington: Indiana University Press, 1994.

Bender, Thomas. Toward an Urban Vision: Ideas and Institutions in Nineteenth-Century America. Lexington: University of Kentucky Press, 1975.

Benjamin, Walter. "The Work of Art in the Age of Mechanical Reproduction." In Illuminations, New York: Schocken, 1969.

Berman, Marshall. All That Is Solid Melts into Air: The Experience of Modernity. New York: Simon and Schuster, 1982.

Bernstein, Laurie. Sonia's Daughters: Prostitutes and Their Regulation in Imperial Russia. Berkeley: University of California Press, 1995.

Berry, Charles R. The Reform in Oaxaca, 1856–1876: A Microhistory of the Liberal Revolution. Lincoln: University of Nebraska Press, 1981.

———. "Ficción y realidad de la reforma: El caso del distrito del centro de Oaxaca, 1856–1867." In María de los Angeles Romero Frizzi, ed., Lecturas históricas del Estado de Oaxaca. Vol. 4, 1877–1930. Mexico City: Instituto Nacional de Antropología e Historia, 1990.

Bhabha, Homi. The Location of Culture. New York: Routledge, 1994.

Bliss, Katherine. "Prostitution, Revolution and Social Reform in Mexico City, 1918–1940." PhD diss., University of Chicago, 1996.

———. "The Science of Redemption: Syphilis, Sexual Promiscuity, and Reformism in Revolutionary Mexico City." Hispanic American Historical Review 79.1 (1999): 1–40.

———. " 'Guided by an Imperious, Moral Need': Prostitutes, Motherhood, and Nationalism in Revolutionary Mexico." In Carlos A. Aguirre and Robert Buffington, eds., Reconstructing Criminality in Latin America. Wilmington, Del.: Scholarly Resources, 2000.

———. Compromised Positions: Prostitution, Public Health, and Gender Politics in Revolutionary Mexico City. University Park: Penn State University Press, 2001.

———. "The Sexual Revolution in Mexican Studies: New Perspectives on Gender, Sexuality, and Culture in Modern Mexico." Latin American Research Review 34.1 (2001): 247–68.

Bonfil Batalla, Guillermo. México Profundo: Reclaiming a Civilization. Austin: University of Texas Press, 1996.

Brading, David. Mexican Phoenix: Our Lady of Guadalupe — Image and Tradition across Five Centuries. Cambridge: Cambridge University Press, 2001.

Brandt, Allan. No Magic Bullet: A Social History of Venereal Disease since 1880. Oxford: Oxford University Press, 1985.

Braverman, Harry. Labor and Monopoly Capital: The Degradation of Work in the Twentieth Century. New York: Monthly Review Press, 1974.

Bretas, Marcos Luiz. "You Can't! The Daily Exercise of Police Authority in Rio de Janeiro, 1907–1930." PhD diss., Open University, 1994.

Brioso y Candiani, Manuel. *La evolución del pueblo oaxaqueño*. Mexico City: Imprenta "A su orden," 1943.

Buffington, Robert. "Revolutionary Reform: Capitalist Development, Prison Reform, and Executive Power in Mexico." In Ricardo Salvatore and Carlos Aguirre, eds., *The Birth of the Penitentiary in Latin America: Essays on Criminology, Prison Reform, and Social Control, 1830–1940*. Austin: University of Texas Press, 1996.

———. *Criminal and Citizen in Modern Mexico*. Lincoln: University of Nebraska Press, 2000.

Buffington, Robert, and William French. "The Culture of Modernity." In Michael C. Meyer and William H. Beezley, eds., *The Oxford History of Mexico*. Oxford: Oxford University Press, 2000.

Buffington, Robert, and Pablo Piccato. "Tale of Two Women: The Narrative Construal of Porfirian Reality." *Americas* 55.3 (January 1999): 391–424.

Burdick, John. *Women, Race, and Popular Christianity in Brazil*. New York: Routledge, 1998.

Camarena Ocampo, Cuauhtémoc, and Teresa Morales Lersch. *Fortaleciendo lo propio: Ideas para la creación de un museo comunitario—Programas de museos comunitarios y eco-museos*. Mexico City: INAH-CONACULTA, 1995.

Cano, Gabriela. "Género y construcción cultural de las profesiones en el porfiriato: Magisterio, medicina, jurisprudencia y odontología." *Historia y grafía*, no. 14 (2000): 207–43.

———. "The *Porfiriato* and the Mexican Revolution: Constructions of Feminism and Nationalism." In Ruth Roach Pierson and Nupur Chaudhuri, eds., *Nation, Empire, Colony: Historicizing Gender and Race*. Bloomington: Indiana University Press, 1998.

———and Georgette José Valenzuela, eds., *Cuatro estudios de género en el México urbano del siglo XIX*. Mexico City: Programa Universitario de Estudios de Género, UNAM, 2001.

Cardoso, Fernando E. [Henrique], and Enzo Falleto. *Dependencia y desarrollo en América Latina*. Mexico City: Siglo Veintiuno, 1971.

Carrera, Magali M. *Imagining Identity in New Spain: Race, Lineage, and the Colonial Body in Portraiture and Casta Paintings*. Austin: University of Texas Press, 2003.

Caulfield, Sueann. *In Defense of Honor: Sexual Morality, Modernity, and Nation in Early Twentieth-Century Brazil*. Durham, N.C.: Duke University Press, 2000.

———. "The History of Gender in the Historiography of Latin America." *Hispanic American Historical Review* 81.3–4 (2001): 449–90.

Ceballos Ramírez, Manuel. *El catolicismo social: Un tercero en discordia*. Mexico City: Colegio de México, 1991.

———. *Historia de Rerum novarum en México, 1867–1931*. 2 vols. Mexico City: Instituto Mexicano de Doctrina Social Cristiana, 1991.

Chambers, Sarah. *From Subjects to Citizens: Honor, Gender, and Politics in Arequipa, Peru, 1780–1854*. University Park: Penn State University Press, 1999.

Chassen-López, Francie R. "Oaxaca: Del porfiriato a la revolución, 1902–1911." Doctoral thesis, Universidad Nacional Autónoma de México, 1986.

———. *Regiones y ferrocarriles en la Oaxaca porfirista*. Oaxaca City: Obra Negra, 1990.

———. " 'Cheaper Than Machines': Women and Agriculture in Porfirian Oaxaca, 1880–

1911." In Mary Kay Vaughan, ed., *Women of the Mexican Countryside, 1850–1990: Creating Spaces, Shaping Transitions.* Tucson: University of Arizona Press, 1994.

———. "The View from the South: An Insurgent Reading of Mexican History." Paper delivered at the Yale Council on Latin American and Iberian Studies, New Haven, Conn., October 2, 2001.

———. "From Liberal to Revolutionary Oaxaca: The View from the South, Mexico, 1867–1911." Unpublished book manuscript.

Chauncey, George. *Gay New York: Gender, Urban Culture, and the Making of the Gay Male World, 1890–1940.* New York: Basic Books, 1994.

Chazkel, Amy. "The Laws of Chance: Persecution and Persistence of the Jogo do Bicho in Rio de Janeiro, Brazil, 1890–1940." PhD diss., Yale University, 2002.

Clancy, Michael. *Exporting Paradise: Tourism and Development in Mexico.* New York: Pergamon, 2001.

Coatsworth, John H. *Growth against Development: The Economic Impact of Railroads in Porfirian Mexico.* Dekalb: Northern Illinois University Press, 1981.

Cohen, Jeffrey H. *The Culture of Migration in Southern Mexico.* Austin: University of Texas Press, 2004.

Collado Herrera, María del Carmen. *La burguesía mexicana: El emporio Braniff, 1865–1920.* Mexico City: Siglo Veintiuno, 1987.

Comaroff, Jean, and John Comaroff. *Modernity and Its Malcontents: Ritual and Power in Postcolonial Africa.* Chicago: University of Chicago Press, 1993.

Connell, R. W. *Masculinities.* Berkeley: University of California Press, 1995.

Cook, Scott, and Martin Diskin, eds. *Markets in Oaxaca.* Austin: University of Texas Press, 1971.

Corbin, Alain. *Women for Hire: Prostitution and Sexuality in France after 1850.* Translated by Alan Sheridan. Cambridge: Harvard University Press, 1990.

Coronil, Fernando. *The Magical State: Nature, Money, and Modernity in Venezuela.* Chicago: University of Chicago Press, 1997.

Corrigan, Phillip, and Derek Sayer. *The Great Arch: English State Formation as Cultural Revolution.* Oxford, U.K.: Basil Blackwell, 1985.

Craib, Raymond B. *Cartographic Mexico: A History of State Fixations and Fugitive Landscapes.* Durham, N.C.: Duke University Press, 2004.

Cronon, William. *Nature's Metropolis: Chicago and the Great West.* New York: W. W. Norton, 1991.

da Costa, Emilia Viotti. *Crowns of Glory, Tears of Blood: The Demerara Slave Rebellion of 1823.* Oxford: Oxford University Press, 1994.

Dalton, Margarita, ed. *Oaxaca: Textos de su historia.* Vols. 3 and 4. Oaxaca City: Instituto de Investigaciones Dr. José María Luis Mora, Gobierno de Estado de Oaxaca, 1990.

Dawson, Alexander. "From Models for the Nation to Model Citizens: Indigenismo and the Revindication of the Mexican Indian, 1920–40." *Journal of Latin American Studies* 30 (1998): 279–308.

Debroise, Olivier. *Fuga mexicana: Un recorrido por la fotografía en México.* Mexico City: Consejo Nacional para la Cultura y las Artes, 1994.

de la Cruz, Víctor. "Las razones de Juchitán." *Hora cero* 35 (1981): 2–5.

Díaz, María Elena. "The Satiric Penny Press for Workers in Mexico, 1900–1910: A Case Study in the Politicisation of Popular Culture." *Journal of Latin American Studies* 22 (May 1990): 497–526.

Dore, Elizabeth. "One Step Forward and Two Steps Back: Gender and the State in the Long Nineteenth Century," in Elizabeth Dore and Maxine Molyneux, eds., *Hidden Histories of Gender and the State in Latin America*. Durham, N.C.: Duke University Press, 2000.

Esparza, Manuel. *Gillow durante el porfiriato y la revolución en Oaxaca, 1887–1922*. Tlaxcala: Talleres Gráficos de Tlaxcala, 1985.

———. "La mediación entre Dios y el poder terrenal: Según el arzobispo Eulogio G. Gillow." *Eslabones* 1 (January–July 1991): 79–83.

———. "Arzobispo Eulogio G. Gillow ¿Un liberal?" In Carlos Martínez Assad, ed., *A Dios lo que es de Dios*. Mexico City: Aguilar, 1995.

———. *Eulogio Gillow y el poder: La correspondencia privada como fuente de la historia*. Oaxaca: Carteles, 2004.

Esparza, Manuel, ed. *Ordenanza para el establecimiento e instrucción de los alcaldes de barrio de la ciudad de Oaxaca*. Oaxaca: Instituto Nacional de Antropología e Historia, Centro Regional de Oaxaca, 1981.

———. *Padrón de capitación de la ciudad de Oaxaca, 1875*. Oaxaca City: Gobierno del Estado de Oaxaca, Documentos del Archivo 1, 1983.

Falcón, Romana. "Force and the Search for Consent: The Role of the *Jefaturas Políticas* of Coahuila in National State Formation." In Gilbert M. Joseph and Daniel Nugent, eds., *Everyday Forms of State Formation: Revolution and the Negotiation of Rule in Modern Mexico*. Durham, N.C.: Duke University Press, 1994.

Ferguson, James. *The Anti-politics Machine: "Development," Depoliticization, and Bureaucratic Power in Lesotho*. Minneapolis: University of Minnesota Press, 1994.

Fernández, Justino. *El arte del siglo XIX en México*. Mexico City: Impresora Universitaria, 1983.

François, Marie. "When Pawnshops Talk: Popular Credit and Material Culture in Mexico City, 1775–1916." PhD diss., University of Arizona, 1998.

———. "Vivir de prestado: El empeño en la ciudad de México." In Anne Staples, ed., *Bienes y vivencias: El siglo XIX mexicano*. Vol. 5, *Historia de la vida cotidiana*. Mexico City: Colegio de México, 2002.

Frank, Andre Gunder. *Capitalism and Underdevelopment in Latin America*. New York: Monthly Review Press, 1967.

French, William E. *A Peaceful and Working People: Manners, Morals, and Class Formation in Northern Mexico*. Albuquerque: University of New Mexico Press, 1996.

———. "Imagining and the Cultural History of Nineteenth-Century Mexico." *Hispanic American Historical Review* 79.2 (1999): 249–67.

García Díaz, Bernardo. *Un pueblo fabril: Santa Rosa, Veracruz, México*. Mexico City: Secretaría de Educación Pública, 1981.

Garon, Sheldon. "The World's Oldest Debate? Prostitution and the State in Imperial Japan, 1900–1945." *American Historical Review*, 98.3 (1993): 710–32.

Gibson, Mary. *Prostitution and the State in Italy, 1860–1915*. New Brunswick, N.J.: Rutgers University Press, 1986.

Gibson, Ralph. *A Social History of French Catholicism, 1789–1914.* London: Routledge, 1989.

Giddens, Anthony. *The Consequences of Modernity.* Stanford, Calif.: Stanford University Press, 1990.

———, and Christopher Pierson. *Conversations with Anthony Giddens: Making Sense of Modernity.* Cambridge, U.K.: Polity, 1998.

———, and Philip Stanworth, eds. *Elites and Power in British Society.* Cambridge: Cambridge University Press, 1974.

Gilfoyle, Timothy J. "Prostitutes in History: From Parables of Pornography to Metaphors of Modernity." *American Historical Review* 104.1 (1999): 117–41.

Gill, Anthony. *Rendering unto Caesar: The Catholic Church and the State in Latin America.* Chicago: University of Chicago Press, 1998.

Goddard, Jorge Adame. *El pensamiento político y social de los católicos mexicanos, 1867–1914.* Mexico City: Universidad Nacional Autónoma de México, 1981.

González, Luis. *San José de Gracia: Mexican Village in Transition.* Austin: University of Texas Press, 1991.

González, Soledad, and Julia Tuñón, eds. *Familias y mujeres en México.* Mexico City: Colegio de México, 1997.

Gordon, Colin. "Governmental Rationality: An Introduction." In Graham Burchell et al., eds., *The Foucault Effect: Studies in Governmentality with Two Lectures by and an Interview with Michel Foucault.* London: Harvester Wheatsheaf, 1991.

Gramsci, Antonio. *Selections from the Prison Notebooks.* Edited and translated by Quinten Hoare and Geoffrey Nowell Smith. London: Lawrence and Wishart, 1971.

Grandin, Gregory. *The Blood of Guatemala: A History of Race and Nation, 1750–1954.* Durham, N.C.: Duke University Press, 2000.

Green, James. *Beyond Carnival: Male Homosexuality in Twentieth-Century Brazil.* Chicago: University of Chicago Press, 1999.

Guerra, François-Xavier. *México, del antiguo régimen a la revolución.* Mexico City: Fondo de Cultura Económica, 1991.

———. *Modernidad e independencias.* Mexico City: Fondo de Cultura Económica, 1993.

Gutiérrez, David G. *Walls and Mirrors: Mexican Americans, Mexican Immigrants, and the Politics of Ethnicity.* Berkeley: University of California Press, 1994.

Guy, Donna. *Sex and Danger in Buenos Aires: Prostitution, Family, and Nation in Argentina.* Lincoln: University of Nebraska Press, 1991.

Haber, Stephen. *Industry and Underdevelopment: Industrialization of Mexico, 1890–1940.* Stanford, Calif.: Stanford University Press, 1989.

Hale, Charles. *The Transformation of Liberalism in Late Nineteenth-Century Mexico.* Princeton, N.J.: Princeton University Press, 1989.

Hall, Stuart, ed. *Modernity: An Introduction to Modern Societies.* Oxford, U.K.: Blackwell, 2000.

Haraway, Donna. "The Persistence of Vision." In Nicholas Mirzoeff, ed., *The Visual Culture Reader.* New York: Routledge, 2002.

Hartch, Todd. "At the Service of the State: The Summer Institute of Linguistics in Mexico, 1935–1985." PhD diss., Yale University, 2000.

Harvey, David. *The Condition of Postmodernity: An Enquiry into the Origins of Cultural Change.* Oxford, U.K.: Blackwell, 1989.

Haslip-Viera, Gabriel. *Crime and Punishment in Late Colonial Mexico City, 1692–1810.* Albu-querque: University of New Mexico Press, 1999.

Henkin, David M. *City Reading: Written Words and Public Spaces in Antebellum New York.* New York: Columbia University Press, 1998.

Hernández Chávez, Alicia. "Origen y ocaso del ejército porfiriano." *Historia mexicana* 39.1 (1989): 257–96.

Hershatter, Gail. *Dangerous Pleasures: Prostitution and Modernity in Twentieth-Century Shang-hai.* Berkeley: University of California Press, 1997.

Higgins, Michael James, and Tanya L. Cohen. *Streets, Bedrooms, and Patios: The Ordinariness of Diversity in Urban Oaxaca.* Austin: University of Texas Press, 2000.

Holloway, Thomas. *Policing Rio de Janeiro: Resistance and Repression in a Nineteenth-Century City.* Stanford, Calif.: Stanford University Press, 1993.

Hondagneu-Sotelo, Pierrette. *Gendered Transitions: Mexican Experiences of Immigration.* Berkeley: University of California Press, 1994.

Howell, Philip. "Prostitutional Space in the Nineteenth-Century European City." In I. S. Black and R. A. Butlin, eds., *Place, Culture and Identity: Essays in Historical Geography in Honour of Alan R. H. Baker.* Quebec City: Presses de l'Université Laval, 2001.

Huntington, Samuel P. "The Clash of Civilizations?" *Foreign Affairs* (summer 1993): 122–49.

Iturribarría, Jorge Fernando. *Oaxaca en la historia: De la época precolombina a los tiempos ac-tuales.* Mexico City: Stylo, 1955.

———. "La política de conciliación del general Díaz y el arzobispo Gillow." *Historia mexi-cana* 14.1 (1964): 81–101.

James, Daniel, and Mirta Zaida Lobato. "Family Photos, Oral Narratives, and Identity For-mation: The Ukrainians of Berisso." *Hispanic American Historical Review* 84.1 (2004): 5–36.

Jay, Martin. *Downcast Eyes: The Denigration of Vision in Twentieth-Century French Thought.* Berkeley: University of California Press, 1994.

Jimenez, Christina. "Making the City Their Own: Popular Groups and Political Culture in Morelia, Mexico, 1880 to 1930." PhD diss., University of California, San Diego, 2001.

Johnson, Lyman L., ed. *The Problem of Order in Changing Societies: Essays on Crime and Polic-ing in Argentina and Uruguay, 1750–1940.* Albuquerque: University of New Mexico Press, 1990.

———, and Sonya Lipsett-Rivera, eds. *The Faces of Honor: Sex, Shame, and Violence in Colonial Latin America.* Albuquerque: University of New Mexico Press, 1998.

Joseph, Gilbert M. "Forging the Regional Pastime: Baseball and Class in Yucatán." In Joseph L. Arbena, ed., *Sport and Society in Latin America: Diffusion, Dependency, and the Rise of Mass Culture.* New York: Greenwood, 1988.

———. *Revolution from Without: Yucatán, Mexico, and the United States, 1880–1924.* Durham, N.C.: Duke University Press, 1988.

———. "On the Trail of Latin American Bandits: A Reexamination of Peasant Resistance." *Latin American Research Review* 25.3 (1990): 7–18.

———. "Close Encounters." In Catherine C. LeGrand and Ricardo D. Salvatore, eds., *Close Encounters of Empire: Writing the Cultural History of U.S.–Latin American Relations.* Dur-ham, N.C.: Duke University Press, 1998.

———. Forward to Ricardo Salvatore, Carlos Aguirre, and Gilbert M. Joseph, eds., *Crime* and Punishment in Latin America: Law and Society since Late Colonial Times. Durham, N.C.: Duke University Press, 2001.

———, Anne Rubenstein, and Eric Zolov, eds., Fragments of a Golden Age: The Politics of Culture in Mexico since 1940. Durham, N.C.: Duke University Press, 2001.

Kalmanowiecki, Laura. "Military Power and Policing in Argentina." PhD diss., New School for Social Research, 1996.

Knight, Alan. The Mexican Revolution. 2 vols. Cambridge: Cambridge University Press, 1986.

Kuecker, Glen David. "A Desert in a Tropical Wilderness: Limits to the Porfirian Project in Northeastern Veracruz, 1870–1910." PhD diss., Rutgers, the State University of New Jersey, 1988.

Lafaye, Jacques. Quetzalcoatl and Guadalupe: The Formation of Mexican National Consciousness, 1531–1813. Chicago: University of Chicago Press, 1976.

Lannon, Frances. Privilege, Persecution, and Prophecy: The Catholic Church in Spain, 1875–1975. Oxford, U.K.: Clarendon, 1987.

Lauderdale Graham, Sandra. House and Street: The Domestic World of Servants and Masters in Nineteenth-Century Rio de Janeiro. Cambridge: Cambridge University Press, 1988.

Lear, John. "Mexico City: Popular Classes and Revolutionary Politics." In Ronn Pineo and James A. Baer, eds., Cities of Hope: People, Protests, and Progress in Urbanizing Latin America, 1870–1930. Boulder, Colo.: Westview, 1998.

———. Workers, Neighbors, and Citizens: The Revolution in Mexico. Lincoln: University of Nebraska Press, 2001.

Levine, Robert M. Images of History: Latin American Photographs as Documents. Durham, N.C.: Duke University Press, 1989.

Lira Vásquez, Carlos Antonio de Jesús. "La Ciudad de Oaxaca: Una aproximación a su evolución urbana decimonónica y al desarrollo arquitectónico porfiriano." Master's thesis, Universidad Autónoma de México, 1997.

———. "La Oaxaca porfiriana: Una ciudad hacia la modernidad." Acervos: Boletín de los archivos y bibliotecas de Oaxaca, July 1997, 12–17.

———. "Los jardines de la Oaxaca porfiriana." Acervos: Boletín de los archivos y bibliotecas de Oaxaca, January 1999, 15–22.

Mallon, Florencia. "The Promise and Dilemma of Subaltern Studies: Perspectives from Latin American History." American Historical Review 99.5 (1994): 1491–515.

Marroquín, Enrique, ed. ¿Persecución religiosa en Oaxaca? Los nuevos movimientos religiosos. Oaxaca City: Instituto Oaxaqueño de las Culturas, 1995.

Martínez Vásquez, Víctor Raúl. Historia de la educación en Oaxaca, 1825–1940. Oaxaca City: Universidad Autónoma "Benito Juárez" de Oaxaca, 1994.

———, and Francie R. Chassen de López, eds. La revolución en Oaxaca, 1900–1930. Mexico City: Consejo Nacional para la Cultura y las Artes, 1993.

Marx, Leo. The Machine in the Garden: Technology and the Pastoral Ideal in America. New York: Oxford University Press, 1964.

Massé Zenejas, Patricia. "Photographs of Mexican Prostitutes in 1865." History of Photography 20.3 (1996): 231–34.

———. Simulacro y elegancia en tarjetas de visita: Fotografías de Cruces y Campa. Mexico City: Instituto Nacional de Antropología e Historia (INAH), 1998.

Massé Zenejas, Patricia. *Cruces y Campa: Una experiencia mexicana del retrato tarjeta de visita.* Mexico City: Consejo Nacional para la Cultura y las Artes (CONACULTA), 2000.

McCreery, David. "'This Life of Misery and Shame': Female Prostitution in Guatemala City, 1880–1920." *Journal of Latin American Studies* 18 (1986): 333–53.

McNamara, Patrick. "'That Time of Unspeakable Hardship': Narratives of War and Popular Nationalism in Mexico, 1855–1911." Paper presented at the 114th Annual Meeting of the American Historical Association, Boston, January 4–7, 2001.

Medina, Cuauhtémoc. "Vigilar y retratar: Dos momentos de la fotografía en Oaxaca." In *Fotografías del Archivo Histórico Municipal "Manuel R. Palacios," Oaxaca: Ramos: aguadores y prostitutas.* Oaxaca: Galería Arvil, 1994.

Medina Gómez, Gloria. "Introducción de la luz eléctrica en la ciudad de Oaxaca: Modernización urbana y Revolución mexicana." Master's thesis, Instituto Nacional de Estudios Históricos de la Revolución Mexicana, 2000.

Miano Borruso, Marinella. *Hombre, mujer y muxe' en el Istmo de Tehuntapec.* Mexico City: Instituto Nacional de Antropología e Historia, 2004.

Mitchell, Timothy. Introduction to Mitchell, ed., *Questions of Modernity.* Minneapolis: University of Minnesota Press, 2000.

———. "The Stage of Modernity." In Mitchell, ed., *Questions of Modernity.* Minneapolis: University of Minnesota Press, 2000.

———, ed., *Questions of Modernity.* Minneapolis: University of Minnesota Press, 2000.

Molony, John. *The Worker Question: A New Historical Perspective on Rerum Novarum.* Hong Kong: Gill and Macmillan, 1991.

Morgan, Tony. "Proletarians, Politicos, and Patriarchs: The Use and Abuse of Cultural Customs in the Early Industrialization of Mexico City, 1880–1910." In William H. Beezley, Cheryl English Martin, and William E. French, eds., *Rituals of Rule, Rituals of Resistance: Public Celebrations and Popular Culture in Mexico.* Wilmington, Del.: Scholarly Resources, 1994.

Morris, Meaghan, and Paul Patton, eds. *Michel Foucault: Power, Truth, Strategy.* Working Papers Collection 2. Sydney: Feral, 1979.

Morse, Richard M., and Jorge E. Hardoy, eds. *Rethinking the Latin American City.* Baltimore: Johns Hopkins University Press, 1992.

Mostkoff-Linares, Aida. "Foreign Visions and National Identity: International Tourism in Mexico, 1821–1921." PhD diss., University of California at Los Angeles, 1999.

Muñoz Cabrejo, Fanni. "The New Order: Diversions and Modernization in Turn-of-the-Century Lima." In William Beezley and Linda A. Curcio-Nagy, eds., *Latin American Popular Culture: An Introduction.* Wilmington, Del.: Scholarly Resources, 2000.

Muro, Víctor Gabriel, ed. *Ciudades provincianas de México: Historia, modernización y cambio cultural.* Zamora: Colegio de Michoacán, 1998.

Nagengast, Carole, Rodolfo Stavenhagen, and Michael Kearney. *Human Rights and Indigenous Workers: The Mixtecs in Mexico and the United States.* San Diego: Center for U.S.-Mexico Studies, 1992.

Nesvig, Martin. "The Lure of the Perverse: Moral Negotiation of Pederasty in Porfirian Mexico." *Mexican Studies* 16 (2000), 1–38.

————. "The Complicated Terrain of Latin American Homosexuality." *Hispanic American Historical Review* 81.3 (2001): 689–729.

Newcomer, Daniel. *Reconciling Modernity: Urban State Formation in 1940s León, Mexico.* Lincoln: University of Nebraska Press, 2004.

Ochoa, Aguilar. *La fotografía durante el imperio de Maximiliano.* Mexico City: Instituto de Investigaciones Estéticas, 1996.

O'Dogherty Madrazo, Laura. *De urnas y sotanas: El Partido católico nacional en Jalisco.* Mexico City: Consejo Nacional para la Cultura y las Artes, 2001.

Olsen, Donald J. *The City as a Work of Art: London, Paris, Vienna.* New Haven, Conn.: Yale University Press, 1986.

Overmyer-Velázquez, Mark. "Espacios públicos y mujeres públicas: La regulación de la prostitución en la Ciudad de Oaxaca, 1885–1911." *Acervos: Boletín de los archivos y bibliotecas de Oaxaca,* February 2001, 20–26.

————. "Tracking the Fugitive City: Recent Works on Modern Latin American Urban History." *Latin American Perspectives* 29.4 (2002): 87–97.

————. "Traspasando las fronteras: Pasado y futuro de los estudios de migración México-Estados Unidos." In Boris Berenzón, ed., *Historia de la historiografía México, Estados Unidos y Canadá.* Mexico City: Universidad Nacional Autónoma de México and Fondo de Cultura Económica, 2004.

Overmyer-Velázquez, Mark, and Yanna Yannakakis. "The Renaissance of Oaxaca City's Historical Archives." *Latin American Research Review* 37.1 (2002): 186–98.

Parameshwar Gaonkar, Dilip, ed. *Alternative Modernities.* Durham, N.C.: Duke University Press, 2001.

————. "On Alternative Modernities." In Parameshwar Gaonkar, ed., *Alternative Modernities.* Durham, N.C.: Duke University Press, 2001.

Parmenter, Ross. *Lawrence in Oaxaca: A Quest for the Novelist in Mexico.* Salt Lake City: Peregrine Smith, 1984.

Pessar, Patricia. *From Fanatics to Folk: Brazilian Millenarianism and Popular Culture.* Durham, N.C.: Duke University Press, 2004.

Piccato, Pablo. "El Paso de Venus por el Disco del Sol: Criminality and Alcoholism in the Late Porfiriato." *Mexican Studies/Estudios mexicanos* 11.2 (1995): 203–41.

————. *City of Suspects: Crime in Mexico City, 1900–1931.* Durham, N.C.: Duke University Press, 2001.

————. "Urbanistas, Ambulantes, and Mendigos: The Dispute for Urban Space in Mexico City, 1890–1930." In Carlos A. Aguirre and Robert Buffington, eds., *Reconstructing Criminality in Latin America.* Wilmington, Del.: Scholarly Resources, 2001.

Poole, Deborah. *Vision, Race, and Modernity: A Visual Economy of the Andean Image World.* Princeton, N.J.: Princeton University Press, 1997.

————. "Tipos 'raciales' y proyectos culturales en Oaxaca, 1920–1940." *Acervos: Boletín de los archivos y bibliotecas de Oaxaca* (April–June 2000): 23–29.

————. "Cultural Diversity and Racial Unity in Oaxaca: Rethinking Hybridity and the State in Post-revolutionary Mexico." Paper presented at the New York City Latin American History Workshop, January 26, 2001.

———. "An Image of 'Our Indian': Type Photographs and Racial Sentiments in Oaxaca, 1920–1940." *Hispanic American Historical Review* 84.1 (2004): 37–82.

Prieur, Annick. *Mema's House, Mexico City: On Transvestites, Queens, and Machos.* Chicago: University of Chicago Press, 1998.

Purnell, Jennie. "Negotiating the Nation: Property and Citizenship in Nineteenth-Century Oaxaca." Paper presented at the 113th Annual Meeting of the American Historical Association, Washington, D.C., January 7–10, 1999.

Quay Hutchinson, Elizabeth. "Add Gender and Stir?: Cooking up Gendered Histories of Modern Latin America." *Latin American Research Review* 38.1 (2003): 267–87.

Raat, William D. "Los intelectuales, el positivismo, y la cuestión indígena." *Historia Mexicana* 20 (1970): 412–27.

Rago, Margareth. *Os prazeres da noite: Prostituição e códigos da sexualidade feminina em São Paulo, 1890–1930.* São Paulo: Paz e Terra, 1991.

Rama, Angel. *The Lettered City.* Edited and translated by John Charles Chasteen. Durham, N.C.: Duke University Press, 1996.

Ramey, James. "Una visión victoriana de Oaxaca." *Acervos: Boletín de los archivos y bibliotecas de Oaxaca* (July 2001): 53–56.

Ramos Escandón, Carmen. "Señoritas porfirianas: Mujer e ideología en el México progresista." In Ramos Escandón, ed., *Presencia y transparencia: La mujer en la historia de México.* Mexico City: Colegio de México, 1992.

Reina, Leticia, ed. *Historia de la cuestión agraria mexicana, Estado de Oaxaca.* Vol. 1. Mexico City: Juan Pablos, 1988.

Riley, Brian. "Liquid Inequity: Historical Drinking Water Crisis in Oaxaca de Juárez, Mexico." Master's thesis, Georgia State University, 1996.

Rivera-Garza, Cristina. "The Masters of the Streets: Bodies, Power and Modernity in Mexico, 1867–1930." PhD diss., University of Houston, 1995.

Rohlfes, Laurence. "Police and Penal Reform in Mexico City, 1876–1911: A Study of Order and Progress in Porfirian Mexico." PhD diss., Tulane University, 1983.

Romo, Ricardo. *History of a Barrio: East Los Angeles.* Austin: University of Texas Press, 1983.

Roseberry, William. "Hegemony and the Language of Contention." In Gilbert M. Joseph and Daniel Nugent, eds., *Everyday Forms of State Formation: Revolution and the Negotiation of Rule in Modern Mexico.* Durham, N.C.: Duke University Press, 1994.

Rubenstein, Anne. *Bad Language, Naked Ladies, and Other Threats to the Nation: A Political History of Comic Books in Mexico.* Durham, N.C.: Duke University Press, 1998.

Rubin, Jeffrey W. *Decentering the Regime: History, Culture, and Radical Politics in Juchitán Mexico.* Durham, N.C.: Duke University Press, 1997.

Ruiz, Ramón Eduardo. *The Great Rebellion: Mexico, 1905–1924.* New York: Norton, 1980.

Ruiz Cervantes, Francisco José. *La revolución en Oaxaca: El movimiento de la soberanía, 1915–1920.* Mexico City: Fondo de Cultura Económica, 1986.

———. "Carlos Gracida, los primeros años difíciles: 1914–1919." *Eslabones* 1 (January–July 1991): 32–35.

———. "Oaxaca ¿Campesinos no revolucionarios? Campesinos en revolución." In *Memoria del Congreso Internacional sobre la Revolución mexicana.* Mexico City: Gobiernos del Estado de San Luis Potosí, INEHRM, 1991.

————. "La Ciudad de Oaxaca: Vista a fines del porfiriato, en el plano de 1903." *Memoria—Colegio de Urbanistas de Oaxaca* 1 (2003): 7–15.

Ruiz Cervantes, Francisco José, and Anselmo Arellanes Meixueiro, "Por los orígenes del movimiento obrero en Oaxaca, 1900–1930." In Angeles Romero Frizzi, ed. *Lecturas históricas del estado de Oaxaca* (1877–1930, Vol. 4). Mexico City: Instituto Nacional de Antropología e Historia, 1990.

————, and Carlos Sánchez Silva. *La ciudad de Oaxaca a través de sus planos.* Oaxaca City: Instituto Oaxaqueño de las Culturas, 1997.

Sagredo Baeza, Rafael. *María Villa (a) La Chiquita, no. 4002: Un parásito social del Porfiriato.* Mexico City: Cal y Arena, 1996.

Said, Edward W. "The Clash of Ignorance." *Nation,* October 22, 2001, 11–13.

Salmerón Castro, Fernando I. "Aguascalientes: De la pequeña ciudad a la ciudad media explosiva." In Victor Gabriel Muro, ed. *Ciudades provincianas de México: Historia, modernización y cambio cultural.* Mexico City: El Colegio de Michoacán, Zamora, 1998. 79–93.

Sánchez, George J. *Becoming Mexican American: Ethnicity, Culture and Identity in Chicano Los Angeles, 1900–1945.* New York: Oxford University Press, 1993.

Sánchez Díaz, Gerardo. "Las ciudades michoacanas: Continuidad y cambios entre dos siglos (1880–1920)." In Víctor Gabriel Muro, ed., *Ciudades provincianas de México: Historia, modernización y cambio cultural.* Mexico City: Colegio de Michoacán, 1998.

Sánchez Silva, Carlos. "La prensa en Oaxaca durante el porfiriato y la revolución, 1876–1920." *Acervos: Boletin de los archivos y bibliotecas de Oaxaca,* (October–December 1997): 8–12.

————. *Indios, comerciantes y burocracia en la Oaxaca poscolonial.* Oaxaca City: Universidad 'Benito Juárez' de Oaxaca, 1999.

————. "Don José Zorrilla Trápaga (1829–1897): El 'Tenorio oaxaqueño.'" In Mario Trujillo Bolio and José Contreras Valdez, eds., *Formación empresarial, fomento industrial y compañías agrícolas en el México del siglo XIX.* Mexico City: CIESAS, 2003.

Saragoza, Alex M. *The Monterrey Elite and the Mexican State.* Austin: University of Texas Press, 1988.

Schell, William. *Integral Outsiders: The American Colony on Mexico City, 1876–1911.* Wilmington, Del.: Scholarly Resources, 2001.

Schwartz, Vanessa. *Spectacular Realities: Early Mass Culture in Fin-de-Siècle Paris.* Berkeley: University of California Press, 1998.

Scobie, James R. "The Growth of Latin American Cities, 1870–1930." In *The Cambridge History of Latin America,* Vol. 4. Cambridge: Cambridge University Press, 1986.

Scott, James C. *Weapons of the Weak: Everyday Forms of Peasant Resistance.* New Haven, Conn.: Yale University Press, 1985.

————. *Domination and the Arts of Resistance: Hidden Transcripts.* New Haven, Conn.: Yale University Press, 1990.

————. *Seeing Like a State: How Certain Schemes to Improve the Human Condition Have Failed.* New Haven, Conn.: Yale University Press, 1998.

Seed, Patricia. *To Love, Honor, and Obey in Colonial Mexico: Conflicts over Marriage Choice, 1574–1821.* Stanford, Calif.: Stanford University Press, 1988.

Sekula, Allan. "The Body and the Archive." *October* 39 (Winter 1986): 3–64.

Sigüenza Orozco, Salvador. *Minería y comunidad indígena: El mineral de Natividad, Ixtlán, Oaxaca (1900–1940)*. Mexico City: CIESAS, 1996.

Sloan, Kathryn A. "Runaway Daughters: Young Women's Roles in Rapto Cases in Nineteenth-Century Mexico." In Anne Rubenstein and Víctor Macías González, eds., *Mexico Uncut: Performance, Space, and Masculine Sexuality after 1810*. Albuquerque: University of New Mexico Press, forthcoming.

Smith, Shawn Michelle. *American Archives: Gender, Race, and Class in Visual Culture*. Princeton, N.J.: Princeton University Press, 1999.

Soja, Edward W. *Postmodern Geographies: The Reassertion of Space in Critical Social Theory*. London: Verso, 1989.

———. *Journeys to Los Angeles and Other Real-and-Imagined Places*. London: Blackwell, 1996.

Sontag, Susan. *On Photography*. New York: Farrar, Straus and Giroux, 1978.

Sowell, David. "La Caja de Ahorros de Bogotá, 1846–1865: Artisans, Credit, Development, and Savings in Early National Colombia." *Hispanic American Historical Review* 73.4 (1993): 615–38.

———. "Political Impulses: Popular Participation in Formal and Informal Politics, Bogotá, Colombia." In James A. Baer and Ronn Pineo, eds., *Cities of Hope: People, Protests, and Progress in Urbanizing Latin America, 1870–1930*. Boulder, Colo.: Westview, 1998.

Spivak, Gayatri Chakravorty. "Can the Subaltern Speak?" In Cary Nelson and Lawrence Grossberg, eds., *Marxism and the Interpretation of Culture*. Chicago: University of Illinois Press, 1988.

Stallybrass, Peter, and Allon White. *The Politics and Poetics of Transgression*. London: Methuen, 1986.

Stephenson, Marcia. *Gender and Modernity in Andean Bolivia*. Austin: University of Texas Press, 1999.

Stern, Steve. *The Secret History of Gender: Women, Men, and Power in Late Colonial Mexico*. Chapel Hill: University of North Carolina Press, 1995.

Stoler, Ann Laura. *Race and the Education of Desire: Foucault's History of Sexuality and the Colonial Order of Things*. Durham, N.C.: Duke University Press, 1995.

Suárez Findlay, Eileen. *Imposing Decency: The Politics of Sexuality and Race in Puerto Rico, 1870–1920*. Durham, N.C.: Duke University Press, 1999.

Swingewood, Alan. *Cultural Theory and the Problems of Modernity*. New York: St. Martin's, 1998.

Tagg, John. *The Burden of Representation: Essays on Photographies and Histories*. Minneapolis: University of Minnesota Press, 1988.

Tamayo, Jorge L. *Oaxaca en el siglo XX*. Mexico City: Editora de El nacional, 1956.

Taracena, Angel. *Apuntes históricos de Oaxaca: Desde los tiempos precortesanos hasta la época actual*. Oaxaca City: Imprenta del Estado, 1941.

———. "La imprenta en Oaxaca." *Acervos: Boletín de los archivos y bibliotecas de Oaxaca* (October–December 1999): 33–35.

Taylor, William B. *Landlord and Peasant in Colonial Oaxaca*. Stanford, Calif.: Stanford University Press, 1972.

Tenenbaum, Barbara A. "Streetwise History: The Paseo de la Reforma and the Porfirian State, 1876–1910." In William H. Beezley, Cheryl English Martin, and William E. French, eds., *Rituals of Rule, Rituals of Resistance: Public Celebrations and Popular Culture in Mexico.* Wilmington, Del.: Scholarly Resources, 1994.

Tenorio-Trillo, Mauricio. *Mexico at the World's Fairs: Crafting a Nation.* Berkeley: University of California Press, 1996.

———. "1910 Mexico City: Space and Nation in the City of the *Centenario.*" *Journal of Latin American Studies* 28 (1996): 75–104.

Thompson, E. P. "Time, Work-Discipline, and Industrial Capitalism." *Past and Present* 38 (1967): 56–97.

Topik, Stephen. "Economic Domination by the Capital: Mexico City and Rio de Janeiro, 1888–1910." In Eric Van Young, Ricardo Sanchez, and Gisela von Wobeser, eds., *La ciudad y el campo en la historia de México.* 2 vols. Mexico City: Universidad Nacional Autónoma de México, 1992.

Torres Bautista, Mario E. *La familia Maurer de Atlixco, Puebla: Entre el porfiriato y la Revolución mexicana.* Mexico City: CNCA, 1994.

Toulmin, Stephen. *Cosmopolis: The Hidden Agenda of Modernity.* New York: Free Press, 1990.

Traffano, Daniela. "En torno a la cuestión indígena en Oaxaca: La prensa y el discurso de los políticos." In Carlos Sánchez Silva, ed., *Historia, sociedad y literatura de Oaxaca: Nuevos enfoques.* Oaxaca City: Universidad Autónoma "Benito Juárez" de Oaxaca, 2004.

Tuñón Pablos, Julia. *Mujeres en México: Una historia olvidada.* Mexico City: Fascículos Planeta, 1987.

Twinam, Ann. *Public Lives, Private Secrets: Gender, Honor, Sexuality, and Illegitimacy in Colonial Spanish America.* Stanford, Calif.: Stanford University Press, 1999.

Urías Horcaditas, Beatriz. "Etnologéda y filantropéda: Las propuestas de 'regeneraci' indios de la Sociedad Indianista Mexicana, 1900–1914." In Claudia Agostoni and Elisa Speckman, eds., *Modernidad, tradición y alteridad: La ciudad de México en el cambio de siglo (XIX–XX).* Mexico City: IIH-UNAM, 2001.

Uribe, Eloisa. "Entre el rosa y el gris: La escultura del siglo XIX en la ciudad de Oaxaca." In *Historia del arte de Oaxaca: Colonia y siglo XX.* Vol. 2. Oaxaca: Instituto Oaxaqueño de las Culturas, 1997.

Vanderwood, Paul. *Disorder and Progress: Bandits, Police, and Mexican Development.* 2nd ed. Wilmington, Del.: Scholarly Resources, 1992.

———. *The Power of God against the Guns of Government: Religious Upheaval in Mexico at the Turn of the Nineteenth Century.* Stanford, Calif.: Stanford University Press, 1998.

Van Young, Eric. "Conclusion: The State as Vampire — Hegemonic Projects, Public Ritual, and Popular Culture in Mexico, 1600–1900." In William H. Beezley, Cheryl English Martin, and William E. French, eds., *Rituals of Rule, Rituals of Resistance: Public Celebrations and Popular Culture in Mexico.* Wilmington, Del.: Scholarly Resources, 1994.

Vargas, Zaragosa. *Proletarians of the North: A History of Mexican Industrial Workers in Detroit and the Midwest, 1917–1933.* Berkeley: University of California Press, 1993.

Vásquez, Genaro. *Para la historia del terruño.* Oaxaca City: Talleres gráficos de la nación, 1931.

Voekel, Pamela. "Peeing on the Palace: Bodily Resistance to Bourbon Reform in Mexico City." *Journal of Historical Sociology* 5.2 (1992): 183–208.

———. *Alone before God: The Religious Origins of Modernity in Mexico.* Durham, N.C.: Duke University Press, 2002.

Wasserman, Mark. *Capitalists, Caciques, and Revolution: The Native Elite and Foreign Enterprise in Chihuahua, Mexico, 1854–1911.* Chapel Hill: University of North Carolina Press, 1984.

———. *Persistent Oligarchs: Elites and Politics in Chihuahua, Mexico, 1910–1940.* Durham, N.C.: Duke University Press, 1993.

Waterbury, Ronald. "Non-revolutionary Peasants: Oaxaca Compared to Morelos in the Mexican Revolution." *Comparative Studies in Society and History* 17.4 (1975): 410–42.

Weeks, Charles A. *The Juárez Myth in Mexico.* Tuscaloosa: University of Alabama Press, 1987.

Wells, Allen, and Gilbert M. Joseph. "Modernizing Visions, Chilango Blueprints, and Provincial Growing Pains: Mérida at the Turn of the Century." *Mexican Studies/Estudios mexicanos* 8.2 (1992): 167–215.

———. *Summer of Discontent, Seasons of Upheaval: Elite Politics and Rural Insurgency in Yucatán, 1876–1915.* Stanford, Calif.: Stanford University Press, 1996.

Whipperman, Bruce. *Oaxaca.* Emeryville, Calif.: Avalon Travel, 2001.

White, Luise. *The Comforts of Home: Prostitution in Colonial Nairobi.* Chicago: University of Chicago Press, 1990.

Williams, Raymond. *The Country and the City.* New York: Oxford University Press, 1973.

Wright-Rios, Edward. "Piety and Progress: Vision, Shrine and Society, Oaxaca, 1887–1934." PhD diss., University of California, San Diego, 2004.

———. "Indian Saints and Nation-States: Ignacio Manuel Altamirano's Landscape and Legends." *Mexican Studies/Estudios mexicanos* 20.1 (2004): 47–68.

Zolov, Eric. "Discovering a Land 'Mysterious and Obvious': The Renarrativizing of Postrevolutionary Mexico." In Gilbert Joseph et al., eds., *Fragments of a Golden Age: The Politics of Culture in Mexico since 1940.* Durham, N.C.: Duke University Press, 2001.

Index

f represents figure, *m* map, and t table.

Albán, Monte, 31
Alberto H. (worker), 139*f*
Aldeco, Lorenzo, 35
Amado J. (worker), 138*f*
American Archives (Smith), 137
Anastacio B. (worker), 138*f*
Anderson, Benedict, 34
Angela H. (prostitute), 140*f*
Antequera. *See* Oaxaca City, Porfirian
Anticlerical laws, 52, 72–74, 78–79, 154; the *Ley Iglesias* and, 73; the *Ley Juárez* and, 72; the *Ley Lerdo* and, 53, 72, 78. *See also* Catholic Church
Antonio Z. (*estupro*, perpetrator), 106, 120
Anxiety and modernity, 1, 3, 40, 136, 153, 157–58
Apuntes históricos de Oaxaca (Taracena), 6
Arbena, Joseph, 32
Architecture, Porfirian, 52–54
Arthur, Charles (U.S. Consular agent), 83, 85, 126, 135
Aubert, François (photographer), 136
Automovilismo (automobile touring) and elites, 32–33

Báez, Victoriano D. (Oaxacan historian), 95–96
Baseball, and elites, 17, 32–33
Batalla, Guillermo Bonfil, 10
Bautista, Juan, 78
Beezley, William, 54
Belmar, Francisco (Mexican Supreme Court judge), 1, 12, 57–58
Benítez, Priciliano (Mexican Colonel), 21–22
Bentham, Jeremy, 65

Bicycling: elites and, 33; in Mexico City, 33
bien público, El (opposition newspaper), 37
Bliss, Katherine, 110
Blood of Guatemala, The (Grandin), 1
Boletín oficial: Revista eclesiástica de la provincia de Antequera (Official Bulletin: Ecclesiastical Magazine of the Province of Antequera), 81. *See also* Catholic Church; Gillow, Eulogio
Bosses, political. *See Jefaturas Políticas*
Breve reseña histórica y geográfica del Estado de Oaxaca (Belmar), 1
Brothels: danger of, 126; the "red zone" and, 98, 116–18, 117*m*; taxation of, 113–16, 118. *See also* Madams; Prostitution and prostitutes
Buffington, Robert, 65

Cacho, Miguel Bolaños (Oaxacan governor), 24
Calderón, Miguel (Oaxacan law student), 103, 108
Calvino, Italo, 34
Campos, Jesús Ramón (Doctor), 131
Capitalist development, Porfirian, 155–56; administrative regulations and, 67–69; modernity and, 1–2, 7–13, 17–32, 53, 82–94; prostitution and, 99–101; support of, by Catholic Church, 71–72, 75, 82–94; workers and, 71–72, 75, 82–96
Cartographic Mexico (Craib), 42
Castellanos, Rafael, 106
Castillo, Ramón (Municipal President in Oaxaca City), 47
Catholic Church, 67; anticlerical laws and,

Catholic Church (*continued*)
52, 72–74, 78–79, 154; Benito Juárez and,
72–74; capitalist development and, 71–
72, 75, 82–94; *Círculo Católico de Obreros de
Oaxaca* and, 38, 86–96, 154; confiscation
of church property and, 52–54, 72–73,
78; family and, 77–78; Fourth Catholic
Congress and, 76–77, 93–94; the "Indian
problem" and, 94; *Ley Iglesias* and, 73; *Ley
Juárez* and, 72; *Ley Lerdo* and, 53, 72, 78;
in Mexico, 70–79, 86, 93–94; moralizing
of workers and, 37, 71–72, 74, 79, 84–94;
newspapers of, 38; Porfirian reconciliation
and, 71–79, 86, 93–94; *The Rerum Novarum*
and, 86; resurgence of, in Oaxaca City,
70–82; social Catholicism and, 93–94;
Sociedad de Artesanos del Estado de Oaxaca
and, 82, 84–85, 87. *See also* Gillow, Eulogio;
Voz de la verdad, La; Workers
Catholic Workers Circle of Oaxaca (*Círculo
Católico de Obreros de Oaxaca*), 38, 86–96,
154. *See also* Catholic Church; Workers
CCOO. *See Círculo Católico de Obreros de
Oaxaca*
Ceballos, Manuel, 86, 94
Cecilia V. (Oaxaca City prostitute), 127–28
Celebrations. *See* Centennial celebration;
Public rituals
Centennial celebration, 56–60, 76, 153. *See
also* Public rituals
Chassen-López, Francie, 6
Chávez, Gregorio (Governor of Oaxaca), 12
Church Law (*Ley Iglesias*), 73. *See also* Catholic
Church
CIPO-RFM (Popular Indigenous Council of
Oaxaca "Ricardo Flores Magón"), 157–58.
See also Indigenous groups
Círculo Católico de Obreros de Oaxaca (Catholic
Workers Circle of Oaxaca), 38, 86–96, 154;
savings banks and, 89–90. *See also* Gillow,
Eulogio; Catholic Church; Workers
Cirilio L. (worker), 139*f*
City council, of Oaxaca City. *See* Elites of
Oaxaca City; Modernity, elite construc-
tion of; Oaxaca City, Porfirian; Prosti-

tution and prostitutes; Regulations, in
Oaxaca City
"City of Oaxaca and Its Principal Buildings,
The" (Torres), 52–53
City space, elite ordering of, 2, 40, 69, 154–
55; administrative regulations and, 41,
67–69; brothels and, 98, 116–18, 117*m*; city
markets and, 68–69; class exclusion and,
42–49, 63–69; *Colonia Díaz-Ordaz* and, 43–
44; the Commission on Avenues, Gardens,
Public Adornment and Carriages and,
50–52; gardens and, 48–52; horticultural
competitions and, 49; maps and mapping
and, 2, 59–62; El Marquesado and, 45–47,
53, 64; the *Oaxaca en el centenario de la
independencia nacional* and, 28, 61; plazas
and, 48–49, 54–55; property ownership
and, 28–29, 29*t*; prostitution and, 100,
103–7, 111–21, 117*m*, 152; race and, 15, 40–
41, 53; renaming of streets and, 61–62;
secular architecture and, 52–54; sexuality
and gender and, 52, 104–6; street lighting
and, 53; symbolic use of, 2, 41, 54–60;
vagrants and, 30–31, 63, 66–67, 69. *See also*
Class; Modernity, elite construction of;
Police in Oaxaca City; Prostitution and
prostitutes; Race; Surveillance
Civic festivals. *See* Public rituals
Clandestinas (clandestine prostitutes), 124,
131–32, 148–49. *See also* Prostitution and
prostitutes
Class: anxiety and, 153; city space and, 42–
49, 63–69; exclusion and, 42–49, 63–69,
84; modernity and, 2–4, 9–11, 40, 52,
84; the photographic registry and, 134–
36, 146; prostitution and, 99–100, 148;
public hygiene and, 63, 65–67. *See also*
Respectability
Class, popular. *See* Class; Indigenous groups;
Madams; Prostitution and prostitutes;
Race; Vagrants; Workers
Colegio de Niñas students, posed as Indians,
57, 58*f*
Colonia Díaz-Ordaz (Oaxaca City neighborhood), 43–44

Comfort, Ignacio (President of Mexico), 73
Comisión de Sanidad Pública (Commission on
    Public Health), 98, 112–13, 119, 124, 128,
    132. See also Prostitution and prostitutes
Commission on Avenues, Gardens, Public
    Adornment and Carriages, 50–52. See also
    City space, elite ordering of
Commission on Public Health (Comisión de
    Sanidad Pública), 98, 112–13, 119, 124, 128,
    132. See also Prostitution and prostitutes
Concepción R. (Madam), 149
Connell, R. W., 106
Consumer culture, 36–37
Conzatti, Cassiano, 50, 52
Córdoza, Luis G. (Civil servant), 78
Coronil, Fernando, 59
Correo del sur, El (newspaper), 45–46, 67
Corrigan, Phillip, 54
Craib, Raymond, 42
Crimen según las leyes naturales, El (Crime Ac-
    cording to the Natural Laws, Calderón),
    103

Daguerre, Louis-Jacques-Mandé, 134
Dependency model, of development, 8
Development, capitalist: dependency model
    of, 8; diffusionist model of, 8. See also
    Capitalist development, Porfirian; Moder-
    nity, elite construction of; Modernity and
    tradition
Deviance, 124; criminal definitions of, 101–3;
    sexual, 101–3, 106–7
Díaz, María Elena, 37
Díaz, Porfirio (President of Mexico), 1, 3, 7,
    11; church-state reconciliation and, 71–
    79; Eulogio Gillow and, 72, 75–76, 79–82,
    88; foreign industrialists and, 23–24; the
    Guardianes de Oaxaca and, 63–64; Insti-
    tuto de Ciencias y Artes and, 27; Mexican
    penal system and, 65; monument to,
    51; Oaxaca City architecture and, 52–54;
    Oaxaca City politics and, 7, 18–23. See also
    Capitalist development, Porfirian
Díaz Quintas, Heliodoro, 37–38
Diffusionist model of development, 8

Discipline. See Regulations in Oaxaca City
Divina Providencia, 83. See also Workers

Elections, municipal, in Oaxaca City, 22–23
Elites of Oaxaca City: automovilismo and, 32–
    33; baseball and, 17, 32–33; bicycling and,
    33; consumer culture of, 36–37; cultural
    and social networks of, 29, 39; foreign
    elite and, 23–27; intermarriage of, 17,
    25–26, 29, 39; middle sector of, 27, 39,
    41; newspapers and, 17, 34–39; political
    dominance of, 17–39, 43, 69, 154; property
    ownership and, 28–29, 29t; sculpture
    and, 51; sports and leisure activities
    and, 17, 31–34, 39; tourist industry and,
    15, 17, 29–32, 39, 157. See also City space,
    elite ordering of; Class; Modernity, elite
    construction of; Oaxaca City, Porfirian
Elites and Power in British Society (Giddens),
    17
Emerald City. See Oaxaca City, Porfirian;
    Oaxaca City, in the twenty-first century
Esparza, Manuel, 79
Espinoza, José (Oaxaca City councilman),
    112–13
Estado de Oaxaca, El (newspaper), 30
Estupro (rape), 106
Ethnicity. See Indigenous groups; Race
Exclusion, race and class. See Class; Race

Factories, 82–83
Falcón, Romana, 18
Family: Catholic Church and, 77–78; dis-
    courses of, 101, 103–4, 106–7; intermar-
    riage of elites and, 17, 25–26, 29, 39;
    prostitution and, 106, 118, 125–26. See also
    Sexuality and gender; Women
Federal Electoral Law, 22
Festivals. See Public rituals
Filio, Isabel (prostitute), 124, 125f
Flores, Adalberto (Political boss), 67
Foreign industrialists, 23–24
Fourth Catholic Congress, 76–77, 93–94;
    the "Indian problem" and, 94. See also
    Catholic Church

Francisca G. (prostitute), 142*f*

French, William, 104, 116

Gardens in Oaxaca City, 48–52; horticultural competitions and, 49. *See also* City space, elite ordering of

Gender. *See* Sexuality and gender

Giddens, Anthony, 17–18

Gillow, Eulogio (Oaxacan Archbishop), 38, 70–83, 86–90, 93, 96, 154; *Boletín oficial* and, 81; *Círculo Católico de Obreros do Oaxaca* (CCOO) and, 86–90; Emilio Pimentel and, 81–82; Fourth Catholic Congress and, 76–77, 93; modernizing of church administration and, 80–81; Porfirio Díaz and, 72, 75–76, 79–82, 88. *See also* Catholic Church; Workers

Gómez, Gildardo (Oaxaca City municipal President), 22, 43, 44

González, Martín (Governor of Oaxaca), 1, 37, 81, 85

Gordon, Colin, 18

Government officials. *See* Elites, of Oaxaca City; Modernity, elite construction of; Prostitution and prostitutes

Gracida, Manuel Martínez (Oaxacan bureaucrat), 49

Gran Círculo Obrero de México (Great Mexican Workers Circle), 84. *See also* Mutual aid societies; Workers

Grandin, Gregory, 1, 3

Grandison, Thomas, 25–26

Great Mexican Workers Circle (*Gran Círculo Obrero de México*), 84. *See also* Mutual aid societies; Workers

Gregoria M. (prostitute), 140*f*

Gremios (guilds), 84–85, 90–91. *See also* Workers

Guadalupe F. (prostitute), 147*f*

Guardianes de Oaxaca, 63–64. *See also* Police in Oaxaca City

Guelaguetza celebration, 31, 157. *See also* Public rituals

Guerra, François-Xavier, 8

Guilds (*gremios*), 84–85, 90–91. *See also* Workers

Harvey, David, 42

Henkin, David, 35

Herlinda M. (prostitute), 144*f*

Hoja del pueblo, La (newspaper), 95–96

Holm, Albert, 134–35

Honor. *See* Respectability; Sexuality and gender

Horticultural competitions, 49. *See also* Gardens in Oaxaca City

Huarache, El (opposition newspaper), 37

ICA (Instituto de Ciencias y Artes del Estado de Oaxaca), 27, 55

Indians. *See* Indigenous groups

Indigenous groups, 6–7, 9–11, 24; centennial celebration and, 56–59, 58*f*; domestic workers, 107–11; Fourth Catholic Congress and, 94; the "Indian problem" and, 94; mining industry and, 12–13; photographic registry of prostitutes and, 2, 43, 84, 99, 108–9, 121–46, 125*f*, 140*f*, 142*f*, 144*f*–45*f*, 147*f*; "¡Pobre Raza!" and, 58–59; Popular Indigenous Council of Oaxaca "Ricardo Flores Magón" (CIPO-RFM) and, 157–58; prostitution and, 99, 107–10, 121; racial categorization in census and, 107–10; *Sociedad Indianista Oaxaqueña* (Oaxacan Indianist Society) and, 58–59; subdivision of land of, 107; tourist industry and, 15, 17, 29–31, 157; Zapotec speakers, 108–9. *See also* Catholic Church; Modernity and tradition; Race; Respectability

Instituto de Ciencias y Artes del Estado de Oaxaca (ICA), 27, 55

Iñurreta, Tirso, 21–22

Invisible Cities (Calvino), 34

Isabel R. (prostitute), 140*f*

Jefaturas Políticas (political bosses), 18–23

Joaquina G. (Oaxacan matrona), 98, 100, 116

Josefina R. (prostitute), 144*f*

Juana A. (prostitute), 147f
Juana G. (prostitute), 105
Juárez, Benito (President of Mexico), 7, 18–20, 27; celebration of, 55–56; reform of Catholic Church and, 72–74

Labor and Labor unions, 83, 85, 93. See also Unions, labor; Workers
Lange, Max (member of Oaxaca City British colony), 44
Lara y Pardo, Luis (Mexican social hygienist), 102, 149
Latin America: Catholic workers circles and, 86; dependency model of development and, 8; diffusionist model of development and, 8; popular credit in, 91
Lawrence, L. L. (U.S. commercial agent), 11
Lawton, Ezra M. (American consular agent), 48, 66
Legibility and modernity. See City space, elite ordering of
Leisure, in Oaxaca City, 31–34
Ley Iglesias (Church Law), 73. See also Catholic Church
Ley Juárez (Juárez Law), 72. See also Catholic Church
Ley Lerdo (Lerdo Law), 53, 72, 78. See also Catholic Church
Libertad, La (newspaper), 104
Lira, Carlos (architectural historian), 53–54
Lombroso, Cesare, 102–3
Luis Mier y Terán Theater and Casino, 26–27, 33, 54
Luisa M. (prostitute), 145f
Luz V. (Madam), 149–50

Madams, 113, 148–51; taxation of, 113–14, 149–50. See also Brothels; Prostitution and prostitutes
Madden, Robert (U.S. citizen), 126
Maps and mapping, of Oaxaca City, 2, 59–62; Oaxaca en el centenario de la independencia nacional and, 61. See also City space, elite ordering of

Markets, regulation of, 68–69
Marquesado, El (Oaxaca City neighborhood), 53, 64; annexation of, 45–47; surveillance of, 45–46
Marx, Karl, 7
"Masters of the Streets" (Rivera-Garza), 111
Matilde C. (prostitute), 140f
Matronas. See Madams
Mauleón, Joaquín (political boss of Oaxaca City), 11
Maximiana G. (Madam), 124
Maximilian of Hapsburg, 73, 75
Medina, Cuauhtémoc, 146
Mendoza, Manuel (Civil servant), 78
Merced V. (prostitute), 126
Mercedes P. (prostitute), 142f
Mexican Revolution, 11, 14, 93, 96, 155–56. See also Mexico
Mexican Southern Railway, 12–13, 20, 40–41, 75, 82–83, 137, 141; Oaxaca City tourist industry and, 30–31; subdivision of indigenous lands and, 107
Mexico: A Difficult Step toward Modernity (de Gortari), xiii
Mexico: anticlerical laws and, 70–73; Catholicism in, 70–75, 77; map of, 3m; 1857 Constitution of, 70, 72, 75, 94; mutual societies and, 84; newspapers and, 34–38; penal system of, 65; photography and, 134–36; population growth and, 6; prostitution and, 101–3, 112; Protestantism in, 94; Rerum Novarum and, 86; state-church reconciliation and, 71–79, 86, 93–94. See also Mexico City; Oaxaca City, in the twenty-first century; Oaxaca City, Porfirian; Mexican Revolution
Mexico City, 68; bicycling in, 33; madams in, 149; modernity and, 8, 10; penitentiary of, 65; political connection to Oaxaca City and, 20; prostitution and, 101, 112. See also Mexico
Mining industry, 3, 41, 141; boom in, 12–13, 23, 99, 107, 110, 155; foreign industrialists and, 23–24; indigenous workers and, 12–

Mining industry (*continued*)
13; prostitution and, 12–13, 23, 107, 110, 137, 141; weakening of, 151
Mitchell, Timothy, 9
Modernity, elite construction of, 7–11, 26–27, 39, 52, 69, 153–55; administrative regulations and, 67–69; anxiety and, 1, 3, 40, 136, 153, 157–58; appropriation of respectability and, 2, 99, 121–29, 137–48, 152, 154; deviance and, 101–7, 124; the female body and, 99–103; gender discourse and, 103–7; morality and, 66–67, 69, 87–97, 99; newspapers and, 34–38; penal system and, 64–65, 69; photography and, 132–36, 148; political dominance of elites and, 17–39, 43, 69, 154; Porfirian capitalist development and, 1–2, 7–13, 17–32, 53, 74–96; public hygiene and, 63, 65–67, 69; public rituals and, 54–60, 76–77, 89; sports and leisure activities and, 31–34, 39; tourist industry and, 15, 17, 29–32, 39, 157; Western-centered assumptions of, 7–9; workers and, 52, 71, 79, 88–97, 154. *See also* City space, elite ordering of; Class; Elites of Oaxaca City; Modernity and tradition; Photographic registries of prostitutes; Prostitution and prostitutes; Race; Regulations in Oaxaca City; Sexuality and gender
Modernity and tradition, 2–4, 8–10; census records and, 107–9; the female body and, 99–103; indigenous population and, 8–10, 29–31, 107–9, 153; newspapers and, 37; prostitution and, 99–101, 122; racial categorization and, 107–10; renaming of streets and, 40, 62; respectability and, 103, 126–29; sexual honor and, 127; tourist industry and, 29–31, 157. *See also* Class; Indigenous groups; Modernity, elite construction of; Race
Mondragón, Luisa (Manager of the watchmen), 127–28
Monte Albán, 31
Monte de Piedad (state pawnshop), 54, 90–91
Morality: class exclusion and, 66–67, 69;

moralizing of workers and, 37, 71–72, 74, 79, 84–94; prostitution and, 99, 104–5, 111–16, 118–20, 127–29, 149–52; sexuality and, 105–6
Mortality rates and public hygiene, 66
Muciño, Marcelino, 33
Mujeres Públicas (Public women). *See* Prostitution and prostitutes
Muñoz Cabrejo, Fanni, 31, 33
Murat, José (Oaxacan Governor), 158
Mutual aid societies, 82–85, 91, 93. *See also* Workers; names of individual societies

"New Order, The: Diversions and Modernization in Turn-of-the-Century Lima" (Muñoz-Cabrejo), 31
Newspapers, 2, 34–39; consumer culture and, 36–37; discourses of sexuality and gender and, 104–5; opposition, 37–38; progovernment, 38; religious, 38. *See also* names of specific newspapers

Oaxaca: illiteracy in, 35; map of, 3m, 4m; proliferation of newspapers in, 34–38; revolutionary movement of, 38, 155–56. *See also* Mexico; Oaxaca City, in the twenty-first century; Oaxaca City, Porfirian
Oaxaca City, in the twenty-first century, 1, 156–59; Popular Indigenous Council of Oaxaca "Ricardo Flores Magón" (CIPO-RFM) and, 157–58. *See also* Indigenous groups; Oaxaca City, Porfirian
Oaxaca City, Porfirian: administrative regulations in, 41, 67–69; alteration of city plazas in, 48–49; annexation of El Marquesado and, 45–47; baseball and, 32–33; capitalist development and, 1–2, 7–13, 17–32, 53, 82–94; centennial celebration of, 56–59; *Círculo Católico de Obreros de Oaxaca* and, 38, 86–96, 154; city census records and, 71, 74, 107–10; *Colonia Díaz-Ordaz* and, 43–44; cultural and social networks in, 29; demographic growth of, 4–5; economic expansion of, 3, 11–13, 99, 107;

elite property ownership and, 28–29, 29t; Eulogio Gillow and, 70–82; experience of modernity and, 2–8; fear of "Yankeeization" and, 80, 94–96; foreign industrialists in, 23–24; gender in, 103–7; Guardianes de Oaxaca and, 63–64; Jefaturas Políticas in, 18–23; legibility of; literacy in, 35; map of, 5m; Mexican Revolution and, 155–56; Monte de Piedad (pawnshop) and, 90–91; mortality rates in, 66; municipal elections in, 22–23; newspapers and, 34–39, 104–5; photography in, 134–36; police of, 63–65; political connection to Mexico City and, 20; political dominance of elites and, 17–39, 43, 69, 154; Porfirian politics and, 7, 18–23; prison in, 63–65, 69; Protestantism in, 95; public hygiene in, 65–67, 69, 112; public rituals in, 54–59, 76–77, 89; resurgence of Catholicism in, 70–82; savings banks in, 90–91; sexuality in, 103–7; sports and leisure in, 31–34, 39; time in, 42–43; tourist industry and, 15, 17, 29–31, 39, 157; Zorrilla Family and, 25–27, 29. See also Catholic Church; Círculo Católico de Obreros de Oaxaca; City space, elite ordering of; Díaz, Porfirio; Elites of Oaxaca City; Family; Gillow, Eulogio; Mexico; Oaxaca; Oaxaca City, in the twenty-first century; Prostitution and prostitutes; Sexuality and gender; Women; Workers

Oaxaca City council. See Elites of Oaxaca City; Modernity, elite construction of; Oaxaca City, Porfirian; Prostitution and prostitutes; Regulations in Oaxaca City

Oaxaca de Juárez. See Oaxaca City, in the twenty-first century; Oaxaca City, Porfirian

Oaxaca en el centenario de la independencia nacional (Portillo), 60–61. See also City space, elite ordering of

Oaxaca Herald (newspaper), 30–31, 34–36, 46, 156

Oaxaca progresista (magazine), 35; and "Sports and Its Utility," 31

Oaxacan Indianist Society (Sociedad Indianista Oaxaqueña), 58–59. See also Indigenous groups

Official Bulletin: Ecclesiastical Magazine of the Province of Antequera (Boletín oficial: Revista eclesiástica de la provincia de Antequera), 81. See also Catholic Church; Gillow, Eulogio

On Photography (Sontag), 122

Orfino D. (worker), 139f

Pawnshops, 90–91

Penal system, in Oaxaca City, 63–65, 69

Periodicals. See Newspapers

Periódico oficial del Estado de Oaxaca, El (newspaper), 52

Petrona O. (prostitute), 122–23, 123f

Photographic registry of prostitutes, 2, 43, 84, 108–9, 121–46; photos of, 123f, 125f, 140f, 142f, 144f–45f, 147f; surveillance and, 135–36. See also Respectability; Trade registries

Photographs and photography, 132–34; images of modernity and, 132–36, 148; interpreting historical, 133–34; as primary documents, 133–34. See also Photographic registry of prostitutes

Pimentel, Emilio (Oaxacan Governor), 12–13, 19, 21, 24, 155–56; Instituto de Ciencias y Artes and, 27; modernization of Oaxaca City and, 41; newspapers and, 37–38; public hygiene and, 65; public rituals and, 55–56; relationship of, with Eulogio Gillow, 81–82; renaming of streets and, 61

Plazas, alteration of, in Oaxaca City, 48–49, 54–55. See also City space, elite ordering of

"¡Pobre Raza!" ("Poor Race!" poem), 58–59. See also Indigenous groups

Police in Oaxaca City, 40–41, 45, 63–65, 69; Guardianes de Oaxaca and, 63–64; public hygiene and, 66–67, 69; sexual displays and, 105; "Special Police Treatise for the Capital of the State of Oaxaca" and, 67; vagrants and, 67, 69. See also Prostitution and prostitutes; Surveillance

Political bosses (Jefaturas Políticas), 18–23

Political dominance of elites, 17–39, 43, 69, 154. *See also* City space, elite ordering of; Modernity, elite construction of

Politics of Oaxaca City: elite dominance of, 17–39, 43, 69, 154; Porfirio Díaz and, 7, 18–23. *See also* City space, elite ordering of; Modernity, elite construction of

Politics and Poetics of Transgression, The (Stallybrass and White), 98

Poole, Deborah, 133–34

"Poor Race!" ("¡Pobre Raza!" poem), 58–59. *See also* Indigenous groups

Popes: Leo XIII, 70, 74, 86; Pius IX, 79. *See also* Catholic Church; *Rerum Novarum, The: On the Condition of the Working Classes*

Popular classes. *See* Class; Indigenous groups; Madams; Prostitution and prostitutes; Race; Vagrants; Workers

Popular Indigenous Council of Oaxaca "Ricardo Flores Magón" (CIPO-RFM), 157–58. *See also* Indigenous groups

Porfirian Oaxaca City. *See* Oaxaca City, Porfirian

"Porfirian Smart Set Anticipates Thorstein Veblen in Guadalajara, The" (Beezley), 54

Portillo, Andrés, 28, 55–56, 60–61

"Portraits of a Possible Nation" (Stepan), 133

Prison, in Oaxaca City, 63–65, 69

Progress. *See* City space, elite ordering of; Modernity, elite construction of

Prostitución en México, La (Lara y Pardo), 102

Prostitution and prostitutes, 63, 69, 97, 103–4, 106–21, 111t; appropriation of elite respectability and, 2, 121–23, 137–48, 152, 154; boom in the mining industry and, 12–13, 23, 107, 110, 137, 141; case histories of, 123–26; city profits from, 114–15; city space and, 103–7, 111–21, 117m, 152; *clandestinas*, 124, 131–32, 148–49; clients of, 150–51; decline of, 110–11, 121, 151; European fashion and, 141, 143, 144t; family and, 106, 118, 125–26; foreign workers and, 141; fugitive prostitutes (*prostituta prófugas*),

151; growth of, and indigenous domestic workers, 99, 107–11, 111t; medico-legal redefintion of, 101–3; migration of, 124; morality and, 99, 104–5, 111–16, 118–20, 127–29, 149–52; nonphotographic registry of, 109–11, 111t; origins of, 143t; perilous life of, 123–26; photographic registry of, 2, 43, 84, 99, 108–9, 121–46; photos from registry of, 123f, 125f, 140f, 142f, 144f–45f, 147f; race and, 84, 99–111, 123, 134–48, 151–52; "red zone" of, 116, 117m; regulation of, 45, 99–137, 152; retirement and, 109, 128–29; sexual deviance and, 101–3, 106–7; subversion of regulations by, 99–100, 122–23, 129–32; surveillance of, 99, 111, 113, 118–21, 126–29, 152; taxation of, 100, 113–15; *La Voz de la verdad* and, 111–12, 130; watchmen and, 111, 118–21, 127–28. *See also* Brothels; Madams; Sexuality and gender; Women; Workers

Protestantism: and fear of "Yankeeization," 80, 94–96; newspapers of, 38

Public hygiene, in Oaxaca City, 63, 65–67, 112; mortality rates and, 66

Public rituals, 2, 41, 54–60, 76, 89; centennial celebration, 56–59, 76, 153; Guelaguetza celebration, 31, 157; Virgin of Guadalupe and, 76; Virgin of Solitude and, 76–77. *See also* City space, elite ordering of

Public women. *See* Prostitution and prostitutes

Puga y Colmenares, Ismael, 37–38

Race: anxiety and, 153; census records and, 107–10; city space and, 15, 40–41, 53; deviance and, 101–3; exclusion and, 107–9, 153, 157; Guelaguetza festival and, 157; modernity and, 4, 9–11, 52, 84; photographic registry of prostitutes and, 84, 99, 123, 134–48; and "¡Pobre Raza!," 58–59; prostitution and, 84, 99–111, 123, 134–48, 151–52; public rituals and, 54–59; racial categorization and, 107–10; regulations and, 84; students posed as Indians and,

57, 58f. See also Indigenous groups; Prostitution and prostitutes; Photographic registry of prostitutes

Rafaela O. (prostitute), 145f

Ramírez, Eduardo (Mayor of Oaxaca City), 115–16

Ramírez, Francisco (Oaxaca City councilman), 116, 118

Ramírez de Aguilar, Ramón, 81

Reform era. See Anticlerical laws

Regalamento de mugeres públicas (Regulations of Public Women). See Prostitution and prostitutes; Regulations in Oaxaca City

Registries, trade. See Registros de oficios;Trade registries

Registros de oficios (trade registries), 84, 108, 136–37, 138f–39f. See also Photographic registry of prostitutes; Workers

Registros de prostitución (registries of prostitution). See Photographic registry of prostitutes; Prostitution and prostitutes

Regulations in Oaxaca City, 41, 67–69; 1890 Plan de Arbitrios and, 68; city markets and, 68–69; prostitution and, 45, 99–137, 152; taxation and, 68; Verification Office of Weights and Measures and, 69; workers and, 84

Rerum Novarum, The: On the Condition of the Working Classes (Pope Leo XIII), 70, 75, 86, 89. See also Catholic Church; Workers

Respectability: appropriation of elite, 2, 99, 121–29, 137–48, 152, 154; photographic registry of prostitutes and, 134–37, 140f, 141, 142f, 144f–45f, 146, 147f, 148; prostitutes and, 2, 99–100, 103–5, 122–23, 126–34

Rituals. See Public rituals

Rivera-Garza, Cristina, 111–12

Romero, Matías, 20–21

Romero Rubio, Carmen, 75

Romero Rubio, Manuel, 75

Rosa B. (prostitute), 142f

Rosa N. (prostitute), 145f

Rosario M. (prostitute), 147f

Rosaura S. (prostitute), 142f

Sánchez Santos, Trinidad (CCOO officer), 91

Sanitation. See Public hygiene, in Oaxaca City

Sara H. (prostitute), 128–29

Savings banks, 90–91

Sayer, Derek, 54

Scheleske y Aguirre, Ernesto, 51

Score, El (magazine), 33

Scott, James, 40, 140

Sculpture, 51

Serafini, Domino, 77

Sex trade. See Prostitution and prostitutes

Sexuality and gender, 1, 118–19; city space and, 53, 104–6; criminal records and, 104; deviance and, 101–3, 106–7; estupro and, 106, 120; female, 105–6, 120; homosexuality, 105–6, 120; male, 101, 105–6, 120; modernity and, 9–11, 99–107, 112–13, 123, 152; in newspapers, 104–5; and "Para las Damas," 103–4; public sexual displays and, 105; sexual honor and, 126–27; sports and, 7–11. See also Family; Prostitution and prostitutes; Women

Sex workers. See Brothels; Prostitution and prostitutes

"Smelling Like a Market" (Coronil), 59

Smith, Shawn Michelle, 137

Social Catholicism, 93–94. See also Catholic Church

Social Class. See Class; Elites of Oaxaca City; Indigenous groups; Madams; Modernity, elite construction of; Prostitution and prostitutes; Respectability; Vagrants; Workers

Social control. See Regulations in Oaxaca City; Workers

Social status, 13. See also Respectability

Sociedad de Artesanos del Estado de Oaxaca (Society of Artisans of the State of Oaxaca), 82, 84–85, 87. See also Catholic Church; Gillow, Eulogio; Workers

Sociedad de Obreros Católicos (Society of Catholic Workers), 87. See also Catholic Church; Gillow, Eulogio; Workers

Sociedad Indianista Oaxaqueña (Oaxacan Indianist Society), 58–59. *See also* Indigenous groups
Society of Artisans of the State of Oaxaca (*Sociedad de Artesanos del Estado de Oaxaca*), 82, 84–85, 87. *See also* Catholic Church; Gillow, Eulogio; Workers
Society of Catholic Workers (Sociedad de Obreros Católicos), 87. *See also* Catholic Church; Gillow, Eulogio; Workers
Sodi, Demetrio, 78
Soja, Edward, 116
Soledad de Vista Hermosa, La (factory), 25, 41
Sontag, Susan, 122
Southworth, J. R., 30
Sowell, David, 91
Space, historical construction of, 42. *See also* City space, elite ordering of
"Special Police Treatise for the Capital of the State of Oaxaca" (Flores), 67. *See also* Police, in Oaxaca City
Spivak, Gayatri, 132
Sports, in Oaxaca City, 31–34
"Sports and Its Utility" (magazine article), 31
Stallybrass, Peter, 98
State formation. *See* Capitalist development, Porfirian; City space, elite ordering of; Modernity, elite construction of
Statues, in Oaxaca City gardens, 50–51
Stepan, Nancy Leys, 133
Streets, in Oaxaca City: paving of, 47–48; renaming of, 61–62. *See also* City space, elite ordering of
Strikes, 85, 93. *See also* Workers
Surveillance, 41, 64; of El Marquesado, 45–46; photographic registries and, 135–36; of prostitutes, 99, 111, 113, 118–21, 126–29, 152. *See also* Police in Oaxaca City; Prostitution and prostitutes; Watchmen, of prostitution

Taracena, Angel, 6
Tejada, Josefa, 25
Tenorio-Trillo, Mauricio, 41, 43

Teodoro V., 105
Thompson, E. P., 42
Torres, Gilberto (Editor of Oaxaca newspaper), 52–54
Tourist industry, 15, 17, 29–31, 157
Trade registries (*registros de oficios*), 84, 108, 136–37, 138*f*–39*f*. *See also* Photographic registry of prostitutes; Workers
Tradition, and modernity. *See* Modernity and tradition
Trápaga, Juan Sáenz, 25–26

Unión, La (newspaper), 67
Unions, labor, 83, 85. *See also* Workers
Urbanization. *See* City space, elite ordering of

Vagrants, 30–31, 63, 66–67, 69
Valencia, José Luz, 106
Vallistocracia, La. See Elites of Oaxaca City
Van Young, Eric, 108
Varela, Juan (Oaxaca City councilman), 119–20
Vargas, Víctor, 37
Vasconcelos, Francisco (President of Sociedad de Artesanos), 84–85
Vásquez, Jesús A., 78
Verification Office of Weights and Measures, 69. *See also* Regulations in Oaxaca City
Vice: moral geography of, 115–16, 117*f*, 118; political economy of, 114–15
Victoriano R. (worker), 138*f*
Violeta G. (prostitute), 147*f*
Viotti da Costa, Emilia, 151–52
Virginia Z. (Oaxaca City prostitute), 124
Virgin of Guadalupe, 75, 76, 89. *See also* Catholic Church
Virgin of Solitude (Patron Saint of Oaxaca City), 76–77. *See also* Catholic Church
Visual order. *See also* City space, elite ordering of
Voekel, Pamela, 74
Voto público, El: Organo del Club central reeleccionista de la Ciudad de Oaxaca (progovernment newspaper), 38

Voz de la justicia, La (opposition newspaper), 37
Voz de la verdad, La (The Voice of the Truth, Catholic newspaper), 75, 77, 80–81, 85, 92, 130; fear of "Yankeeization" and, 95–96; "Para las Damas" and, 103–4; and prostitution, 111–12, 130. See also Catholic Church
Voz de México, La (Catholic newspaper), 75. See also Catholic Church

Watchman, of prostitution, 111, 127–28; corruption of, 118–20. See also Surveillance
Weber, Max, 7
White, Allon, 98
White, Luise, 124
Women: discourses on role of, 101–7; intermarriage of elites and, 17, 25–26, 29, 39; property ownership and, 28–29, 29t; respectability and, 127–29; workers, 83, 85, 90. See also Family; Madams; Prostitution and prostitutes; Sexuality and gender; Workers
Workers: artisans, 82, 87; capitalist development and, 71–72, 75, 82–96; *Círculo Católico de Obreros de Oaxaca* and, 38, 86–96, 154; displacement from city plazas and, 48–49; *Divina Providencia* and, 83; in factories, 82–83, 93; the *Gran Círculo Obrero de México* and, 84; and *gremios*, 84–85, 90–91; indige-

nous, and growth of prostitution trade, 107–11; indigenous, and mining industry, 12–13; labor unions and, 83, 85, 93; market regulations and, 69; moralizing of, and Catholic Church, 37, 71–72, 74, 79, 84–94; mutual aid societies and, 82–85, 91, 93; newspapers of, 37; public sexual displays and, 105; regulations and, 84; *Rerum Novarum* and, 86; savings banks and, 90–91; *Sociedad de Artesanos del Estado de Oaxaca* and; 82, 84–85, 87; strikes and, 85, 93; time and, 42; trade registries and, 84, 108, 136–37, 138f–39f; unrest of, 93; wage inequality and, 83; women, 83, 85, 90; work ethic and, 52, 71, 88, 91, 154; working conditions of, 83, 85. See also Catholic Church; Class; Prostitution and prostitutes

"Yankeeization," fear of, 80, 94–96

Zapatistas, 157. See also Indigenous groups
Zapotec speakers, and city census records, 108–9. See also Indigenous groups
Zeferina G. (*estupro* victim), 106
Zertuche, Albino (Governor of Oaxaca), 21, 44
Zorrilla Family, 25–27, 29, 44
Zorrilla, Federico, 26
Zorrilla, José, 25–26, 38, 84
Zorrilla, José Jr., 26

Mark Overmyer-Velázquez is assistant professor of history
at the University of Connecticut.

Library of Congress Cataloging-in-Publication Data

Overmyer-Velázquez, Mark.
Visions of the Emerald City : modernity, tradition, and the
formation of Porfirian Oaxaca, Mexico / Mark Overmyer-Velázquez.
    p. cm.
Includes bibliographical references and index.
ISBN 0-8223-3777-0 (cloth : alk. paper)
ISBN 0-8223-3790-8 (pbk. : alk. paper)
1. Oaxaca de Juárez (Mexico) – History – 19th century.
2. Mexico – History – 1867–1910. I. Title.
F1391.O12094 2006
972'.7404 – dc22
2005028237